Daughters of Gaia

DAUGHTERS
OF GAIA

Women in the Ancient Mediterranean World

Bella Vivante

UNIVERSITY OF OKLAHOMA PRESS
NORMAN

Library of Congress Cataloging-in-Publication Data

Vivante, Bella.
    Daughters of Gaia : women in the ancient Mediterranean world / Bella Vivante.
        p. cm.   (Praeger series on the ancient world, ISSN 1932–1406)
    Includes bibliographical references and index.
    1. Women—History—To 500.   2. Women—Mediterranean Region—History.
3. Civilization, Classical.   4. Women—Mediterranean Region—Social conditions—
History.   5. Sex role—Mediterranean Region—History.   I. Title.   II. Title: Women in the
ancient Mediterranean world.
    HQ1127.V56   2007
    305.4209182'2–dc22   2006026026

Library of Congress Catalog Card Number: 2006026026

British Library Cataloguing in Publication Data is available.

ISBN: 978–0–8061–3992–0 (paper)

1 2 3 4 5 6 7 8 9 10

Streams of sacred rivers flow backwards …
for Phoibos, the master of music, did not endow my mind
with the lyre's sacred melodies, or I would have sung out my song
in answer to the male race.

Chorus of Women, Euripides' Medea

Those who do not have the power over the story that dominates their
lives—power to retell it, rethink it, and change it as times change—truly are
powerless, because they cannot think new thoughts.

Salman Rushdie, radio interview

Ts'its'tsi'nako, Thought-Woman,
is sitting in her room …
thinking of a story now

I'm telling you the story
she is thinking.

Leslie Marmon Silko, Ceremony

Contents

Illustrations

Preface

This book is a labor of love, the fruit of years of research that reveals that ancient women's lives were far richer, more diverse, and often more powerful than has commonly been thought. Two works form significant stages in this work: one was my edited collection, *Women's Roles in Ancient Civilizations: A Reference Guide*, which examined separately 12 ancient civilizations around the world. In all these pre-state societies women universally received positive valuation, while the cultural pressures of developing patriarchal states resulted in the progressive erosion of women's powers and status. In the second, the publication of my lectures in *The Colorado School of Mines Journal* monograph (2006), I began the thematic exploration of ancient women's roles that set a foundation for this book.

Of inestimable value have been the radically different perceptions of woman's identity and cultural standing I have been privileged to learn from many indigenous American peoples. These perceptions have provided me invaluable models for fashioning my own sense of identity and for framing research questions distinct from familiar Western ones, enabling a far greater understanding about ancient women's lives than conventional Western lenses allow. These empowered modes of perceiving and thinking about women's status permeate this book's approach and provide distinctive and insightful ways of examining ancient women's lives.

Figure 0.1 "Warka Vase," Inanna receiving offerings, limestone low relief. Mesopotamia, 4th mil. B.C.E. Erich Lessing/Art Resource, NY, Iraq Museum, Baghdad, Iraq.

Acknowledgments

Over these many years many people have significantly helped my learning or provided crucial support towards this research, most of whom I cannot name individually. These include professors, colleagues, students, friends, acquaintances, and people I communicated with at conferences, workshops, and lectures. I want to recognize the many indigenous American individuals I have been privileged to meet and learn from. I name only a few: Roberta Blackgoat, Fanny Tiger Bruner, Margaret Downs, Viola Hatch, Kolani Coker Short, Bill Wahpepah, Margaret Whitewater, Zelima Xochiquetzal.

I wish to acknowledge the people instrumental to bringing this book to production, starting with the then-editor at Greenwood Press, Dr. Barbara Rader, for inviting me to edit the *Women's Roles* book, Dr. Heather Staines, who accepted this book for Praeger Press, and my current editor at Praeger, Dr. Elizabeth Demers, for guiding the book into publication. I thank Dr. Juana Simpson for her careful reading and insightful comments on earlier drafts and for our many stimulating conversations. I thank Arlene Riley for help with the art selection. I thank Dr. Richard Wilkinson and Diane Wolkstein for graciously permitting me use of photograph and poetry. I thank the Tucson and Denver folk dancers, the swimming swans, and the women of the gifting circles for providing regular occasions for spiritual, emotional, physical, and mental renewal and for their unflagging, enthusiastic support. Foremost, I thank my partner, Riley, my true *âme soeur,* "sister spirit," for love and support throughout this book's long emergence.

Figure 0.2 Cycladic figurine, marble. ca. 2700–2500 B.C.E. The British Museum/Art Resource, NY, London, Great Britain.

Ancient Mediterranean Civilizations Timelines

Dates are B.C.E., "Before the Common Era," and C.E., the "Common Era."

From 40,000 B.C.E.	Paleolithic, "Old Stone" Age: European "Venus" figures, cave paintings
7000–3500 B.C.E.	Neolithic, "New Stone" Age: Çatal Höyük

EGYPT

3000–2680 B.C.E.	Archaic Period/Early Dynastic: Unification of Egypt, Dynasties 1–2 ca. 2900 Queen Meryt-Neith, possibly 3rd king of 1st Dynasty
2680–2145	Old Kingdom, Dynasties 3–8
ca. 2500	Queens Hetepheres, Meresankh, 4th Dynasty
ca. 2150	Queen Nitocris, end of 6th Dynasty
2020–1645	Middle Kingdom, Dynasties 11–13
ca. 1789	Queen Sobeknofru, end of 12th Dynasty
1550–1070	New Kingdom, Dynasties 18–20
1473–58	Queen Hatshepsut, 5th ruler of 18th Dynasty
14th c.	Queens Tiye, Nefertiti, late18th Dynasty
13th c.	Queen Nefertari, early 19th Dynasty
1190	Queen Twosret, end of 19th Dynasty
ca. 1045–955	Queen Makeda of Sheba/Ethiopia
332–30	Ptolemaic Greek Rule
51–31	Kleopatra VII rules Egypt

MESOPOTAMIA

3000–2350	B.C.E. Sumerian Civilization: invention of writing
ca. 2500	Queen Ku-Bau, 1st Dynasty of Ur
2350–2193	Sargon I unifies Sumer and Akkad, Akkadian dynasty Priestess and Poet Enkheduanna, 1st known world author
21st c.	Queen Abi-Simti, wife of King Shulgi of Ur
1900–1595	Old Babylonian/Old Assyrian periods
1779–1745	King Zimri-Lim: Queen Mother Addu-diri, Queen Shibtu Royal daughters Inib-sharri, Kiru, et aliae
1760	Hammurabi reunites lands, 1st Babylonian dynasty
911–823	Assyrian rule
539–330	Persian period
6th c.	Queen Tomyris of Massagetae defeats King Cyrus of Persia
330	Alexander the Great of Macedon conquers Babylon and Persia

GREECE

3500–1400	Minoan civilization centered on Crete: Theran frescoes
1600–1150	Mycenaean civilization
12th c.	Queens Helen, Klytaimestra
ca. 1200	the legendary Trojan War
11th–9th c.	Dark Ages: Geometric art
8th–6th c.	Archaic Period
8th–7th c.	Greek colonization to west and east; 1st Greek temples to Hera, Artemis
8th–6th c.	Poets Homer, *Iliad, Odyssey;* Hesiod, *Theogony;*Sappho, Kleoboulina
ca. 600	1st Greek coins found at Temple of Artemis at Ephesos
6th c.	Philosophers Pythagoras, Theano, Arignote, Damo, Myia **509** beginnings of Athenian democracy
5th–4th c.	Classical Period
5th c.	Naval commander Artemisia Poets Korinna, Praxilla, Telesilla, Pindar
	Tragedians Aeschylus, Oresteia; Sophocles, Antigone; and

Euripides, Medea, Hippolytus, Trojan Women, Helen

Comic playwright Aristophanes, Lysistrata, Women at the Thesmophoria, Women at the Assembly

Philosophers Arete, Aspasia, Diotima, Sokrates; possibly Aisara, Periktione I, and Phintys Historians Herodotos, History of the Persian Wars, and Thucydides, History of the Peloponnesian War

4th c.	Philosophers Plato, Aristotle, Diogenes the Cynic Queen Olympias of Macedon, mother of Alexander
356–23	Alexander the Great conquers lands east to Persia
323–30	Hellenistic Period
4th–3rd c.	Hellenistic Queens Arsinoë I and II and Berenike I and II Philosophers Epicurus, Hipparkhia, Leontion, Zeno founder of Stoicism **300** Ptolemy I builds Library and Museum in Alexandria
3rd c.	Poets Anyte, Erinna, Nossis, Kallimakhos, Theokritos
3rd–1st c.	Philosophers Periktione II, Theano II
51- 31	Kleopatra VII rules Egypt
30	Kleopatra and Antony commit suicide after defeat by Octavian
1st C. C.E.	Greek biographer and historian Plutarch, *Sayings of Spartan Women*
2nd c.	Female inscriptional poets Damo, Dionysia, Trebulla, Julia Balbilla
5th c.	Neoplatonist Philosophers Asklepigenia, Hypatia, Plotinus
5th–15th c.	Byzantine Empire centered in Constantinople
6th c.	Theodora, wife of Emperor Justinian Building of Hagia Sophia, Church of Holy Wisdom
1453	Ottoman conquest of Constantinople, name changed to Istanbul

ROME

8th–6th C. B.C.E.	Etruscan rule
	Legendary heroines Lucretia, Sabine Women
510–30 B.C.E.	Roman Republic [the dates are from 510 to 30 BCE] 491 Women stop Coriolanus's attack against Rome
3rd–2nd c.	Punic Wars, Rome against Carthage

	195 Women protest for repeal of Oppian Law
190s–121	Cornelia, ideal Roman matron 146 Final defeat of Carthage; Roman conquest of Greece
1st c. B.C.E.	Poets Catullus, Ovid, Sulpicia I, Vergil
47–44	Dictatorship and assassination of Julius Caesar
42	Hortensia's speech in Roman Forum
31	Battle of Actium—Rome conquers Egypt
30 B.C.E.–476 C.E.	Roman Empire
20s	Queen Amanishakhete of Kush resists Roman emperor Augustus
1st C. C.E.	Wives and mothers of emperors Livia, Agrippina I and II Poet Sulpicia II; civic benefactor Eumachia
60s	Queen Boudica of Celts first defeats then is conquered by Romans
2nd c.	Emperor's wife and philosopher, Julia Domna
3rd c.	Christian martyr Vibia Perpetua
306–37	Emperor Constantine makes Christianity the official religion of the Roman
	Empire, capital moved to Byzantion, its name changed to Constantinople
378–95	Emperor Theodosius ends Olympic Games, Eleusinian Mysteries, other Greek and Roman religious practices
5th c.	Jewish alchemist Maria; Christian travel writer Egeria
476	End of Roman Empire in the West

Introduction

"DAUGHTERS OF GAIA": THE MEANING OF THIS BOOK

In the *Theogony*, the ancient Greek poet Hesiod told the story of the creation of the gods. Chaos was the first deity to come into being. Second came Gaia, Goddess of the Earth, followed by Eros, God of Erotic Desire. Although Eros loosened the limbs of mortals and gods with erotic passion, he did not engender any beings. From the neuter Chaos emerged the Underworld and Night, from whom in turn Day and the Upper Air arose. But it was the female Gaia that produced the divine genealogy. After giving birth by herself to the landscape, sea, and sky, Gaia mated with Ouranos, "Sky," and initiated the cycle of sexual reproduction that created the succeeding generations of gods and ultimately humans. Despite some brief, yet significant appearances, Gaia recedes in Hesiod's creation tale, which highlights the increasing power of male deities, with the god Zeus ultimately gaining supreme authority.

The situation differed dramatically in the realm of rituals and belief, where the "Homeric Hymn to Gaia" calls her

> Gaia, mother of all, well founded,
> the oldest being, who nurtures all that exists upon the earth—
> all that moves upon the divine earth or on the sea,
> and all that fly, all beings feed from your abundance.[1]

In the "Hymn to Gaia," the Goddess of the Earth upon whom all life depends remains essential in the Greeks' fundamental belief system, which is expressed through both hymns and ritual actions. By favoring mortals with good offspring and successful crops, Gaia confers all human blessedness.

The hymn also describes the social manifestations of the blessedness Gaia bestows—prosperity, wealth, and "well-ordered cities of beautiful women" where boys and girls delightfully play in a secure environment. The material prosperity Gaia grants blossoms into blessedness in the family and community, and all those whom Gaia, "Sacred Goddess, Spirit of Abundance," honors flourish. The hymn thus portrays Gaia as a goddess who could not be ignored but was necessary for life to exist and for one to prosper in all forms of abundance.

Hesiod's creation tale and the "Hymn to Gaia" seem to portray contradictory images. Did the Greeks believe both, or did they prefer one above the other? These distinct views of Gaia and the differing purposes for these stories' composition vividly exemplify the goal of this book—to gain meaningful appreciation of the fullness of women's lives in the ancient Mediterranean world. As these varying tales of Gaia illustrate, we must make sense of documents whose meanings are rarely self-evident. Instead, all items need to be seen in a broad cultural background and in relation to other, apparently contradictory sources of evidence.

These two tales about Gaia also portray the dual visions needed for this investigation. The *Theogony* presents the mythological stories about the gods, which project human social relations onto the divine realm by depicting the gods organized into patriarchal familial and social structures, with a male figure, Zeus, in charge. As tales, these stories developed a life of their own in the mythological tradition and were frequently transmitted in the literature. But the two portrayals of Gaia show that these mythologically oriented tales did not encompass the full range of views the Greeks held about their deities. Often the mythological tales had little or no connection with the people's religious beliefs and forms of worship, as the "Hymn to Gaia" represents.

Consequently, we must first identify the views about women and female dimensions that people held in their root belief systems. We can then examine what happened to these perceptions in the stories that became canonical in the official cultural lore. The "Hymn to Gaia" displays a valuing of the female from her physical aspects to the cultural, an esteem for women that is shown through religious observance and recognition of women's indispensable role in the continuity of the community. The mythological tales stressed the social institutions that supported various hierarchical relations—by class, age, and gender. While they assumed the superiority of the elite over other classes, these tales conscientiously detailed the imposition of male superiority in various arenas—marriage, economic control, and political governance. The hymns indicate the ways ancient peoples constructed ideas about the female and actual women's status; the mythological tales reveal what happened to these originary beliefs as ancient civilizations developed.

Gaia the original female Earth spirit gave birth to all, enables all life to exist, and generates all human blessedness with her bounty. The Daughters of Gaia encompass all divine and human female beings descended from Gaia, who exhibit in multiple ways her essential female powers—birth, nurturance, sustaining of life, transformation, joy, creativity, death, wisdom, social order, beauty, inner harmony, and more. This book explores the divine figures and the actual women who embodied the various transmutations of the concepts of femaleness.

SCOPE OF THE SUBJECT

This book examines women's lives in the ancient world via four Mediterranean civilizations—Egypt, Mesopotamia, Greece, and Rome. The geographical range of these ancient cultures encompassed the fertile valleys of the Tigris and Euphrates Rivers in modern Iraq to the lands ringing the southern, eastern, and northern coasts of the Mediterranean Sea viewed across four thousand years of time. These were distinct, neighboring cultures that had extensive contact. The earliest records date to the development of Egyptian and Mesopotamian dynasties in the third millennium B.C.E., each of whose ancient kingdoms lasted two to three millennia. Greek ascendancy emerged in distinct stages in the second to first millennia B.C.E. Rome began its expansion through Italy in the first millennium B.C.E., and the Roman Empire reigned across all these lands and those of central and western Europe until the fifth century C.E., the general ending point of this study.

This scope provides a compelling, cohesive window for examining women in the ancient Mediterranean. The chronological span permits us to observe the evolution of women's roles over time, both within a given civilization and, because of their interrelations, from one society to another. From this diverse and interactive cultural range and the extensive time span, a wealth of resources emerges pertaining to women. This comparative treatment displays clearly the relative valuation different cultures accorded to women and shows how women's prerogatives expanded or diminished across cultures connected by space and time.

Finally, modern researchers regard all these ancient civilizations as contributing to the development of the ideas central to Western thinking. We derive from these ancient civilizations the ways we perceive ourselves and the world, and the language and images we use to describe what we see. Consequently, appreciation of women's lives in these particular ancient cultures provides first of all a historical picture of how the women lived who are regarded as the ancestresses of women in the modern West. It also enables us to observe the changes that occurred in the development of women's roles from ancient times to the present, which makes possible a deeper understanding of the forces shaping women's lives today.

At the same time that the crescent of ancient cultures around the Mediterranean provides this tight focus, occasional comparisons with other African, Asian, and indigenous American societies help to illuminate the Mediterranean material by furnishing valuable perspectives that deepen our understanding of the primary material. Resources on indigenous American women help to establish women-centered ways of perceiving female roles, while women rulers and warriors from indigenous American and African societies expand the scope for examining these dimensions of women's activities. These occasional wider comparisons permit insights into the features that characterize women's lives in cultures globally, further enriching our principal exploration.

The evidence for this examination includes archeological, artistic, dramatic, historical, inscriptional, literary, medical, philosophical, poetic, and theological material. Understandably, extant remains of this varied evidence are unevenly distributed across these different cultures and periods. For various reasons, all documents require careful analysis within their cultural contexts in order to appreciate their meanings. The evidence comes largely from historical periods when patriarchal social institutions, which severely restricted women's activities in political, legal, and often economic arenas, were well established and written documents used to legitimate their normalcy. Concurrently, cultural artifacts increasingly delineated women's negative attributes, and openly misogynistic male writings suppressed earlier positive valuations.

Finally, the remaining texts come overwhelmingly from men, who themselves hailed from the elite class and lived in particular times. As noted, these texts rarely present self-evident descriptions of women's lives. Rather, they tend to reflect the thinking of the select individuals or class that produced them. Consequently, we must bear in mind what function the projection of female figures in the male-authored texts played in the larger social framework. This book's aim is to strike a meaningful balance among these projected images in order to retrieve genuine features of actual women's lives.

THEORETICAL PERSPECTIVES

The analytical framework for this book derives from an interweaving of feminist and multiethnic analyses across numerous disciplines (see Suggestions for Further Readings at the end of this book).

Contemporary scholarly trends seek to situate one's subject in its fuller cultural background. Consequently, the book's chapters each explore the significance of its topic within its cultural and historical placement. Thus, chapter 2 presents not only the evidence for goddess worship, but also explores what it meant to the members of the community to be worshipping female deities. Chapter 4 presents also the moral and cultural implications of women's health issues. And chapter 6 on female rulers first examines different decision-making structures and the various ways women have actively participated in their societies' governance. From this larger perspective we then view the few exceptional ruling women in ancient dynastic kingdoms.

Particularly important are the interwoven effects of women's centered and multiethnic analyses. This book takes a gynocentric approach that seeks to understand women's lives as much as possible from their own perspectives. It examines the ways women were active agents in their own lives, endowed with value and meaning, and not only the objects of societal repression. Hence, while the book reveals the restrictions their societies imposed on women, it accentuates the features that empowered women and that affirmed their active cultural participation. Most of the extant historical record derives from ancient cultures whose social institutions reflected the patriarchal thinking of the ruling social factions. This entailed, as Gerda Lerner well showed, the privileging of men throughout most cultural arenas, including familial, political, economic, religious, intellectual, and creative realms of activity.

However, it would be a mistake to think that the patriarchal forms these ancient societies exhibited were identical with the patriarchal shape of modern Western cultures. The time span covered by this book reveals various stages in the early development of patriarchal institutions. Thus, even if certain dimensions of contemporary society correspond to their analogous ancient features, we cannot automatically assume they carried the same boundaries, meanings, and values that we accord those aspects today. Rather, we must again examine our subject as fully as possible within its own cultural setting.

Pivotal for the approach of this book is research into indigenous American women's roles.[2] Whatever their influence on the subsequent development of Western culture, none of the ancient societies examined here exhibited features identical with those of modern Western society. Precisely because of their radical difference—meaning from the fundamental roots of cultural thinking—the indigenous American images present valuable alternative models for understanding women's placement within their cultural environments. In particular, certain concepts emerge as significant for the study of women in antiquity. These begin by according primacy to the spiritual realm, and by recognizing the centrality of female deities and of women's concerns as pivotal to the well-being of the community. These perceptions set the foundation for the various ways the society expressed its valuing of women's cultural roles.

The indigenous American material further displays a cultural outlook that recognizes women as autonomous human beings in complementary relationships with men, both sexes important for their contributions to the society. Because the valuation of women in the West has suffered severe deterioration, models from cultures that accord inherent value to women and to their social roles furnish essential other lenses for our historical examination of ancient women. This examination also gives attention where appropriate to men's roles and the relations between the two genders, both of which often serve to illuminate particular aspects of women's lives.

TOPIC ORGANIZATION

Chapter 1 looks at goddesses and their qualities in each culture, while chapter 2 examines the diverse ways women worshipped goddesses. From these fundamental cultural perceptions of divine female figures and the female rites that honored them the specific features of women's varied social roles developed, rooted in women's place in the family and the reproductive perpetuation of the community. Chapter 3 examines a woman's personal life from birth to death, while chapter 4 presents the ancient perceptions of women in the fields of health and medicine. Chapter 5 explores women's economic roles, from domestic-based unpaid and paid labor, to the diverse economic activities women performed.

Chapter 6 examines ways women participated in civic governance, and then spotlights the few women who reigned outright. Chapter 7 examines women's connection with war, from being its victim to highlighting the few women who actively engaged in warrior activities to exploring the legendary images of the Amazons. The final two chapters present women's own voices about their lives, beginning with ancient women's philosophical writings and concluding with women's poetry, which looks first at the varied range of subjects on which women wrote and ends with love poetry. Since women's own works represent a small percentage of the ancient sources, having the fuller understanding of women's lives first permits us to place women's own texts into their appropriate cultural background. This in turn enables us to see how women responded to and influenced the various aspects of their societal roles. This examination of the historical record includes artistic, literary, and mythic sources that help to animate and elucidate the artifactual evidence, and that provide connecting motifs throughout the narrative.

HISTORICAL BACKGROUND

Each chapter discusses the background pertinent to that chapter's topic. This section presents a general historical overview, which the timelines that directly precede- this introduction supplement. By the end of the third millennium, political developments in both Egypt and Mesopotamia resulted in the establishment of large monarchical kingdoms whose rule extended over ever-increasing territorial boundaries. These earliest world civilizations exhibited some similar features—a central hierarchical organization consolidated by the king who reigned at its apex; belief in the divine sanction of the king's right to rule; development of societal institutions that increasingly privileged men in all arenas of social activity; and evolution of a view of the gods that validated the hierarchical, patriarchal social organization. Historians identify two eras by their prevailing metallurgy—the second millennium is called the Bronze Age, followed by the Iron Age in the early first millennium.

These expanding ancient kingdoms kept the kinds of enduring records that enable us to investigate ancient cultures, including monumental building programs, increased production of durable material goods, and most importantly, writing. Writing crucially permits us to discern more specifically ancient peoples' ideas, beliefs, and institutions. Ushering in the "historical period," this new technology advanced the administration of these increasingly complex societies. From its functional, commercial origins, writing quickly developed into a literary poetic recording of religious, mythological, and cultural lore.

Also significant is the ancient development of social structures that characterize what come to be known as state societies, which differ substantially from tribal societies. A tribal community tends to be small, a collection of related family groups that work together as a cohesive entity for the good of the whole. State societies exhibit a centrally organized, hierarchical societal structure that typically has a single ruler or select group of rulers who command large groups of people across vast territories. Whatever their familial, clan, or regional networks of support, in state societies people owe their allegiance to the ruler or upper class, for whose benefit they labor. These basic characteristics emerge in the ancient monarchical kingdoms as well as in the representative forms of government developed by the Greek city-states and by the Roman Republic.

Changes in dwellings, residential and burial patterns, and other evidence in the prehistorical archaeological record contrast sharply with that deriving

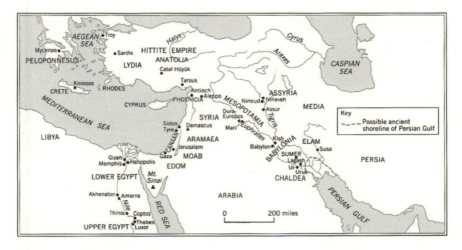

Ancient Anatolia, Egypt, Levant, and Mesopotamia. Reproduced from Fiero, Gloria K., *The Humanistic Tradition*, vol. 1, 3rd edition, 1998, McGraw-Hill, p. 27. Reproduced by permission of The McGraw-Hill Companies.

from the later known state societies. Like more recently documented pre-state societies, the ancient ones largely had loosely organized, egalitarian social structures, and they generally valued women highly for their essential procreative, productive, and creative contributions to the society. The ancient evidence from both pre-state and state societies shows that patriarchal social systems, far from being the norm, were new developments often closely tied to state formation. Remarkably, analogous shifts in societal formation and in women's roles have been documented in cultures worldwide, and sharp distinctions emerge in the perception of women and their cultural roles between pre-state societies and the complex structures of state organizational systems.

Egyptian history is identified by its ruling dynasties, which are grouped together into distinct periods. The principal divisions include the Old Kingdom—third to eighth dynasties, 2650–2135 B.C.E.—Middle Kingdom, eleventh to thirteenth dynasties, 2040–1640 B.C.E.—and New Kingdom, eighteenth to twentieth dynasties, 1550–1070 B.C.E. The first centuries B.C.E. and C.E. are known as the Late Period, when different foreign nations ruled Egypt, including the Ethiopians, Persians, Ptolemaic Greeks, and Romans. Dating to the Old Kingdom are Egyptian hieroglyphics, the pictographic system of writing called by the Greek term that means "sacred markings." The word reveals the sacred and mysterious way the later Greeks, and probably the Egyptians too, regarded the distinct shapes of the written characters and the ritualized purposes for which they were used.

Two linguistically distinct peoples comprised the ancient Mesopotamians. Sumerian civilization dates to the early third millennium B.C.E., when the Babylonians, a Semitic people speaking a language called Akkadian, appeared

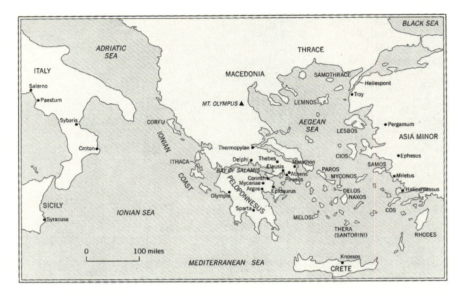

Ancient Greece. Reproduced from Fiero, Gloria K., *The Humanistic Tradition,* vol. 1, 3rd edition, 1998, McGraw-Hill, p. 63. Reproduced by permission of The McGraw-Hill Companies.

in the region. Mesopotamian ruling periods began with the Babylonian Sargon, the first to dominate the two groups of people, 2350–2193 B.C.E., followed by the Neo-Sumerian period, 2110–2004 B.C.E. Subsequently, the south was divided into Old, Middle, and Neo-Babylonian periods, while another Semitic group, the Assyrians, ruled the north, analogously divided into Old, Middle, and Neo-Assyrian periods. Like Egypt, later Mesopotamian history witnessed domination by the Persians, Greeks, and Romans. The Sumerians' cuneiform, wedge-shaped characters, may be the earliest system of writing in the world.

Ancient Greece experienced a more variegated political history. In the third to early second millennia B.C.E. the basically peaceful Minoan civilization on Crete and the nearby islands, where women held important cultural roles, maintained powerful contacts with Egypt and the Levant. Although the warlike, Indo-European Mycenaeans conquered the Minoans in about 1450 B.C.E., they adopted many features of Minoan civilization, including ruling structures, religious ideas, art, and writing. The Mycenaeans transformed the Minoan syllabary, which represented consonant and vowel combinations, into their Linear B, an early form of Greek. All later Greek mythological tales and the foundation of most Greek cities and religious institutions may be traced to the Mycenaean civilization, 1600–1100 B.C.E. Unlike the Egyptians and Mesopotamians, the Mycenaeans remained distinct, sovereign principalities under locally ruling monarchs, never uniting into a large, consolidated kingdom.

Concurrent with the Mycenaeans, another Indo-European civilization, the Hittites, ruled over north central Anatolia, the land base also known as Asia Minor, modern-day Turkey. The Hittites at various times conquered parts of Mesopotamia, the Levant, and Egypt, and they wrote in a cuneiform script. Their documents relate battles on their western frontier that correspond to the Trojan War of legendary Greek fame, circa 1200 B.C.E. This war for material gain and territorial expansion epitomizes the central activities of Mycenaean rulers, and it augurs the demise of all Bronze Age civilizations. Later Greek oral traditions privileged the Trojan War as the momentous event through which they perceived their past and fashioned their identity five hundred years later.

After the collapse of Mycenaean civilization, historical Greek material emerged in the Archaic period, eighth to sixth centuries B.C.E., during which time distinctive Greek institutions developed. Writing was reintroduced from Phoenicia as an alphabet, the prototype of the current Greek, Cyrillic, and European alphabets. Coinage was introduced from Lydia in Anatolia. Greeks embarked on massive colonization—in the east on the western coast of Anatolia, known as Ionia; to north Africa at Kyrene, west of Egypt; and in southern Italy, Sicily, and the south coast of France in the west. The Greek political system of distinctive, sovereign city-states—the *polis*—emerged. Most important were two *poleis:* Sparta, which had the longest, most stable polity ruled by a diarchy—two kings—and elite male citizens. Athens endured a more turbulent history of kings and tyrants until it developed an incipient democracy in 509 B.C.E. These cultural developments were consolidated during the Classical period, fifth to fourth centuries B.C.E., and Greek civilization—Hellenism—spread to Egypt and Mesopotamia after Alexander's conquests in the Hellenistic period, third to first centuries B.C.E.

Roman sources dated their origins to the eighth century B.C.E., when the Etruscan civilization, which had much contact with the Greeks, reigned in central and northern Italy. A monarchy of mostly Etruscan kings was overturned and the Roman Republic established in 510 B.C.E. Rome first expanded its rule over Italy and then aimed to conquer other Mediterranean lands. It defeated its mighty rival Carthage, in modern Tunisia, in three Punic Wars, and by the beginning of the Roman Empire, 30 B.C.E., Rome's rule extended over north Africa, the Levant, Anatolia, Greece, and central and western Europe. At its farthest extent within the next two centuries Roman imperial rule reached from Persia to Scotland, before it too dissolved by the late fourth century due to internal breakdowns and repeated incursions from foreign invaders. In 324 C.E., Constantine, the first emperor to declare Christianity the official imperial religion, founded Constantinople on the ancient site of Byzantion, modern Istanbul, where flourished the Greek Byzantine Empire until its conquest by the Ottoman Turks in 1453.

The material from across these diverse ancient civilizations provides an illuminating portrayal of the evolution in ancient social perceptions of women. We can historically trace the diminishing value accorded women and notions of the female from the earliest documents in the historical record to those

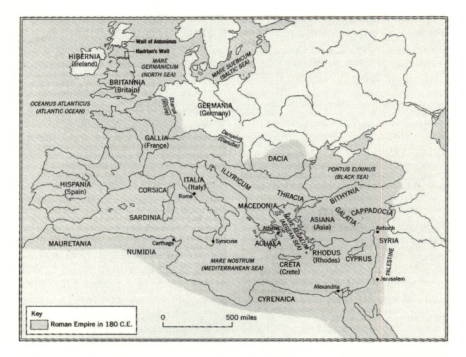

The Roman Empire in 180 C.E. Reproduced from Fiero, Gloria K., *The Humanistic Tradition*, vol. 1, 3rd edition, 1998, McGraw-Hill, p. 131. Reproduced by permission of The McGraw-Hill Companies.

emerging later in antiquity, when patriarchal ideas increasingly predominated in shaping people's lives. This book's beginning focus on goddesses and women's rituals provides a foundation comprised of the widest possible positive views ancient peoples held of women and of female figures, views that almost certainly persisted from earlier times. This foundation supplies an edifying perspective from which to observe the subsequent changes in the conception of goddesses and in women's social roles. These changes in turn reveal the shifts in cultural thinking that found concrete expression in the types of activities these ancient cultures permitted to women.

SPELLING AND ABBREVIATIONS

In the interest of understanding each people on their own terms as far as possible, I commonly transliterate Greek terms rather than using the conventional Latin forms. Thus, I use "k" not "c" for Greek kappa, and render Greek syllables as "ai," "oi," "on," and "os," rather than the Latin forms of "ae," "oe," "um," and "us." These more direct renditions of the Greek yield: Kleopatra for Cleopatra, *hetaira* for *hetaera*, Byzantion for Byzantium, or Ephesos for Ephesus. However, common place names or names that would entail too many changes remain unchanged, such as Aeschylus, Corinth, and Mycenae.

In accord with modern scholarly practice, the dating classification used in this book is B.C.E., "Before the Common Era," and C.E., "the Common Era." These provide neutral designations that correspond to the Western calendrical divisions of B.C. and A.D., respectively.

Figure 0.3 Earring with Nike driving a two-horse chariot, gold. Greek, ca. 350–325 B.C.E. Henry Lillie Pierce Fund 98.788, Museum of Fine Arts, Boston.

Figure 0.4 Goddess Nut spreading her wings in protection over the deceased, detail of painted coffin, painted wood. Egyptian New Kingdom, 21st or 22nd dynasty. Werner Forman/Art Resource, NY, The British Museum, London, Great Britain.

One

Ancient Goddesses—The Primacy of Female Divinity

"In the beginning, the Creator made our Mother Earth. Then came Selu, Grandmother Corn." Thus Cherokee poet Marilou Awiakta, quoting a Cherokee medicine man, sets the spiritual basis for her portrait of Selu, the Cherokee Corn-Mother, in *Selu: Seeking the Corn-Mother's Wisdom*. Awiakta elaborates, "Used in this ritual sense, 'Grandmother' connotes 'Mother of Us All,' a spirit being who is eternally wise."[1] Awiakta's book shows the primal centrality of Selu to Cherokee beliefs and conduct, both as traditionally conceived and as those traditions may be relevantly and valuably applied to the modern world. Such ongoing dynamic belief systems in the primacy of female deity, characteristic of many cultures around the world, provide a valuable modern entry point for an exploration of ancient goddess worship.

PREHISTORIC REPRESENTATIONS

Paleolithic Images: Female Fertility and Wild Nature

Archaeological and early historical records worldwide reveal that the first deities human beings worshipped were female. Goddesses characteristically oversaw the spheres of fertility, birth, nurturance, sustenance, and protection. The oldest depictions of female figures accentuated their fertile capabilities. This emphasis persisted throughout Europe, the Near East, and North Africa across thousands of years of time. Unclothed Paleolithic figurines from about 25,000–20,000 B.C.E., called "Venus" figures, epitomize the concept of the fertile female—rotund figures with full breasts, belly, and buttocks that exemplify a body-centered focus on female fecundity.

Early peoples perceived the natural world as sacred and female. The many cave paintings by the pastoral-hunting-incipient agricultural peoples living in the Tassili N'Ajjer range of the eastern Sahara, western Libya, about 7000–5000 B.C.E. show female and male figures herding, hunting, fighting, and spending time with their families. A painting of superb quality called the "Horned Goddess of Aouanrhet" (Figure 1.1) depicts a dancing female figure filled with

1

Figure 1.1 Horned Goddess of Aouanrhet, cave painting. Tassili N'Ajjer range, western Libya. By permission of the Flammarion Groupe.

ritual symbols. White dots of scarification swoop across her shoulders, torso, breasts, and calves. She sports a fringed loincloth and long-fringed bands on her upper arms and around her calves, while fringed mittens encase her hands and wrists. The effect of these accoutrements is striking: magical, mysterious, intimating ritual status and supernatural powers.

Through the millennia goddesses of animals and wild nature will bear the horns of the cow or the crescent moon depicted behind this figure's head. Researchers interpret the row of bristles over her head as a wheat field showering forth its grains. In light of the other cave paintings and of the time period—right on the threshold of the Neolithic—this figure may literally represent the divine female's transition from a goddess of the wild into the female deity that instead cultivates the wild and thus imparts this sacred, life-sustaining knowledge to human beings. The later over-painting of the smaller, headless figures seem intended to invoke the female image for her divine warrior powers.

Neolithic Images: Female Fertility and the Cultivated Earth

The emphasis on fertility in the Paleolithic "Venus" figurines is evident in early Neolithic representations, superbly illustrated by the full-bodied seated female figure from Çatal Höyük, south central Turkey, seventh millennium

B.C.E. (Figure 1.2). Almost twenty thousand years after the earliest known "Venus" image, this Anatolian statue displays both the ample breasts, belly, and buttocks of the former figures and the goal of the long-lasting visual spotlighting of the fertile female body. Seated on a birthing throne, the Çatal Höyük figure is depicted in the process of giving birth, a scene repeated in some wall paintings. Flanked by two panthers, the statue perpetuates the female divinity's connection with the wild.

Whether representing a human or divine being, the Çatal Höyük birthing images depict a valuing of women's fundamental biological activities that their communities considered important enough to display visually. Like paintings of the hunt, portrayals of females giving birth may have held magico-religious and ritual significance, the prominence of the goddess's act of giving birth critical to insure a mortal woman's successful labor.

The Çatal Höyük figure well illustrates the perception of female fertility in agricultural societies, when goddesses of fertility were strongly identified with the bounty of the earth. The earth was personified as a mother, a living, nurturing female being who sustained life through her produce, and to

Figure 1.2 Seated female figure with panthers, terracotta, with reconstructed head. Çatal Höyük. By permission of the Museum of Anatolian Civilizations, Ankara, Turkey.

whom human women were likened. Conflating the two realms, goddesses represented both the fertility of the earth and of women, both major concerns to ancient societies. Consequently, people regarded the earth, together with her bounty and her divine and human female incarnations, all as sacred. Worship of earth goddesses was fundamental to the belief systems and the ritual calendars of these ancient civilizations.

Further emblematic of female fertility and emphasizing a woman's nurturant powers are the frequent depictions of the nursing mother, known by the Greek name, *kourotrophos,* "child-nurturer." With roots reaching deep into the Neolithic Period, these images span the Mediterranean throughout antiquity. Egyptian Isis nursing Horus (Figure 1.3) well illustrates the type.

Bronze Age Images: Female Desire and Sexuality

Bronze Age statuettes exhibited new, slenderized bodies, which might reflect changing cultural ideals of the feminine. Despite the slenderizing of the female body, these figures remained connected to the earlier, more obvious fertility

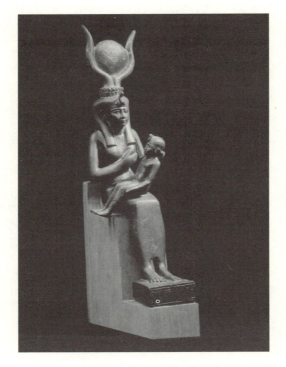

Figure 1.3 Isis and Horus, bronze. Serapeum, Sakkara, Egypt. Photographer, J. D. Dallet. By permission of the Egyptian Museum of Cairo, Egypt.

images. The thousands of early third millennium B.C.E. marble female Cycladic figurines portray this slimmer and yet pregnant female body, exquisitely exemplified by Figure 0.2. An early second millennium Mesopotamian clay plaque, called "Queen of the Night" (Figure 1.4), sensually portrays a winged goddess, probably Ishtar, facing forward with full breasts and a marked pubic triangle. Characterizing her deep connection with animals, she stands on two panthers, holds hooped snakes in each hand, and large owls, also facing front, flank her on either side. The pose of these female figures continues to draw the viewer's gaze to the breasts, belly, and pubes, emphasizing their sexuality.

The distinctive marking of the pubic triangle reveals a crucial dimension in ancient notions of fertility. Considering more than the end result of crop or baby production, ancient thinking encompassed the range of activities that resulted in fertility. As later literary records articulated, concepts of beauty, seduction, erotic desire, and sexuality were embedded in the realms

Figure 1.4 Queen of the Night, clay plaque. Old Babylonian, ca. 1800–1750 B.C.E. The British Museum/Art Resource, NY, London, Great Britain.

overseen by goddesses of fertility. All these features were valued not only as markers of fertility but also for the distinctive pleasures they provided. Consequently, ancient peoples celebrated goddesses and their human incarnations for bringing to humankind the divine delights of eroticism and sexuality, prized for their own sakes and for the offspring they engendered.

Ample-bodied, nude Paleolithic and early Neolithic depictions of the female appeared to emphasize the reproductive and maternal aspects of a woman's body. Sensuous Bronze Age portrayals of full-figured goddesses visually display the delights of erotic desire and sexuality that suggest a more sensual glorification of the female body. Nude portrayals of these presumably divine female figures of desire and sexuality did not continue after the development of patriarchal civilizations. Although goddesses of sexuality and fertility continued to be openly praised for their erotic and reproductive powers in both ritual and literature, their visual portrayals conformed to the proper dress of their society's elite women.

HISTORICAL PERIOD

The introduction of writing discloses the cosmologies ancient cultures developed, and the many roles female deities played. All these ancient civilizations were polytheistic, worshipping many gods and goddesses who were seen to be immortal and more powerful than human beings, but who often exhibited human traits. The world was perceived as alive and animated by divine spirits, and the principal deities were responsible for major forces of nature, society, or human activity. Uniquely, the Egyptian pharaoh, Akhnaten, mid-fifteenth century B.C.E., promoted the worship of a single, male god. But Akhnaten's successors immediately rejected his religious revisions, nor did monotheism take hold even among Jewish worshippers until a much later period. Each society's pantheon, that is, its arrangement of all the gods, unmistakably reflected their patriarchal social organization with a male deity as the hierarchical head of the divine assembly. Although male gods reigned in the cosmological tales, the worship of female deities, typically associated with the most fundamental aspects of life, were vital to people's spiritual and religious lives and to the well-being of the entire community.

Creation Goddesses

Everywhere goddesses were the original creators, who formed features of the landscape, created human beings, and often gave birth to other gods. Illustrative is the ancient Babylonian tale describing the creation of the first human beings by the Mother Goddess Ninhursag, who mixed blood from a slain god with clay, from which she then pinched off fourteen pieces to form seven pairs of humans, female and male. The text indicates that the song Ninhursag sang over her newly created beings developed into a chant sung for women in labor. This provided a powerful connection between the mythic and the everyday, by situating both the birth giver and the infant in a sacred context.

The earliest layers of all stories reflect the primacy of female deity in the origin of the cosmos—Mesopotamian Tiamat, "Salt Water," Egyptian Neith, Greek Gaia, "Earth." Neith initially ruled supreme, while Gaia first produced a few offspring on her own before she created her own consort Ouranos, "Sky." In all these tales the power of the originating female deity was soon overcome, and the official accounts of cosmic or divine creation did not develop from the stories of these original creator goddesses. However the original deities came into being, once they are sexually paired into female and male, they inaugurate the sexual reproduction of the gods, which produces the deities important in that culture's historical ideologies and beliefs. Moreover, in all these stories the succession of ruling gods proceeds violently.

Official Egyptian theology showed a supreme male Atum supplanting the original creating goddess Neith. The emerging canonical tales related that Atum came into being of himself, embodying both female and male principles, and that he then spit out the first paired divinities, male Shu, "Air," and female Tefnut, "Moisture." This pair initiated sexual copulation to produce the next generations of deities—Geb, "Earth," and Nut, "Sky," from whose mating Nut gave birth to Isis and Osiris, Nephthys and Seth, deities crucial for the maintenance of Egyptian society, rulership, and ideas about the afterlife.

In the Egyptian tale, violence erupts between the two brothers, as Seth kills Osiris to seize the rule for himself and discards Osiris' dismembered body into the Nile. Reflecting perhaps different sororal relations enjoyed by girls, together with her sister Nephthys, Isis temporarily resurrects the body of her brother Osiris, and, getting impregnated by his sperm, bears Horus, the falcon, who grows to avenges his father's death and claim the rule, establishing before the other gods his legitimate right to the throne. From this tale of male sibling rivalry and female collaboration emerged major figures of Egyptian cosmology—Osiris reigns over the underworld, and Horus represents every living Egyptian pharaoh. Isis and Nephthys, maintaining the image of mutual female assistance, together with other goddesses aid the dead on their journey to the next world.

Differing from the Egyptian creation account, the Mesopotamian and Greek creation tales displayed similar patterns of gender and generational conflicts, with a marked diminution over the generations of the female's power and the ascendancy of a single male to supreme authority. Greek Gaia, as seen, gives birth to her consort Ouranos, and she helps her son and grandson defeat their fathers in the subsequent generational battles. But Gaia's greater originating power ultimately yields to the supreme authority of her grandson Zeus.

For the Mesopotamians the initial mingling of Tiamat with her consort Apsu, "Fresh Water," culminates in the fifth generation with the supremacy of the god Marduk, who kills Tiamat and cuts her body in two to form the earth and the sky. The beginning of Genesis linguistically echoes this mythologized act of creation—the substance from which the biblical God fashions the heavens and earth, called *t'hom,* often translated as "the deep," is derived from the name Tiamat.

The violence characterizing the succession of the gods no doubt reflects bloody transitions in dynastic rule. The same fundamental sociohistorical dynamics, with their distinctive cultural variations, emerge throughout these tales—after the greater power of the primal female deity and several generations of paired deities, the final generation culminates in the supreme rule of a male deity. The stories severely attenuate or entirely suppress the role of the original goddesses, and they portray the goddesses important in later generations as subordinate to the reigning male deity. Buttressed by archaeological and documentary evidence, these stories portray the expanding power of patriarchal thinking and the correspondingly decreasing valuation of actual women that marked the fourth to first millennia B.C.E. Nevertheless, these mythological scenarios of cosmic succession do not fully represent how the ancients thought about their gods and goddesses. These stories highlight the greater authority accorded to men in political terms, and to some extent to male deities in cultural belief and ritual practice. Despite the social restrictions imposed on women, belief in and rites for goddesses long continued fundamental to cultural practices. Egyptian Hathor and Mesopotamian Ishtar, both central to their respective culture's religious observances, are missing from the official accounts of creation, while the ritual importance of Greek goddesses like Demeter or Hera never emerges from the elaborate genealogy of the Greek gods Hesiod presented in his *Theogony*. These tales also ignore the fundamental role of goddesses like Egyptian Nut in maintaining cosmic order. Hence, these official creation accounts had a complex relationship to their societies' actual beliefs and practices that display only in part the perceptions people held about their goddesses.

Goddesses—Diverse Associations

Besides the association of goddesses with the fertility of the earth, animals, crops, and human women that continued throughout antiquity, ancient cultures attributed various qualities to their goddesses. Goddesses represented the sky and prominent celestial bodies. In ancient Egyptian cosmology Nut and her male counterpart Geb contrast with the almost universal association of female deities with the earth and male ones with the sky. Likewise, Egyptian Hathor was a sun goddess, an association she had to share with the Egyptian sun god, Re. Hathor and Isis had connections with both the sun and the moon, which was also represented by a male deity, Hathor's son, Khonsu. Although the Mesopotamians too had a god of the moon, Sin or Nanna, it was the moon god's untamed daughter, Inanna/Ishtar, who visually and mythologically represented this heavenly body.

A Minoan gold ring from Crete depicts female deity in association with the sun, moon, and the whole sky. The later Greeks and Romans represented the moon as female—Greek Artemis or Hekate and Roman Diana. The observable lunar cycles presented powerful analogies for women's own monthly cycles. Furthermore, a tripartite division of the moon's changes into waxing, full, and waning metaphorically represented what were seen as the three major stages of a woman's life—girlhood, mature, fertile womanhood, and postchildbearing age.

Female spirits often represented natural features, perceived as divinely animated trees, water, plants, and stars. The Tree of Life was a central image in ancient goddess-worshipping cultures, prominently depicted in all art. Egyptian Hathor was invoked as the Sycamore Tree Goddess, Mesopotamian Inanna/Ishtar was always shown either by her tree, the palm, or with identifying palm fronds, and Greek Athena was known by her signature tree, the olive. The Greeks also believed in numerous female nature spirits called nymphs, who were further identified by their location—oreads, mountain nymphs, dryads, wood nymphs, and so forth.

Several goddesses illustrate the concept presented by Laguna Pueblo scholar Paula Gunn Allen that to call the female creating deity only a fertility goddess limits our perception of her powers.[2] Many ancient goddesses represented creative activities, including the arts, language, knowledge, wisdom, and social harmony. For the Greeks, Mnemosyne, "Memory," and her daughters, the Nine Muses, inspired all creative activity, including the proper governance of the society, a scope also embraced by the Egyptian goddess of music, Merit. Interestingly, female divinities often oversaw areas of activity from which actual women were excluded. Mesopotamian Nisaba and Egyptian Seshat were their respective culture's goddesses of writing, even though in both societies men held formal scribal positions.

Similarly, despite actual women's almost total exclusion from formal avenues of political governance, goddesses often insured the proper functioning of the society. Egyptian Ma'at and Nut and Greek Themis represented the cosmic order of society. Ishtar was an important city deity for the ancient Mesopotamians, supporting the king in his rule and insuring the well-being of the community. A carved plaque from the middle of the third millennium B.C.E. portrays a crowned, enthroned Inanna, holding a branch of her date palm in her right hand, her long locks curling over her shoulders, gazing powerfully out at the viewer. Likewise, the prevalent image of the "Goddess in the Window," such as Figure 1.13, also depicts her powerful role as protector of the home and city. The Greek goddesses Athena and Hera enjoyed similar civic oversight, while at public sanctuaries ancient Greeks worshipped, as divine, entities that we regard as abstract personifications, like Dike, "Justice," and Peitho, "Persuasion." Gaining the favor of these divine female powers enabled men to achieve their political goals.

Goddesses of Destruction and Death

Goddesses were commonly perceived as embracing the totality of life's processes, the ongoing cycle of life, death, regeneration, and transformation. Consequently, people regarded these primal goddesses as the source of everything, both the beneficial blessings humans received and the fearsome events of disease, punishment, and death they suffered. The powers encompassed by Mesopotamian Inanna/Ishtar and Egyptian Hathor well represent this range. On the one hand they were honored for their fundamental life-producing powers of fecundity, while other images revealed their violent, fearsome qualities. Inanna's warrior aspects will be treated in chapter 7. For the Egyptians, Hathor figured as one of several "Angry Goddesses" who stops her human-killing rampage in the myth of "The Destruction of Mankind" only when she gets drunk on beer colored with red ocher to resemble blood. These tales portray these destructive sides of female divinities as merely one aspect in the broad span of a goddess's power. Indeed, Hathor's bloody rampage turns into the vehicle for how beautiful women came to be.

In their association with death, goddesses appeared as kindly or maleficent depending on the culture's view of the afterlife. In Egyptian beliefs in a splendid afterworld, at least for society's elite, several goddesses held important funerary roles. Images of Neith, Isis, Nephthys, and Selket were placed at the head and foot of coffins to protect the deceased and to insure their rebirth in the underworld. Paintings of a voluptuous, nude Nut adorned lids of coffins to welcome the dead into their new life (Figure 1.5).

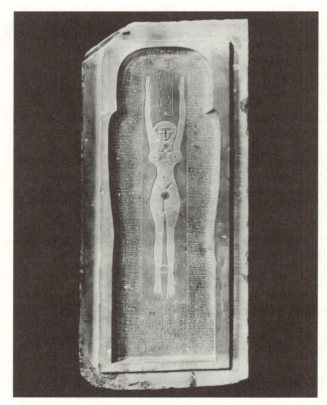

Figure 1.5 Nut inside coffin of God's wife Ankhnesneferi-bre. 2400 B.C.E. Copyright © The Trustees of the British Museum.

Hathor, so strongly associated with fertility in this world, was also known as "Mistress of the Desert," the place for burials, or "Mistress of the West," the realm of the dead. Believed to protect the dead, nude female figurines representing Hathor were placed in the burials of men, women, and children in order to facilitate their rebirth into the next life. The Egyptians further celebrated Hathor's key role in supplying the crucial link between the living and the dead by sharing ritual meals with the deceased at funerals and annual festivals for the dead. By contrast, in the gloomier Mesopotamian view of the afterlife, Ereshkigal, the queen of the underworld, loomed as another embodiment of harmful forces.

In time, rather than embracing a spectrum of life-producing, degenerative, and transformative powers, increasing division into discrete powers for good or harm characterized the evolution of ancient Greek and Roman goddesses, who became emblematic of fearsome, negative forces, such as the Greek powers of vengeance called the Furies, and Nemesis, "Punishment." These negative female powers turned increasingly monstrous, like the hideous, screeching creatures, the Harpies, who befouled and stole their victims' food.

INDIVIDUAL GODDESSES

Egypt

Goddesses held immense importance in ancient Egyptian religious cosmology, beliefs, and practices. Different goddesses rose to central prominence in Egypt's four-thousand-year ancient history. While goddesses had their own distinctive qualities, they encompassed multiple aspects and shared many attributes. Far from being problematic, this overlap seemed to reinforce the powers each goddess held. In their association with the natural world, many held some connection to the annual flooding of the Nile, from which they were goddesses of fertility—of land, crops, animals, and humans.

Egyptian goddesses represented diverse animals. Many were depicted with a lion's head, perceived as embodying the power, strength, and fierceness that lions possess. Several were conceptualized as a cow goddess, often depicted as suckling the future king and as welcoming the dead to their new realm, portrayals that accentuated the cow's nurturant qualities. Others carried the traits of snakes, which were looked on as sacred, beneficial animals, as elsewhere throughout the ancient Mediterranean. The power of the snake goddess took shape as the uraeus, which the pharaoh wore on his crown for protection and as a sign of power. Another common association was as a tree goddess, notably as Egypt's oldest hardwood tree, the sycamore.

Egyptian goddesses fulfilled two critical social roles. The principal goddesses were at all times supporters of the royal line, often portrayed as mother of the king and as sanctioning the pharaoh's right to rule. In their tomb paintings, rulers had themselves depicted as being nursed by one of these goddesses. Queens and queen mothers identified with the principal female deities and typically served as their priestesses. Moreover, the insignia of the pharaoh's power as Lord of the Two Lands incorporated the vulture image of Nekhbet in the White Crown of Upper Egypt (the Nile headwaters in the south) and the cobra image of Wadjet in the Red Crown of Lower Egypt (the delta in the north). The predynastic powers of these two goddesses did not continue in the later canon. However, as frequently occurs, in establishing a new dynastic rule over combined northern and southern lands, the new king could not completely eradicate their memory but had to appropriate their power into his in order to legitimate his rule.

Most significantly, all goddesses played crucial roles in guiding the dead on their journey to the next world and enabling their blessed rebirth. Although early in the dynastic period the land of the dead was identified as the realm of Osiris, female deities were worshipped for protecting the dead and for warmly receiving them in the next world into their womanly embrace, which underscored the goddesses' highly revered benign power.

This broad power of Egyptian goddesses experienced a steady decline across four thousand years of ancient Egyptian history. The original female creator goddesses were eclipsed as the official divine canon was formed, which accorded the role of primary creator to a male deity. By the first millennium, the status of many shifted from a mother goddess to a daughter of the male deity, with the consequent loss in power and authority such changes imply.

Hathor

For much of ancient Egyptian history Hathor was the most important goddess worshipped. She embraced numerous powers—she was connected with the sun, sexuality, fertility, women's concerns, prostitutes, well-being of the community, war, and death. The earliest references to Hathor (ca. 2600–2500 B.C.E.) emphasize her role as a solar goddess. The Pyramid Texts of that period, which call her "the Eye of the Sun," portray her as embodying the light and warmth that radiate from the center of the sun's disk. As the consort of the chief Egyptian deity, the sun god Re, Hathor was called God's Wife and was considered the divine mother of the king of Egypt. Egyptian queens down to Kleopatra VII identified with Hathor and served as her priestesses.

Hathor embraced the powers essential for both the living and the dead. Revered as a goddess of fertility, her images and rituals emphasized the delights of the activities that result in reproduction—sexuality, music, dance, and drunkenness. All are ecstatic activities prized for the sensual enjoyment they provide as much as for the offspring that will result. Hathor brought these same powers that insure the happiness and continuity of the living to the dead, who required Hathor's support in order to be reborn in the next world. Tomb paintings typically show her holding—alone or together—a sistrum (a hand-held percussive instrument), the ankh, and the *menat* necklace, both symbols of life. All three items iconographically identified Hathor, and they signified the aid and blessings she bestowed on the deceased as they made their journey into the next world. Figure 1.6 depicts Hathor holding up her *menat* necklace with her right hand to the dead king Sety I while taking him by his right hand. He reaches for the necklace with his left.

During the time of her preeminence, Hathor was represented as the Sycamore Tree Goddess, as the uraeus, and especially as the cow goddess, an image that stressed her beneficence to the living and the dead. She was also a major lion goddess—it is as a lion that Hathor as the "Angry Goddess" ravages humankind, a potent force for both destruction and growth.

Isis

Isis was mentioned in the earliest references, and she played a major role in the canonical divine succession, but her importance as a deity worshipped came much later, from the second millennium B.C.E. Isis's powers included fertility, successful harvest, women's concerns, motherhood, making of kings, magic, cures, destiny, and death. Isis was identified with Sirius, the Dog Star, whose rising in midsummer heralded the inundation of the Nile. Thus Isis embodied this inundation and the renewal of the parched land just as she revived her brother-consort Osiris in the stories. As the mother of Horus, Isis too was considered a mother of kings, perhaps equated with the highly important role of Queen Mother. In this capacity Isis was the per-

Figure 1.6 Hathor as Mistress of the Western Desert greets the dead King Sety I, painted plaster on limestone. Réunion des Musées Nationaux / Art Resource, NY, Louvre, Paris, France.

sonified throne, the one who transformed the prince into king. In contrast to Hathor, whose connection with fertility emphasized the sexual ecstasies that lead to regeneration, Isis was identified as a mother, and her images typically portrayed her as nursing her son Horus (Figure 1.3).

This different emphasis of the two may explain the rising appeal of Isis as Hathor's popularity declined by the end of the second millennium B.C.E., a shifting dynamic that no doubt reflected changes in cultural thinking. With advancing patriarchal notions of female sexual chastity, open celebrations of female sexuality appeared increasingly problematic, and it became correspondingly difficult to sustain belief in the wholesomeness of such rites or of the goddesses who sanctioned them.

In Egypt, Isis' focus on motherhood allowed the concern with fertility to shift from the erotic delights of sexuality to the child that results from intercourse and to the maternal, nurturing qualities of the goddess. The images of Isis offering her breast to the infant Horus exemplified this focus. Whereas Hathor epitomized the sensual joys of sexuality and erotic desire, Isis stressed maternal and familial love. By spotlighting Isis's motherhood, female sexuality accorded with changing social mores. Moreover, since Isis impregnated herself magically from the body of the temporarily revived Osiris and not from normal copulation, her story supplants the role intercourse plays in reproduction. One late source attributes to Isis the invention of marriage, the socially legitimate arena for sexual expression. The Christian story of the mortal Mary's immaculate conception of the divine Jesus demonstrates the consequences of this process, which now bypasses sexual intercourse entirely and focuses on a sorrowing, mournful mother figure. Perhaps Mary's sadness is at the loss of the exuberant celebration of female sexuality that Hathor, Inanna/Ishtar, Ashtarte, and others so gloriously embodied for millennia.

This shift from worship of Hathor to Isis emerged in other ways as well. Expanding from the New Kingdom through the late antique period, Isis was increasingly portrayed with the iconographical insignia that had formerly identified Hathor. She is only once represented as a cow, but she supplanted Hathor in the sun bark and appeared with the sun disk and cow's horns headdress characteristic of Hathor (see Figures 1.3, 1.6–1.7). As noted, Isis and her sister Nephthys played crucial roles in guiding and protecting the dead, and their images, sometimes together with those of other goddesses, were placed at the head and foot of coffins for this purpose. As Isis came to ascendancy, she overtook Hathor's central role as official greeter of the deceased and the one who would insure the dead's blessed transition to the next world— Figure 1.7 portrays her greeting the dead Queen Nefertari with the ankh in her right hand.

Isis was also invoked for medicinal cures and for magical charms for both blessings and curses. Those seeking physical or psychological cures slept overnight at Isis's temples, and temple officials interpreted their dreams the next day. Isis's blood, which probably represented menstrual blood, was considered powerful, and red cloths symbolic of her blood were wrapped around the mummy for protection. Isis proclaimed the destiny of the newborn; such predictions characterized the New Year, known as Isis's

Figure 1.7 Queen Nefertari offering to Isis, her tomb wall painting. By permission of The Getty Conservation Institute. Copyright © The J. Paul Getty Trust 1992. All rights reserved.

Birthday. Late texts called her "Mistress of life, ruler of fate and destiny"— her ability to overcome destiny augmented her appeal as a savior goddess. With few exceptions, Isis did not appear in animal form, and so stood out as a more human, less strange or fierce deity than others.

By the end of the ancient period, Isis had absorbed the powers of many other goddesses to be considered supreme over all. Isis's appeal climbed steadily among the ancient Egyptians, who revered her for her multiple qualities, and soon spread beyond the borders of Egypt, as first Greeks and then Romans avidly adopted her worship. Remains of her temples can be found across Europe as far as northern England. Besides the music, dance, and cultic drama characterizing other Egyptian rites, distinctive features of Isis worship included a professional priesthood, who were identified by their shaved heads and pure white linen dress and who mounted elaborate public processions.

One may well ask what made Isis so universally appealing in the ancient Mediterranean polytheistic world filled with powerful goddesses. First, in the ancient religious perceptions that frequently separated concepts of divinity and human morality, Isis brought morality to religious belief, a movement that had been growing throughout the Near East and Greece since the Bronze Age. Secondly, Isis's Egyptian promise of a comforting afterlife would have attracted many followers, the same promise that made Jesus's teaching so appealing several centuries later. This promise of salvation was a distinctive new feature among ancient Mediterranean religious practices, which focused foremost on maintaining public rites for community deities.

Moreover, Isis's promise of salvation seemed more assuring than the mystery religions' offers of blessedness in the next world.

Neith

A New Kingdom text calls Neith "the eldest, the Mother of the gods, who shone on the first face,"[3] suggesting that she was the first deity of the Egyptian cosmos—her symbols appeared on late fourth-millennium predynastic pottery. An even later text invokes her as the mother of Re who began the process of reproduction by birth, and she may well have figured as an original creator goddess before the official dynastic divine genealogy was established. Never paired with a husband, Neith created land features and other gods with her heart. Neith was associated with the inundation of the Nile, oversaw weavers, and was represented both as a rising cobra, a protective image, and as a crocodile, a dangerous and terrifying one.

Known as Mistress of the Bow and Ruler of Arrows, Neith had as her symbol two crossed arrows, marking her as a warrior deity invoked for success in battle. Associated with the Delta city of Sais, Neith represented the predynastic political entity of the north. Once the pharaoh of Upper Egypt conquered Lower Egypt, it was Neith's red crown that he wore together with the south's white one to signify his status as Lord of the Two Lands. Neith also appeared as a protector of the living and the dead king, while the deceased were believed to acquire Neith's power.

By the early third millennium, Hathor began to eclipse Neith as the goddess of central religious importance. However, the memory of Neith's original role persisted, as she provided important benefices, reemerging as the creating mother goddess in the mid-second millennium B.C.E. When the rulers of Sais eventually commanded both Upper and Lower Egypt in the sixth century B.C.E., Neith briefly replaced the long-reigning chief of the gods, Amun-Re, as head of the divine pantheon.

Nut

Nut, the Sky, another ancient goddess, was the daughter of the first couple in the official genealogy. Impregnated by her brother-consort Geb, Nut bore the important deities Isis, Nephthys, Osiris, and Seth. Nut also bore the sun god Re, the supreme god of the Egyptian pantheon for most of its ancient history. Hence, she was addressed as mother of the gods, one who was already powerful in her own mother's womb. Paintings typically depicted Nut bent over the earth, which her toes and hands touch while her body spans the sky. Each night Nut swallows the sun, whom she bears anew each morning from her birth canal. Both visual and literary imagery portrayed her as providing the framework of the world and as maintaining the fundamental order of the cosmos, while in her association with the natural world, Nut was frequently portrayed as the Sycamore Tree Goddess.

Nut, the original cow goddess, represented the annual flooding of the Nile; hence her fertilizing powers. Moreover, the sky was originally the land of the dead, so Nut too was an important funerary deity. Recall the voluptuous, nude images of Nut painted within coffins, sensuously welcoming the dead into their new life (Figure 1.5). Other images (see Figure 0.4), depicted this protective Nut with outspread or folded wings. Coffin inscriptions accompanied the visuals: "O my Mother Nut, stretch yourself over me, that I may be placed among the imperishable stars, which are in you, and that I may not die."[4]

Mesopotamia: Inanna/Ishtar

Several female creator deities appeared in ancient Mesopotamian literature—Tiamat, the original deity, Ninhursag and Aruru, creators of human beings. However, these goddesses did not seem to figure significantly in the worship and belief of the historical period. Rather, for over two millennia of ancient Mesopotamian history the goddess known as Inanna to the Sumerians and Ishtar to the Semitic Babylonians and Assyrians reigned as the most important female deity. Although differences must have existed across these cultures and over time, the two were identified in antiquity.

Numerous hymns to and poems about Inanna/Ishtar, which include the earliest literature by a known author, the priestess Enkheduanna (chapter 9), depict her wide range of powers. Known as a goddess of sex and war, Inanna/Ishtar's powers began with sexuality, erotic desire, and the pleasures of lovemaking. From this base her powers radiated out to include fertility, women's concerns, women's and men's gender identities, protection, social harmony, the political rule of kings, prostitutes, and warfare.

One of the earliest representations of Inanna, dating to the fourth millennium B.C.E., is the low-relief carving of the goddess on the limestone ritual vessel known as the "Warka Vase" (Figure 0.1) from Uruk in southern Iraq. On the left a worshipper is presenting a basket of fruits to the goddess, who greets him with a smile. Clothed in a ceremonial robe and wearing an elaborate headdress over her long, flowing hair, she stands before her ritual symbols, two sheafs of reed adorned with two long fillets, which often identify her presence even when she herself is not depicted.

An early "Hymn to Ishtar" vividly illustrates her range of powers. The hymn begins with the sensuous physical description of the goddess, extolling her for the powers of sexuality and erotic desire, activities necessary for fertility and highly prized for their joyful pleasures.

Praise the goddess, the most awesome of the goddesses.
Let one revere the mistress of the peoples, the greatest of all the gods …
Ishtar is clothed with pleasure and love.
She is laden with vitality, charm, and voluptuousness.
In lips she is sweet; life is in her mouth.[5]

Just as Ishtar's power begins with her sexuality, her oversight of human activity begins with women, as the hymn identifies Ishtar's concern for various women's roles, across all social classes and stages of a woman's life:

Be it slave, unattached girl, or mother, she preserves (her).
One calls on her; among women one names her name.[6]

After extolling her supreme status among all the gods, the hymn's concluding five stanzas praise Ishtar for sanctioning the king's rule. She is the one who makes possible his reign, who has enabled the king to conquer and subject other nations to his authority, thereby granting him dominion over the multitudes he rules. In short, Ishtar's oversight of the king sets the conditions for his glorious deeds and accomplishments. Mesopotamian literature and art both reinforced this civic dimension of Ishtar as the city's guardian deity. Early sealstone images depicted Inanna/Ishtar enthroned or carrying objects of political power, such as a scepter.

Inanna/Ishtar's spectrum of powers encompassed many oppositions— sex and war, building and destroying, raising up and suppressing, wealth and poverty, and so forth. The insights to concepts of gender identity are especially interesting. Her festivals entailed "ritual head-overturning, priest to become woman, priestess to become man," while Inanna's great powers included the ability "to turn man into woman, woman into man."[7] These passages show that on a ritual level, the ancient Mesopotamians recognized the malleability of gender roles. Although based on biological sex, societal gender roles are socially constructed, distinguished by the prescribed social gender expectations and visually marked by fashions of hairstyle and dress. Through her rites, awareness of one's gender identity and of gender-related qualities emerges as a further gift this goddess bestows.

Greece

The portrayal of historical Greek goddesses almost two millennia later than the earliest descriptions of Egyptian and Mesopotamian goddesses reveals the expansion of antifemale patriarchal thinking and practices. In contrast to the broad powers embraced by Egyptian and Mesopotamian female divinities, Greek and Roman goddesses were overwhelmingly associated with only one or very few qualities. Notably, the earlier, linked features of sexuality and fertility diverged to delineate the goddesses' separate spheres. Although they maintained some ritual ties, the Greek goddess of fertility, Demeter, was differentiated from their goddess of sexuality, Aphrodite, a distinction maintained by their Roman counterparts, Ceres and Venus.

Minoan

Like their Egyptian and Mesopotamian contemporaries, Minoan goddesses probably encompassed a broad spectrum of powers. Depictions of divine female figures—or their mortal priestesses—show the goddess atop a mountain, known as the Mountain Mother, or in association with snakes and trees, both symbols of life. One superb gold sealing ring shows the goddess sitting underneath her sacred tree. She is identified as divine by her much greater size than her votaries floating before her. Double axes, the iconic symbol of Minoan ritual practices, as well as a representation of the sky, sun, and moon, elaborate the image.

Minoan goddesses and ritual practices greatly influenced the Mycenaean Greeks, who conquered the Minoans about 1450 B.C.E., but who were profoundly captivated by the highly developed Minoan culture. Visual imagery shows that Minoan perceptions of female divinity and women's ritual practices shaped Mycenaean ideas. Many goddesses of historical Greece were descended from these Bronze Age Minoan and Mycenaean antecedents.

Aphrodite

Aphrodite was the Greek goddess of sexuality and erotic desire, her name derived from the Semitic Canaanite goddess Ashtarte. Aphrodite's principal sanctuary was on the island of Cyprus, whose location in the eastern Mediterranean functioned as a bridge between the civilizations of the ancient Near East and Greece. Like her Near Eastern and Egyptian counterparts, Aphrodite was a goddess of eroticism and sensuality, worshipped for the pleasures sexuality provides. "What is life, what is love, without golden Aphrodite?" begins an early Greek poem. However, the fierce, warrior traits that characterized the goddesses Ishtar and Hathor have been transposed as Aphrodite maintained connections with warrior activities through her liaisons with the male god of war, Ares. These stories preserved the connections between the passions of sex and war but removed from Aphrodite's purview the fierceness or ability to pursue these martial activities herself.

Visual and literary representations of Aphrodite reveal the Greeks' discomfort with open celebrations of female sexuality. In Homer's epic poem the *Iliad,* Aphrodite's mortal incarnation, Helen, rebels against the goddess, refusing to be the human embodiment of divine sexuality in a society concerned with patriarchal codes of morality that required women to uphold sexual fidelity. Aphrodite likewise underwent a moral transformation in the highly influential trilogy of plays, *The Oresteia,* produced by Athens' premier tragedian Aeschylus in 458 B.C.E. The trilogy dramatizes the human effects of a cosmic shift from gynocentric to androcentric values and rule. In the third play Aphrodite is invoked not as the goddess who symbolizes the joys of sexuality, but as a prim, chaste deity who oversees the societal institution of marriage within the moral framework of Zeus's patriarchal rule. This shift in Aphrodite's portrayal parallels the shift from Hathor to Isis in Egyptian ideology since Aeschylus's portrayal of Aphrodite placed female sexuality within the restricted sphere of marriage, and it concentrated on the fruitful outcome of sexual intercourse, not on the sensual pleasures that goddesses of sexuality bestow.

Early Greek visuals, which portrayed Aphrodite as a properly attired, respectable Greek matron, perpetuated this moralistic image. In the fourth century B.C.E. Greek artists struck a bold new course when they began to depict Aphrodite in the nude, thereby challenging an artistic tradition that for centuries portrayed only male nudes. These early nude female sculptures contrast sharply with the open display of the female body, breasts, and pubic area befitting a goddess of beauty and sexuality in Bronze Age images. Instead, these artists sculpted their nude Aphrodites to look as though they were embarrassed to be caught undressed, contracting their torsos and covering their breasts and genitals with their hands. The missing arms of the Aphrodite from Melos (Venus de Milo, Figure 1.8) accentuates this failed attempt. This fashioning of a nude female trying to hide her nakedness from view may reflect the artist's unease in pushing against artistic conventions, as he both dared openly to depict female nudity while he showed at the same time how serious a challenge such a portrayal presents to social expectations.

Such portrayals also cast the viewer into the role of voyeur, who appears to spy upon the goddess in an intimate, unprotected moment, which feeds the prurient interests of pornography. These nude Aphrodites were not necessarily pornographic in and of themselves. However, casting female sexuality in order to titillate the notional male observer reflects a further shift in cultural attitudes. If female sexuality was no longer celebrated openly, what happened to it in the social fabric? We have observed the shift from joyous celebrations of sexuality to a focus on the outcome of intercourse and the presumably more decorous feelings of maternal love for the newborn, seen for both Isis and Aphrodite.

The late nude Greek Aphrodites indicate another development. The portrayal of these embarrassed Aphrodites trying to hide their nude bodies reaffirms patriarchal notions that considered female sexuality to be the source of women's shame and that should therefore be concealed. Even as women and

Figure 1.8 Aphrodite of Melos, marble. Réunion des Musées Nationaux / Art Resource, NY, Louvre, Paris, France.

men continued to worship Aphrodite in rituals that promoted intercourse and fertility, her public image illustrates the problematic status goddesses of sexuality posed to patriarchal ideologies that increasingly demonized female sexuality.

Finally, like many other goddesses, Aphrodite also served as a city deity, principally in the port city of Corinth, where her sanctuary and temple stood on the Acrocorinth overlooking the city. In contrast to the lions accompanying other Mediterranean goddesses of sexuality, Aphrodite was associated with small, tame birds—sparrows and mourning doves.

Artemis

Diametrically opposed to Aphrodite, a goddess for adult women and men, Artemis was the goddess of the young par excellence, both of animals and of humans. In this capacity she was depicted as a *kourotrophos,* and her rituals oversaw the maturation rites of girls and boys. Together with Athena, Artemis was called a "maiden" goddess. "Maiden," however, at an early date probably meant unmarried rather than signifying one's sexual status, for ritually Artemis had associations with sexuality. Interestingly, the fifth-century Greek writer Herodotos named Artemis as the Greek equivalent to Hathor, rather than Aphrodite as one might expect for the Egyptian goddess of sexuality.

However, like Hathor, Artemis was a goddess of the wild, expressed by her epithet *Potnia Theron,* "Mistress of the Animals," an image beautifully illustrated by a late second millennium Mycenaean ivory carving from Minet-el-Beida, Syria (Figure 10.6). Presumably echoing her Paleolithic ancestor, Artemis was both a protector of animals and their hunter at the same time, her most frequent representation in the art. This deep connection to nature probably made Artemis appear similar to pre-Greek goddesses whose identities she absorbed as she took on their names as her epithets—for example, Artemis Britomartis in northern Greece and Artemis Diktinna in Crete. The wide scope of these names evokes the many goddesses whose worship waned after Greek conquest, but who were too important to be dismissed outright.

The statue of Artemis at her major sanctuary at Ephesos, on the west coast of Turkey (Figure 1.9), which the Amazons had founded, illustrates both her immense importance as a Greek deity and the effects of Greek–Near Eastern syncretism in the Hellenistic period. Located on the eastern border of Greek lands, the influence of Near Eastern goddess imagery emerges in Artemis's high crown and her column-like skirt decorated with rows of animals. The depiction of Artemis of Ephesos with multiple breasts suggests fertility, and the image invokes Artemis as protector of the young who insures their increase.

The statue of Artemis at Ephesos may also carry ritual associations. She may be wearing a trophy mantle of strung-together bulls' testicles, which were given as offerings to Artemis and other Near Eastern ecstatic deities. This necklace dramatically projects the goddess's power, for Artemis would be perceived both as absorbing the bulls' power and as capable of controlling it. Similar to rites of fertility, Artemis was worshipped with ecstatic rites that celebrated her wild, untamed, and untamable elemental qualities that were as potent as the male fertility of a bull.

Figure 1.9 Artemis of Ephesos. Photograph
by B. Vivante.

Athena

Athena in Athens epitomized a patron city deity. In contrast to other Greek
goddesses, Athena held a variety of associations. Her roots as a nature goddess are evident through her integral connection to her symbols, the olive
tree and the owl. The tree accentuated her promotion of the olive's fertility
and productivity, and the owl signified her wisdom. Athena was also considered a "maiden" goddess, associated with prepubescent rituals.

Athena was a goddess of crafts, overseeing both women's craft of weaving and men's bronze working. She was also considered a goddess of battle,
perhaps in origin as fierce as Ishtar or Hathor. But by the Greek historical
period the male war god Ares represented the fierceness of war. Athena became rather the goddess of victory in battle, so identified through her epithet, Nike, "Victory," visually portrayed as winged.

Athena's image developed into what some observers interpret as a willing token advocate for the ruling male elite. As told in Hesiod's *Theogony*,
afraid that she would bear a son who would overthrow him, Zeus swallowed
the goddess Metis, "Cunning" or "Cleverness," whom he had already impregnated with their daughter Athena. Consequently, Zeus gave birth to Athena

from his head, which, together with the meaning of her mother's name, emphasized Athena's intellectual qualities. Hesiod's tale acknowledged Athena's mother, even as Zeus appropriated her powers of birth to deliver Athena in this unique manner.

However, in the final play of Aeschylus' *Oresteia,* Athena proclaims that since she was born from a father without a mother, she is for the male in all things. Just as Aeschylus transformed the focus of Aphrodite's powers in the trilogy, he also elided out the memory of Athena's mother. Outside of Aeschylus' drama, it appears unlikely that Athena presented such an image to her ancient followers. Rather, she was feted annually as the patron deity of Athens who guaranteed the well-being of its citizens. Universally identifying the city of Athens is Athena's temple on the Acropolis, the Parthenon, a marvel of ancient design and construction, which took into account the optical effect of being seen from the ground below so as to appear perfectly straight and symmetrical. The forty-foot-high, gold and ivory statue of Athena by the sculptor Pheidias—Figure 1.10 offers a reconstructed image— exquisitely reveals the depth of the Athenians' reverence for their city goddess. The statue portrays her with elaborated, identifying attributes—four-horse chariot on

Figure 1.10 Athena Parthenos, reconstruction of the 40-foot-tall, gold and ivory cult statue of Athena by Pheidias. With permission of the Royal Ontario Museum © ROM.

her helmet, protective Gorgon face in the middle of her mantle, spear, shield, and snake, and holding her winged aspect as Nike in her right hand.

Demeter and Persephone

Demeter was goddess of grain, more specifically goddess of the cultivated grain, her integral connection to agriculture. As a goddess of the earth's and women's fertility, worship of Demeter was fundamental to the continuity and well-being of the community, and her rites were among the oldest and most widespread of Greek women's ritual observances. Although the two were originally separate deities with separate realms, once Persephone, goddess of the underworld, was tied to Demeter as her daughter, the two became a holy dyad, known as *Hai Semnai,* "the Revered Holy Ones."

The story of Persephone's abduction by her uncle Hades, god of the underworld, and of Demeter's grief at the loss of her daughter was fundamental to Greek religious and cultural thinking. In the "Homeric Hymn to Demeter," by arrangement with her father Zeus, Hades abducts Persephone while she gathers flowers in a meadow with her girlfriends—a characteristic metaphor for the adolescent girl's readiness for marriage. Demeter's anger at her daughter's abduction causes the earth to wither. Forced to yield to Demeter's demands, Zeus agrees to allow Persephone's return. But Hades tricks her into eating pomegranate seeds—three or nine depending on the version—which compels her to spend that many months under the earth. Thus the hymn explains the origin of the seasons. The joyful reunion of mother and daughter prefigure the blessings the two goddesses bestow on their human worshippers.

Besides its symbolic reflections of the seasonal fertility and fallowness of the earth, this story provides unique insights into female bonds and gender relations. First is the strength of the mother-daughter dyad, rare in world cosmologies, where divine mother-son pairs predominate. This tale stresses Demeter's maternal bond with her daughter, the strongest relationship in the hymn, which the earth goddess, who alone has the power to do so, will see restored at any cost. As sister and aunt, the goddess Hekate—the only one of all the deities whose original powers Zeus could not diminish—aids Demeter in her search and accompanies Persephone after her return. The hymn thus reflects a constellation of close female relationships.

But gender conflict drives the plot. Zeus engineered the abduction- marriage without Demeter's knowledge, and their standoff illuminates the kinds of power each possesses. Demeter's is the power of the earth's fertility. Zeus bribes and cajoles Demeter to release her anger and permit the earth to be fruitful, but alone he cannot generate life. While Zeus must capitulate to Demeter's essential powers, as supreme god he ultimately establishes his authority over Demeter's power. The story succinctly portrays the gender dynamics operating on several societal levels—women possessed fundamental life powers over which men imposed their social control. Nevertheless Demeter remained a potent symbol of women's generative powers until late antiquity.

A distinctive feature of Demeter's sanctuary and worship at Eleusis was that she shared both with her daughter Persephone, often referred to simply as Kore, daughter. Among the votive offerings dedicated to the two Holy Ones at Eleusis is a large fifth-century marble relief depicting Demeter, Persephone, and a boy, perhaps Ploutos, "Wealth" (Figure 1.11). Demeter on the left, holding a scepter, faces the boy and may be giving him something, perhaps the seed and instructions for its sowing. Behind him stands Persephone, her hair cut short and with a torch to light her way out of the underworld.

Hera

Hera's associations with cows, oxen, the Near East, women's concerns, fertility and pre-Greek deities indicates her ancient and widespread powers, perhaps akin to those displayed by the Egyptian cow goddess Hathor. In historical times, Hera was principally a goddess of marriage, portrayed in the stories as the sister and wife of Zeus, with whom she had a stormy relationship. But, no doubt reflecting her pre-Greek eminence, the vitality of her rituals and worship far surpassed the shrewish image the patriarchal stories made of her. From western to eastern boundaries, the earliest temples were built for Hera and Artemis, which became the prototypes for Greek temple architecture—the later temple to Artemis at Ephesos was considered one of the seven wonders of the ancient world. Further attesting to her importance, Hera functioned as a city deity for several cities throughout Greece, notably Argos in the northern Peloponnesos and on the island of Samos in eastern Greece.

Kybele

In Anatolia, Kybele was the great Mother Goddess, variously portrayed as a goddess of the mountains, animals, wild nature, fertility, war, healer, and protector of her people. Worshipped by ecstatic rites, the Greeks associated her with Demeter. The ecstatic nature of her rites became legendary, and she may have offered immortality to her initiates.

Rome

Due to their admiration of Greek culture, from the late third century B.C.E. the Romans adapted their own gods and stories to fit Greek models—thus, Ceres for Demeter, Diana for Artemis, Juno for Hera, Minerva for Athena, and Venus for Aphrodite. Although the powers of Roman goddesses appear diminished, they did not entirely vanish. The strongest beliefs and worship often perpetuated earlier, native Italian practices. Roman goddesses continued to oversee women's fertility, successful childbirth, and especially motherhood—ever the principal purposes of a woman's life.

Bona Dea

Bona Dea, whose name literally means "Good Goddess," was a native Italian fertility goddess, associated like Demeter with successful agricultural

Figure 1.11 Demeter, Persephone and child, mar-
ble votive relief from the sanctuary of Demeter at
Eleusis. Erich Lessing / Art Resource, NY, National
Archaeological Museum, Athens, Greece.

production and human fertility. Like Demeter, Bona Dea was celebrated by
ecstatic, all-women's rites.

Ceres

Another old Italian earth goddess who also in time became associated with
Demeter, Ceres's elemental connection with the earth's and women's fertility persisted at the core of her worship. In earliest times she was associated
with Tellus, "Mother Earth," in overseeing fertility, motherhood, and marital
fidelity. Ceres protected married women—the property of men who wrongly
divorced their wives was confiscated, half given to their wives, the other half
consecrated to Ceres. The goddess welcomed the dead back into her earthly
embrace. A pit in the earth called the *mundus Cereris,* "world of Ceres," sacred
to the goddess and considered the entryway to the underworld, was uncovered three times a year to allow the spirits of the dead to visit the living.

Ceres's centrality for the continuity of all life transformed into symbolic
political meanings. A temple dedicated to Ceres on Rome's Aventine hill in
493 B.C.E. to win her favor against famine became central to popular political

activities. Gaining important supervisory roles in administering Ceres's observances at her new temple, the plebeian magistrates known as aediles oversaw the distribution of grain to Rome's urban population, an enormously influential position. Politicians stamped Ceres's image on coins to show their support of this popular grain dole, and Julius Caesar honored Ceres on coins marking his military victories as a way to identify with his plebeian supporters.

With the founding of empire, the imperial family adopted Ceres's imagery to exemplify the qualities of motherhood and marital fidelity promoted as women's highest virtues. A cameo of Augustus's wife Livia depicts her with Ceres's crown, a wreath of fertile grain. One panel of the Ara Pacis, the "Altar of Peace" that the Senate erected in honor of Augustus' victories and end to civil war, spotlights Ceres as Mother Italy (Figure 1.12). She is seated on a throne in a natural landscape, holding two infants, surrounded by domesticated animals and flanked by female spirits of water, plants, and possibly air. By fusing notions of material prosperity with political success—as does the introductory hymn to Gaia—Ceres's images potently symbolized key political issues.

Juno

In Rome Juno received secondary cultic worship as consort of Jupiter, the chief male god. Mythological stories cast Juno and Jupiter into the roles of the archetypal quarreling couple like the principal divine Greek couple Hera and Zeus. But Juno's powers were older and more widespread than these tales. Juno was a goddess of women, presiding over childbirth as Juno Lucina, their protector as mothers. Coins from a city near Rome depict Juno armed as a warrior goddess wearing a goatskin headdress and represented by her sacred snake. If the snake accepted a young girl's offerings, it proved

Figure 1.12 Ceres, as Mother Italy, Ara Pacis, marble. Rome. Scala / Art Resource, NY, Museum of the Ara Pacis, Rome, Italy.

Figure 1.13 Goddess
Astarte in a window,
ivory relief. Arslan Tash,
ancient Hadatu, Syria,
ca. 8th c. B.C.E. Erich
Lessing/Art Resource,
NY, Louvre, Paris,
France.

she was a virgin. As a warrior deity Juno appeared to oversee girls' transitions
to marriage and adulthood.

Juno was also a civic deity. Reflecting Etruscan origins, she was called
Regina, "Queen," at her earliest temples in Rome, which served key roles
in solemnizing Rome's political organization, an epithet she held through
imperial times. Rome's first mint may have been within the temple of Juno
Moneta, whence derives the word money.

Venus

While still retaining some of the aspects of the older goddesses of eroticism
and sexuality in ritual, Venus became a goddess of love rather than of sex. Vergil's monumental epic poem about the founding of Rome, *The Aeneid*, portrays
Venus's powers negatively. As a goddess of sex she appears merely as a wanton
deity who imposes a destructive passion of lust upon the hapless Carthaginian
queen, Dido. Any association Venus might have had with love emerges as hyp-
ocritical and self-serving in the poem. This total denunciation of the goddess
of sex, desire, and fertility depicts an extreme development from the openly
joyous celebrations of sexuality and all its pleasures so prominent in earlier ancient cultures and periods. It also reflects yet another stage in the shifts noted
from Egyptian Hathor to Isis and in the perception of the Greek Aphrodite.

Interestingly, at the height of the moralizing of the incipient Roman Empire, end of first century B.C.E. to first century C.E., Venus was the patron deity
of the city of Pompeii, a bustling port and commercial center, like Aphrodite
in Corinth. One impressive Pompeiian store sign depicts a properly dressed
and crowned Venus entering the city astride a team of four elephants, an
image that underscores her importance in overseeing foreign trade.

Two

Sanctifying Women's Lives—Ancient Women's Rituals

Worship of female deities was foundational to ancient polytheistic religious systems. Spiritual belief and ritual practices permeated the lives of ancient peoples, and rites for both female and male deities filled the calendar year. Rituals had the primary function of obtaining the deity's blessings, often in connection with agricultural and human fertility, and with personal or civic prosperity. Many of the same features characterized the worship of female and male deities—prayers, offerings, processions, songs, dances, and animal sacrifices. In Greece, athletic comptetitions like the Olympian games for Zeus, and poetic and dramatic festivals like those for Athena and Dionysos, presented major occasions for expressing one's reverence to the deity. Animal sacrifices were a means of ritually killing an animal, offering a symbolic part to the deity, and providing the human community with an opportunity to eat meat.

Besides the spiritual dimension, religious festivals offered worshippers opportunities for much-needed respite from labor in societies that did not have regularly scheduled days off from work. The fundamental role of women's rites and worship of goddesses in the larger cultural fabric persisted for millennia alongside the officially promoted canons of male creator and ruling deities. Sex-segregated worship typified ancient Greek and Roman religious practice—with some exceptions, men mainly worshipped male deities and women female deities in male- and female-only rites. Significantly, two of the few practices observed by women and men together honored female deities—the Panathenaia for Athena and the Eleusinian Mysteries for Demeter and Persephone, to be discussed below.

SIMILAR RITUAL FEATURES

Dancing

Some of the earliest pottery and paintings show women dancing in settings that are clearly sacred. Dancing formed women's principal means of spiritual expression throughout antiquity. Studies show that the physical activity of dancing with its accompanying physiological sensations generates feelings of euphoria that many peoples have associated with spiritual fulfillment and ecstasy. The whirling dances of Sufi dervishes present a vibrant contemporary example.

Dancing figured prominently in rituals of fertility, where it contributed substantially to the sensuous, ecstatic practices believed to promote agricultural and human fertility. Ecstatic dancing characterized the fertility rites of Mesopotamian Inanna/Ishtar, Egyptian Hathor, and Greek Demeter, and it figured prominently in rituals for Greek Artemis and Anatolian Kybele, goddesses of wild nature. The Spartan goddess Helen was considered a sacred leader of the dance, and characteristic of the Greek rites for Artemis and Demeter was the *pannykhis*, women's all-night ecstatic dancing. Dancing was especially significant in the worship of Hathor, in whose observances female musicians, singers, and dancers held valued positions. Hathor was invoked as "Mistress of Music, Queen of Harp-playing, Lady of the Dance." Hathor's musical instruments—harp, sistrum, and tambourine—were considered sacred items, replete with the goddess's magical properties.

Minoan art portrayed dancing as central to spiritual expression. The intricate imagery engraved on many small gold sealing rings used to seal storage jars or communiqués depicts women and men engaged in ecstatic dance rituals. One painting on a narrow wall between doorways portrays a woman spinning, as her braids fly out around her head. Modeled on Minoan prototypes, Figure 2.1 shows a Mycenaean terra-cotta group of women engaged in a sacred circle dance. The backward lean of the women's bodies suggests a naturalistic portrayal as the women's torsos are propelled back from the centrifugal force of their spinning. A miniature wall fresco highlights the seated, individually distinguished female spectators watching women dancing in the foreground, the entire composition underscoring women's significant social and ritual roles in Minoan society.

Sacred Marriage and Fertility Rites

These ancient Mediterranean societies joyously celebrated the importance of fertility—of people, animals, and crops—to the entire community. In the annual Sacred Marriage rites, known by the Greek term *hieros gamos,* the king or high priest engaged in sexual intercourse with the priestess of the goddess of sexuality and fertility. Hymns and stories from these cultures describe the same basic scene—in preparation to lovemaking, and with the aid of various attendants, the goddess bathes and anoints herself with scented oils and perfumes, adorns herself in gleaming clothing, make-up, and jewelry, and proceeds to seduce her lover/consort. The hymns celebrating the Sacred Marriage rites of Inanna and her male consort Dumuzi (Babylonian Tammuz) evoke their mating with explicit sexual imagery. After receiving her mother's help in the preparatory adornment, Inanna greets Dumuzi, vividly proclaimed in Wolkstein and Kramer's evocative translation:

"My vulva, the horn,
The Boat of Heaven,
Is full of eagerness like the young moon.
My untilled land lies fallow.
As for me, Inanna,
Who will plow my vulva?
Who will plow my high field?
Who will plow my wet ground?"

Dumuzi replied:
"Great Lady, I Dumuzi, the King, will plow your vulva."

"Then plow my vulva, man of my heart!
Plow my vulva!"[1]

Such unabashed imagery emerged also among the ancient Egyptians, who addressed Hathor as Mistress of the Vulva. From the earliest records, Baubo images that graphically depict female figures squatting with open legs and fully exposed genitalia gave visual expression to such explicit

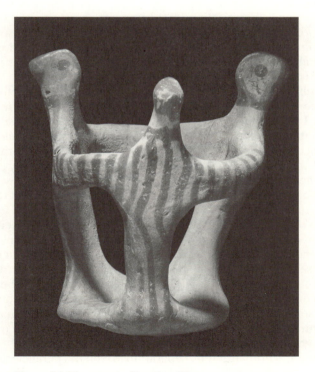

Figure 2.1 Mycenaean Dancing Women, terra-cotta. ca. 1300 B.C.E. Copyright © The Trustees of the British Museum.

honoring of female genitalia. Although some artists were still carving Shelaghs, the Irish versions of the Baubo figures, as late as the tenth century C.E., already in antiquity such open displays first became covert, and then disappeared.

Agricultural imagery permeated sacred marriage hymns, which integrally connected agricultural and human reproduction. By what anthropologists call sympathetic magic, these rites were believed to transpose magically the success of human intercourse to the fertility of the fields. By performing these acts of ritualized sexual intercourse the king and the priestess of the goddess of sexuality insured the successful fertility of the earth and of humans.

While select royal and religious individuals embodied the forces of cosmic fertility by enacting the sacred marriage rites of divine beings, people were able to express their joyous recognition of the sacred power of intercourse in fertility rituals. The Egyptians and Mesopotamians openly, exuberantly, and ecstatically celebrated their goddesses of sexuality and fertility, Hathor and Inanna/Ishtar, respectively. Entire communities of women and men together worshipped these goddesses in raucous festivals that lasted two to three weeks, and that included much gaiety, exuberant music, feasting, dancing, drinking, sexually suggestive joking and play, and sexual inter-course. The jocularity entailed rituals of insult, known by the Greek term *aiskhrologia,* literally "shame talk." Within a ritual context, these periods of mocking ritual insults and "obscenities" functioned as a kind of spiritual venting to cleanse the mind and emotions of harmful feelings in order to enable full concentration on the ritual practices.

The fertility rites for Greek Demeter and Roman Ceres exhibited many of the same features as those for the Egyptian and Mesopotamian fertility goddesses. Interestingly, the early Greek poet Hesiod asserts that the secret mystery rites for Demeter were once performed openly in the fields of Crete, an idea that perhaps recalls Minoan practices. But Greek and Roman women celebrated the fertility Demeter and Ceres bestowed primarily in women-only rites, held apart and in secret from the men.

The performance of fertility rituals in sex-segregated rites that were also to be kept secret reveals some fundamentally different conceptual approaches to the place of female sexuality in the cultural ideology. The gendered separa-tion of what once could be openly revered with unabashed sexual practices restricted the expression of female sexuality. While women still celebrated their own sexuality and fertile abilities among themselves—and were cul-turally encouraged to do so—raucous, public celebrations by both women and men conflicted with new concepts of social morality, rendering them no longer socially acceptable. Nevertheless, even in this changed ideologi-cal environment, some festivals for Demeter and for Dionysos continued to entail anonymous ritual intercourse down to the late period.

The Greek and Roman gender separation in worship paralleled sharpened social demarcations as elite citizen women did not generally engage in ritual practices with slaves, prostitutes, or women of lower classes. The exchange of gender, age, class, and status roles in Inanna/Ishtar's festivals encouraged temporary breakdowns of social distinctions and perhaps elicited valuable insights into the positions of those different from oneself. Scholars usually regard this breaking down of social barriers in ritual performance as a means of reinforcing these distinctions by allowing a brief spate of exuberant inversion. For the Greeks and even more so for the Romans, however, ritual practices reiterated other social divisions and did not commonly allow women of different social class and status to intermingle even for ritual purposes. The Greek and Roman ritual practices seemed therefore to endorse conceptions of an identity whose gender and class distinctions appear as fixed not fluid components of one's persona.

One offshoot of Greek women's-only rites resulted in reinforcing concepts of female solidarity. Such ritual and divine sanction to women's mutual support may by the Greek historical period have formed a significant balance to the restrictions imposed on women in other areas of social activity, since probably from the earliest times the religious arena provided Greek women with deeply embedded sources of cultural authority.

All these aspects of fertility rites were further attenuated by the Roman period, the fewer ecstatic rites practiced with far greater secrecy. The ecstatic fertility rites for both male and female deities were considered contrary to Roman moral sexual standards and were declared illegal at various times. Elite Roman women may have continued practices for the Bona Dea similar to Greek women's observances for Demeter. But Roman women expressed their concern with fertility far more through rituals that emphasized motherhood. This emphasis reveals another step in the shift in attention from sexuality to motherhood, now clearly seen in the almost total disappearance of the celebration of sexuality and a preponderance of rites praising motherhood. Rather than participating together in life-affirming fertility celebrations, Roman women's and men's energies were diverted into the role of spectator at violent, bloody exhibitions.

Mourning Customs

In all these ancient Mediterranean civilizations, women prepared the dead for the funerary rites that properly sent the deceased on their journey to the next world. In Egyptian funerals, two women assumed the roles of the goddesses Isis and Nephthys to escort the dead. Both Egyptian and Greek painted funerary scenes prominently portrayed female mourners, as one Greek vase illustrates (Figure 2.2). A significant female occupation was the professional mourner, hired to enhance the status and esteem of the deceased.

Women's funerary associations were ritually expressed through the Mourning Rites for the dying god of vegetation that were central to the religious practices of the ancient Mediterranean. While their mythological stories differed, the intent of these rites was similar—to mourn the dead vegetation, usually after the harvest, and to offer prayers for its return the following year. Some stories associated the annual disappearance of vegetation with

Figure 2.2 Female Mourners, black figure *loutrophoros*, terra-cotta. The Metropolitan Museum of Art, funds from various donors, 1927 (27.228). Photograph, All rights reserved, The Metropolitan Museum of Art, New York.

a female deity. In the Mesopotamian tale "The Descent of Ishtar," the disappearance of vegetation is due to the goddess's absence from the world of the living when she descends, of her own volition, to the underworld. Greek tales split the causes of the earth's barrenness between Persephone's absence, like Ishtar's, from the living world and Demeter's anger and grief at the kidnapping of her daughter. Both the Mesopotamian and Greek stories culminated in the goddess's return, symbolic of the renewal of the earth's vegetation.

The tales about a male vegetation deity provided the occasion for the formalized mourning rites, as they describe the god's death and mourning by his lover, the goddess of sexuality. In the tale of her descent, after Ishtar returns to the upper world, her wayward lover Tammuz is condemned to death, and the tale ends with the lament of the female deities. Among the Sumerians Inanna mourned Dumuzi, for the Babylonians Ishtar mourned Tammuz, Isis mourned Osiris for the Egyptians, and Aphrodite mourned Adonis for the Greeks. A biblical passage illustrates the profound importance of these rites. Railing against the missionary fervor of Jeremiah in that book, the Judean women assert their right to continue practicing, with their husbands' support, the mourning rites for Tammuz. In their view, it is because Jeremiah prevented their performance of this all-important ritual that they ended up in their present condition of exile. Echoes of the ancient importance of these mid-summer mourning rites persist today—the month corresponding to July in Arabic, Hebrew, and Turkish is named Tammuz or Temmuz.

DISTINCTIVE RITUAL EXPRESSIONS

Mesopotamia

Naditum and Temple Priestesses

Mesopotamian priestesses served both gods and goddesses. Those serving the chief god of Babylon, Marduk, could keep their dowries, were typically supported by their brothers, and engaged in commercial activities. A group known as the sacred women bore or nursed children for the sky god Adad. Interestingly, it was for the Old Babylonian sun god Shamash that female religious structures arose that afforded women who so chose—or were so chosen—a formal means to avoid marriage, childbearing, and rearing. In perhaps the earliest illustration of such a select group of women, in the early second millennium B.C.E., cloistered *naditum*, "fallow," women dedicated to Shamash in Sippar lived celibately in a segregated community.

In Babylon, however, *naditum* priestesses could marry but had to remain celibate, and some engaged in business and domestic affairs. As in other instances in which women forewent childbirth and motherhood for religious purposes, the idea that a wife could remain celibate within marriage underscores the sacredness of the *naditum* priestess's role.

A different role was that of the temple priestesses of Ishtar. The biblical word "harlot" or the former scholarly epithet "temple prostitute" have obscured rather than helped our understanding, for they cast the Mesopotamian priestesses in the derogatory light of later misogynistic and erotophobic perspectives. Sources reveal that sexual intercourse was part of service that women, men, and eunuchs fulfilled for the goddess Ishtar. Who served as Ishtar's sexual temple priestesses and for how long is not clear. The Greek author Herodotos claims that all women, single or married, served Ishtar in this way as part of their rites of passage, while other sources suggest only a select few performed this service. A mid-third millennium statuette of a seated woman from the temple of Ishtar at Mari in present-day Syria well depicts the high status of a priestess of Ishtar without, however, indicating her precise priestly role (Figure 10.2). Seated on an imposing throne, her feet resting on a footstool, and covered in a shawl and skirt of ceremonial feathers, the woman gazes forward with an air of confident authority.

Some of Ishtar's priests were eunuchs and male homosexuals whose dancing talents and cross-dressing antics provided entertainment during religious festivals. Men who did not develop normally or who were castrated for ritual purposes comprised the eunuchs serving Ishtar. Castration rarely functioned as a punishment. That homosexual activity functioned as integral parts of ritual activity demonstrates that the ancient Mesopotamians, characteristic of all these ancient Mediterranean cultures, did not stigmatize nonprocreative sexual practices, but rather prized the pleasures sexual diversity offered.

Although they engaged in sexual intercourse with men who then left offerings for the goddess, Ishtar's temple priestesses were distinct from prostitutes. The priestesses performed a ritual act in honor of the goddess imbued with a sense of sacredness. Prostitutes engaged in sexual activity for commercial purposes. Although the two categories overlapped, the Mesopotamians distinguished between them. The later denunciations of the sexual activities of these temple priestesses reveal the advancing demonization of female sexuality.

Egypt

Royal Priestesses

Egyptian goddesses were characteristically identified with royal queens, both the queen mother and the king's wife. These royal women were seen to incarnate the goddess's divine authority. Identified by their priestly roles in inscriptions and visual portrayals, the women's royal priestly offices functioned to secure the goddesses' continued support for the well-being of the royal dynasty and the entire land, as Nefertari's tomb painting illustrates (Figure 1.7).

Royal women may have been the principal dancers and musicians at Hathor's festivals, where her hand-held percussive instrument, the sistrum, gave concrete expression to the magical and emotive qualities of music. The Egyptians regarded the women who played these musical instruments as transmitting the goddess's divine powers. Elite women held important roles as the chief dancers and musicians in the temples of various gods and possibly also at feasts. Exercise of these fundamentally ecstatic dimensions of spiritual expression by the women of highest status demonstrates the valued place accorded these activities in ancient Egyptian society.

Greece

While Egyptian and Mesopotamian evidence portrays major fertility festivals that all people celebrated and particular priestly offices performed by a select few, Greece presents a unique picture of elaborate, lifelong, women-only rituals.

Greek Forerunners—Minoan Rites

Minoan wall paintings from ancient Thera, present-day Santorini, depict young girls' puberty and adolescent transition rites, with the girls shown at different stages of physical development and at different steps of the ritual processes. The crocus flower and the yellow-tinged saffron dye derived from its stigmas figure prominently in these paintings. Crocus designs adorn the clothing and jewelry of the female figures, such as Figure 2.5, while crocus buds dot the walls and landscape. The youngest girls gather the crocus flowers from wild, rocky terrains in specially designed baskets, which they bring to the reigning female deity, possibly a Mistress of Animals, judging from the distinctive animals flanking her on her throne.

These paintings imbue the economic and medicinal values of saffron with ritual meanings. Saffron is high in carotenes, absorbed by the body as vitamin A, which promotes high birth weight, a significant factor contributing to infant survival and successful reproduction. Saffron was also used as an aphrodisiac, an emmenagogue, to ease menstruation, and in larger doses to induce abortion. The red tinge of men's eyes in other Minoan paintings may further reflect the red streaking of the cornea caused by a lack of vitamin A, which suggests that the women did not share the saffron with the men. By connecting the crocus with female activities, from which men were excluded, these paintings suggest Minoan women's awareness of saffron's health and medicinal properties and their probable control of its collection and consumption. If women were generally in better physical condition than men in Bronze Age Minoan society, that factor too would have contributed to Minoan women's central cultural role. The Theran frescoes of girls' ritual practices seem to affirm female identity, providing women and girls strong validation of their important cultural roles.

Girls' Transition Rites

Possibly echoing earlier Minoan practices, the ancient Greeks ritually sanctified what they perceived as pivotal developmental stages in a girl's life. These included prepuberty, puberty, adolescence, and the culminating transition from adolescence to adulthood, commonly exemplified by marriage. The Greeks developed elaborate rites of transitions for girls unparalleled in the ancient Mediterranean, and indeed with rare comparanda almost anywhere in the world.

Current research suggests that societies that hold girls' puberty or adolescent rites often stand at a transitional stage in their own social development, as they experience changes from a matrifocal, often tribally based social system to one establishing patriarchal values and practices. These girls' rites then serve to recall the powers of the mature female divinities that have now been subsumed under the rites of immature girls. A similar transformation in social dynamics may underlie the demotion of the Egyptian mother goddesses Hathor and Mut to the status of daughter with the consequent diminution of the powers each was seen to wield.

The roles ancient Greek female transition rites played in their cultural ideology support this interpretation. The performance of these rites instilled into the girls the idea that their physical changes prepared them for their upcoming wifely role—submission to their husbands. The rites thus functioned to embed the girls within the patriarchal social structure that framed their lives. At the same time these rites also furnished occasions for affirming female identity and value to the community. Most of the evidence from historical Greece describes rites practiced by elite girls in ancient Athens and Sparta. Rites for young, unmarried women were apparently conducted by a select few, either on behalf of the larger group, or as the privileged honor reserved for the chosen elite.

Even if these rites were performed only by the elite, they still held a critical place in the social fabric and were deeply connected with the community's well-being. The goddesses Artemis, Athena, Helen, and Persephone oversaw different stages of girls' maturation rituals. Of especial significance were the rituals marking the two passages from childhood into adolescence, that is puberty rituals, and from adolescent to adult woman. Puberty rituals were apparently not held for boys in ancient Greece; boys' rites centered on the latter stage of transition.

Puberty and Adolescence

Puberty rituals sanctified a girl's entry into adolescence, celebrating the onset of menstruation and a girl's reproductive potential. Whether held annually or quadrennially, these rites occurred prior to menarche, so that the girls participating in the rituals, whether directly or by proxy of group leaders, ranged from 6 to 10 years of age. Actual rites differed greatly. In Aristophanes' comedy *Lysistrata* the Chorus of Women proudly recall different prepubertal rites they performed as young Athenian girls.

When I turned seven I straightaway carried the sacred *hiera* for the Arrephoria
Then at age ten I ground barley for Athena
and shedding my *krokotos* dress I played the bear at the Brauronia.
And I carried the ritual basket at the Panathenaia when my beauty developed.[2]

The first three refer to prepuberty rites, two for Athena, the third for Artemis. The reference to grinding barley identifies the kind of activities considered prized skills. To show that she excels at ordinary tasks both prepares the girl for her adult activities and demonstrates her industriousness to her kin and potential mate.

As with most female rites, the details of these rituals are mostly unknown. In the secret Arrephoria, which means "the carrying of unspeakable things," two prepubescent girls resided in Athena's sanctuary on the slopes of the Acropolis for a year, learning and possibly weaving the designs for the sacred robe to be presented to Athena in her major festival, the Panathenaia. At some point, the girls solemnly exchanged certain *hiera*, "holy things," with others buried in a pit in a grove sacred to Aphrodite. Both the ritual exchange and the transfer from the goddess overseeing the young to the one who valorizes the sexuality of adult women mark the girls' symbolic passage into a new state.

Athenian girls celebrated the Brauronia on the eastern coast of Attika in honor of Artemis, the goddess of the young and of transitions par excellence. In these rites, animal and human converged, as the girls assumed the aspect of Artemis' sacred animals, the bear or deer. The girls thereby symbolically played out ancient Greek cultural belief that regarded girls, especially adolescents, as resembling wild animals, not yet tamed and harnessed into their roles as adult, married women. Reinforcing the girls' identification with the wild, sources describe the girls who participated in the Brauronia as "playing the bear," without, however, explaining what "playing the bear" meant. Pottery fragments from Brauron show girls in short tunics racing, a feature typical of many ancient Greek rites, which the bronze statuette of a girl runner from Dodona in northwest Greece finely illustrates (Figure 2.3).

Both the Brauronia for Artemis and the Arrephoria for Athena ritualized the girls' transformation from one life stage to another. These prepubescent transition rites spiritually prepared the girls in advance for the physical changes that would eventually take place and that would mark their entry into adolescence, *partheneia*, a stage of a girl's life that the Greeks highly ritualized. The myths that signaled a girl's entry into the ambivalent period of *partheneia* often symbolically portrayed the death of the child as the girl entered a new social and age-related status. Greek myths and cultural customs marked this period as dangerous, when the adolescent girl, the *parthenos*, was perceived as biologically capable of having a child, but not yet under the control of, in Greek literally "tamed by," a husband to legitimate any children she might have. The very potential in a young, unmarried woman's sexuality and fertility rendered a *parthenos* dangerous, not yet transformed into the controlled, productive fertility of a *gyne*, a married woman.

Figure 2.3 Girl Runner, bronze. Sparta, Greece, 6th c. B.C.E. The British Museum/Art Resource, NY, London, Great Britain.

Cultural attitudes idealized a *parthenos*' virginity, hence the frequent translation as "maiden," which may not be entirely accurate. The story of Kallisto, whose name means "Most Beautiful," illustrates the Greek sense of danger. The setting typifies many myths that accompany the transition from adolescent to adult woman as it portrays the adolescent girl's abduction from Artemis' choral band, the mythic ideal of the girls' adolescent group referred to frequently in Greek literature. In this tale Zeus, lusting after Kallisto, disguises himself as Artemis to rape her. Unable to hide her pregnancy, Kallisto is ostracized from Artemis' choral band, while Hera, jealous of Kallisto's beauty and of Zeus's attention to her, changes her into a bear. The story ends with Kallisto and her son transformed into the Big and Little Dippers, known in antiquity as the Big and Little Bears. Despite this concluding explanatory tag, in this and other stories, the mythology shows its disapproval of the pregnant adolescent and depicts the dire consequences of this dangerous period for the young woman.

Athenian practice kept this period short by marrying girls shortly after menarche. By contrast, *parthenoi* in Sparta were encouraged to marry at the more mature age of 18. Some controversial evidence suggests a *parthenos* in Sparta could bear a child without incurring social disapproval. The entire stage of *partheneia* appears as a time of symbolic death. This ill-defined, liminal condition well represents the status of the adolescent who is no longer a child but not yet a full-status adult within the community.

Passages to Adulthood

Throughout the ancient Greek world, a girl's passage from adolescent to a marriageable woman received public recognition. Many rites celebrated girls' and boys' attainment of adult status. Processions, races, and public performances marked the final transition, when the young were formally introduced to the community. In Sparta, girls' public performance celebrated their attainment not only of marriageable maturity but also of adult citizen status in the community, independent of their marital status.

In contrast to the generally secretive nature of the prepubertal rites, this public recognition was an important dimension of this later transitional stage as both girls and boys publicly enacted their readiness to assume their adult social roles. The public displays of the girls' beauty and dancing offered them a way to come to terms with their own changing bodies and sexual readiness while they received public recognition for their value to the community. In Athens, dedication of statues of adolescent girls known as Kore figures, such as Figure 2.6, visually commemorated this transition. This public validation of the girls' personal experiences in turn provided them a sanctioned outlet for expressing their personal feelings. These celebrations therefore imparted various public and private meanings to the girls.

The fourth rite Aristophanes mentions above evokes the annual celebration of the Panathenaia for their patron city deity, Athena, which Athenians observed with greater ceremony every four years. The frieze around the outer edge of the interior wall of the Parthenon depicts the spectrum of participants, from gods to mortals. Central to the frieze is the presentation of the robe woven for this occasion, the *peplos,* to be presented to the goddess, and which perhaps adorned the cult statue of Athena within the temple.

In time, celebration of the Panathenaia expanded from honoring a local Athenian goddess of the young to a Panhellenic, "all Greek," rite that attracted participants from throughout Greece to its renowned poetic and athletic competitions. The prizes for these contests, a particular type of vase, known as a Panathenaiac amphora, became distinctive in both shape and illustration—most depict Athena on one side and a mythological or athletic scene on the other. It is noteworthy that it was a festival originally marking adolescent girls' passage to adulthood that transformed into a Panhellenic celebration intended to increase Athens' cultural importance in the larger Greek world. Statues of young women about two to three feet high called *kore* (sg.) or *korai* (pl.), from the Greek for girl or daughter, found on the Athenian Acropolis may have been dedicated to commemorate this transitional stage.

Altogether, the impact of these various girls' transition rites, from the prepubertal to the passage into adulthood, provided important cultural sanctions for the physical and emotional changes the girls were experiencing and for the community value of their evolving personal and public status. Except for some groups, such as the Jewish bat mitzvah or the Mexican quinceañera, there is generally a dearth of public recognition for the tumultuous changes female adolescents go through, and wild, unsupervised prom nights often serve as the only public marker of the adolescent's important passage to her adult status. Thus, the community attention ancient Greece gave to this turbulent period by ritually marking these stages and transitions would have provided the young person with major social support and validation for their many changes. These would have been of inestimable value for the young women, who were empowered by these rites to have confidence in their bodies, themselves, and their crucial roles for their communities.

Marriage

The most characteristic marker that a woman had attained adult status was marriage, and wedding rites were designed to provide public recognition of what was essentially a private event. Greece, like other ancient Mediterranean cultures, provided no religious sanction for marriage, which was fundamentally a financial transaction between two families. The ritual dimensions of ancient Greek wedding ceremonies stressed the bride's attainment of the erotic powers of Aphrodite. Some cities elaborated the ritual attention to the new bride, such as Sparta, which identified the bride with Helen. Athenian vase paintings also frequently portray Helen as the embodiment of the bride's eroticism and desirability, valued qualities that signify the bride's fertile potential.

To celebrate this new status and the couple's fertile potential, wedding ceremonies entailed much feasting—among the Mesopotamians, wedding feasts given by the groom's family could last a week or longer. The ancient

Greeks held joyous processionals accompanied by song and torchlight that took the bride from her father's home to her husband's, where her mother-in-law formally welcomed her into her new home. In many cultures, friends of the bride and groom celebrated the couple's first night with bawdy songs, both to encourage the couple in their new lovemaking and, as some sources state, to cover the bride's wedding night screams.

Adult Women's Rites

Adult, married, citizen women celebrated their valued familial and civic roles in various rituals throughout the year. The frequency of these rituals provided women numerous opportunities to move about in their communities. They thereby offset to some extent the legal and political restrictions many ancient Greek cities imposed on women. Most were women-only rites for predominantly female deities, but women also worshipped the male deities Dionysos and Poseidon.

Although each goddess had a slightly different emphasis, women honored Aphrodite, Demeter, and Hera for their oversight of women's sexuality, fertility, and marriage. While Greek custom, and in some cases law, imposed rules for appropriate sexual behavior, there was no denunciation of sexuality, especially female sexuality, as bad in itself. To the contrary, the ancient Greeks, like the Egyptians and Mesopotamians, delighted in the pleasures of sexuality and regarded both women and men as active, sexual beings. Hence, married, citizen women, men, prostitutes, and women of lower socioeconomic status all celebrated Aphrodite for her powers of sexuality and eroticism, but typically in separate rituals.

Rituals in the Home and the City

Largely ignored in the mythological tradition, Hestia played a crucial role as goddess of the hearth. Upon entering her husband's home at marriage, an Athenian bride was led three times around the central hearth fire to introduce her to the goddess of the hearth and home and to establish her role as the new mistress of the household. Likewise, each morning, the matron dedicated prayers and offerings to Hestia, invoking her protection for a successful household with many sons. Hestia's central importance is shown by the fact that at the major sanctuary for Zeus at Olympia, daily offerings were made first to Hestia before Zeus and the other deities honored there.

An early painted plaque from Corinth, sixth century B.C.E., depicts the mother and children, all wearing wreaths, engaging in a household ritual at the central hearth of the home (Figure 2.4). One adolescent girl pours a libation at the hearth, a boy brings in an animal for sacrifice, two other boys provide the music, while the mother and oldest daughter approach from behind. Since there were no official priestly positions—aristocratic families perpetuated their caretaker roles of certain sanctuaries—women and men equally engaged in sacred activities, including prayers, sacrifices, and other offerings. Here, the mother will officiate at the animal sacrifice.

Figure 2.4 Women's rituals in the home, painted plaque. Corinth, Greece. 7th c. B.C.E. Nimatallah / Art Resource, NY, National Archaeological Museum, Athens, Greece.

In Athens, Athenian women played a central, honored role in the annual Panathenaia for Athena, and they wove the new ceremonial robe, *peplos*, for Athena's cult statue in the Parthenon for the quadrennial celebrations. Hera served as a powerful city deity in Argos, Samos, and other places. It is likely that in their rites for Hera, the women affirmed their important civic status as well as their crucial roles in the cycle of regeneration. At Elis, in the northwest Peloponessos, a council of 16 women elders from the surrounding communities organized races for Hera that antedated the men's races for Zeus in neighboring Olympia, and continued to be held parallel to the men's rites.

Women's Rites for Demeter

Holding a central place in women's worship was the annual cycle of festivals for Demeter, celebrated throughout the Greek world. Best known from the Athenian calendar, her rites occurred at pivotal moments in the solar, agricultural year. The *Haloa* was celebrated near the winter solstice and the *Skira* around the summer solstice. The oldest rites for Demeter with roots well back into Mycenaean and pre-Greek times was the *Thesmophoria,* a mid-fall festival.

Rites typical of vegetative, fertility deities, including the god Dionysos, characterized all these festivals for Demeter. The ancient Greeks perceived these two deities as parallel. Both were deities of cultivation, fertility, and prosperity—Demeter as goddess of the cultivated grain, of women, and of bread, and Dionysos as god of the cultivated vine, of male fertility, and of wine. Both were intimately linked to the agricultural basis of Greek life and ritual. Rites for Demeter centered on activities designed to insure plant growth. Some required fasting or abstinence from certain foods before periods of open displays of sexuality that included baked images of female and male genitalia, songs, dances, same-sex sexual play, and *aiskhrologia.*

Most significant was the Thesmophoria, "the bringing of the sacred (law)," which was the most widespread and possibly the most important of all women's festivals for Demeter. Though practiced throughout the ancient Greek world, our most specific evidence comes, as often, from Athens. For three days, Athenian women occupied a prime downtown location, otherwise considered male by virtue of being public space, but to which no men were allowed during the festival. In the rites the women celebrated their own and the earth's powers of fertility, sexuality, and abundance. Moving from fasting and reflection to joyous and raucous celebration of their child-producing abilities, on the last day, known as *Kalligeneia*, "Fair Birth," the women's adolescent daughters may have joined them. At some point during these rites, the remains of pigs, the prolific animal sacred to Demeter, that were buried in special pits during the summer rites of the Skira, were dug up and mixed with the seed for the fall planting. In a rite of sympathetic magic the decayed flesh from Demeter's animal was thought to fertilize the seed and insure an abundant crop.

Eleusinian Mysteries

Emanating from this rich cycle of female ritual, Demeter's worship in the late-summer observance of the Eleusinian Mysteries developed into the most important religious practice in the ancient Greek and Roman worlds that lasted for two thousand years. According to Greek belief, Eleusis, about 13 miles northwest of Athens, was the site of the first agricultural production in Greece, with barley, Demeter's grain, the first to be cultivated. While the mystery rites to different deities at times converged and became interwoven, the rites for Demeter maintained a central importance. Two features distinguished Demeter's worship in the Eleusinian Mysteries from other Demetrian observances—the central role of Persephone and the fact that both men and women participated.

The practices of the Eleusinian Mysteries were meant to be kept secret. The word "mysteries" derives from the Greek verb *muô*, "to keep closed," as the eyes or mouth, that is, to keep silent. The initiate, known as *mustês*, under penalty of death took a vow of silence not to reveal the secrets of the rites, a vow that they overwhelmingly kept. Preparatory rites in Athens included a raucous day when worshippers washed their pigs in the sea—no doubt a squealing, shrieking melee—then returned home to perform the solemn sacrifices to Demeter. A ritual procession in a specified order along the Sacred Way brought worshippers to Eleusis. Along the way participants held an unknown ritual at a sanctuary to Aphrodite, reinforcing the connections between the two goddesses' realms of sexuality and fertility, and they were subjected to the ritual mockery of *aiskhrologia* at a bridge crossing before Eleusis. Upon arrival, the women engaged in a *pannykhis*, ecstatic all-night women's dance, while the men prepared the camps.

After a day of rest and possibly fasting, the rites proceeded with recitations and enactments of Persephone's story of abduction and return, such as told in the "Homeric Hymn to Demeter." A natural cave in the small hill overlooking Eleusis has a man-made trap door in the floor, which could have been used to stage Persephone's abduction into the underworld, while a worked passage around the back of the cave may have served as her route back.

The highest stage of initiation into the Eleusinian Mysteries was the *epopteia,* the sacred viewing, which secured for the initiate the blessings of the worship of Demeter and her daughter. Most scholars believe a sheaf of grain, Demeter's plant, was shown during the *epopteia.* The grain was no doubt familiar to most people, who would have been directly involved in its growing, harvesting, and preparation into food. Hence, its importance as an object shown at the highest viewing would remind the congregants of the sacred mystery of transformation that occurs when the seed develops into a plant that can be cultivated and processed for human sustenance. As the highest object of the viewing, grain therefore symbolized the initiates' appreciation for the gifts the goddess of grain bestowed on humankind.

The relationship of the Eleusinian Mysteries with women's winter festival for Demeter, the Haloa, suggests another possibility for the object shown during the *epopteia.* Athenian women observed the Haloa in Eleusis, with the fertility rites characteristic of Demeter's festivals. Some sketchy evidence intimates that on the last day of the festivities, men joined the women, who together celebrated their powers of fertility by engaging in anonymous ritual sexual intercourse. This winter-solstice renewal ritual occurred nine months before the Eleusinian Mysteries, a timing that assimilates the rituals celebrating the cycles of nature to the term of human gestation.

An early Christian source reinforces the suggestiveness of this timing, by reporting that at the *epopteia* a bright light suddenly blazed out in the darkness, while the high priest uttered the words, "Io, Io, the Goddess has given birth to a mighty child." The priest's words converge with the nine-month interval between the Haloa and the Mysteries to indicate that the object displayed at the *epopteia* was a child who had been conceived during the ritual sexuality of the Haloa. This sacrally conceived infant together with the sheaf of grain would well represent the two principal arenas encompassed in Demeter's realm of fertility—that of the earth and of human women, both being celebrated by the men and women of the community.

Persephone brought another dimension to this worship—her status as Queen of the Underworld extended Demeter's blessedness to a new realm, shaping not only life on earth but in the afterlife as well. Consequently, the Eleusinian Mysteries bestowed dual blessings on the initiates—the blessings of fertility in this world and of a joyous place in the next life. Thus Persephone, the daughter whose return from the underworld inaugurated the cycle of the seasons, a necessary alternation in the agricultural year, was also invoked for her role in promoting human blessedness.

In contrast to most Greek ritual practice, which focused on the practical trade-off of offering to a deity in exchange for their concrete support in this world, mystery religions offered a transcendent experience to their practitioners, a belief in some blessing to come. These transcendent beliefs, if not salvation exactly, furnished a concept of enlightenment withheld from non-initiates that gave worshippers hope of an improved lot in the next world. It is very likely that this emphasis on ideas of transcendence in the Eleusinian worship of Demeter and Persephone resulted in these rites becoming open to both men and women.

However mysterious particular aspects of Demeter's Eleusinian rites may be, their significance throughout Greek and Roman antiquity is not at all in doubt. Greek poets sang of the blessedness that initiation into the Eleusinian Mysteries brought, beginning with the late seventh-century "Homeric Hymn to Demeter," which proclaims,

Blessed are those of earthbound mortals who have seen these rites.
But whoever has not been initiated into the rites lives unfortunate with a different
  lot,
wasting away in the deadening darkness.[3]

At the end of the fifth century, the Chorus in Aristophanes' comedy *Frogs* portrays a group of initiates in the underworld who joyously celebrate the two goddesses' rites:

Forward now, to the Goddess' sacred circle-dance,
to the grove that's in blossom,
and play on the way for we belong to a select company.
And I shall go where the girls go
and I shall go with the women who keep the nightlong rites
of the Goddess and carry their sacred torch[4]

Many centuries later, the Roman orator Cicero claimed that Greece gave nothing to the world so wonderful as the Eleusinian Mysteries. It is due in fact to the great power and appeal of these rites that they were targeted for destruction by early Christian zealots. Many sanctuaries, like Eleusis, were destroyed under the antipagan measures of the militant Christian emperor Theodosius at the end of the fourth century C.E. Thus, a two-thousand-year-old religious belief and practice came to an end, pointedly opposed and in time superseded by a belief that claimed the superiority and primacy of a distant male deity.

Rome

Roman women's rituals strongly distinguished the class, marital, and moral status of the participants. Some festivals for Venus permitted women of lower classes and prostitutes to celebrate their own sexuality and fertility, but most rites were restricted to upper-class matrons, and some specific only to women who had been married to only one man, a *univira*. Roman women's rites accentuated women's ideal qualities of motherhood and marital sexual fidelity, and like those of Greek women, their rites were closed to men.

Sexuality and Fertility

Elite Roman women had some limited opportunities for celebrating their own sexuality and fertility through the ecstatic, female-only rites for the Bona Dea and for Ceres. Women of the lower classes and prostitutes celebrated their sexuality on April 1 in honor of the one aspect of Fortuna, "Good Fortune," that was open to them—Fortuna Virilis, "Virile Fortune." Emphasizing the different conduct expected of the upper class, on April 1 patrician matrons honored the Roman goddess of sexuality Venus as Verticordia, "Changer of Hearts," that is, toward virtue, a cult established during the war against Carthage to warn women against adultery. These religious epithets stress that sexual fidelity and motherhood are the only valid aspects of sexuality that should concern elite Roman women.

Motherhood

Most Roman women's ritual observances concentrated on proper enactment of their roles as mothers and matrons of the household and community, which they performed for different goddesses. A major festival for Juno, goddess of women, marriage, and childbirth, was the Matronalia, celebrated on March 1 to commemorate the building of Juno's temple on the Esquiline Hill, one of the seven hills of Rome. For the Matronalia, husbands gave their wives gifts and words of respect, while the matrons in turn served and entertained their own slaves. The festival emphasized the matron's honored place within the home and the responsibility entailed in her position. Since the festival marked a civic event—the building of Juno's temple—it connected the matron's domestic roles with her standing in the civic community.

On June 11 Roman matrons celebrated a festival with a similar name, the Matralia, to the native Italian goddess Mater Matuta, whose name may reflect biological growth. In these rites, the women emphasized their domestic roles by baking ritual cakes, and they underscored their class standing by driving a slave woman out of the temple. The rites interestingly accentuated an aunt's preference for her sister's children over her own.

Elite Roman women worshipped Fortuna in various guises. At marriage, brides dedicated their girlhood clothing to Fortuna Virginalis, "Virgin," and passed to the protection of the oracular deity Fortuna Primigenia, "Firstborn," who watched over mothers and childbirth. Only *univirae*, women who had only one husband, could honor several aspects of the goddess, beginning with Fortuna Virgo. Only *univirae* could touch the veiled statue in the temple of Fortuna in the cattle market that was connected with a cult of Patrician Chastity. In 295 a separate shrine to Plebeian Chastity was dedicated, offering plebeian women the same religious sanctions for leading sexually faithful lives as elite women. Likewise restricted to *univirae*, the cult of Fortuna

Muliebris, "Woman's Fortune," memorialized women's stopping a potential rebel invasion in 491, another example of the close ties between women's ritual and civic roles.

Vestal Virgins

Publicly perpetuating the central importance of the hearth, the institution of the Vestal Virgins was a salient feature of Roman civic religious practices. Dedicated to the Roman goddess of the hearth, Vesta, six girls from the most elite Roman families tended the fire of the public hearth of Rome. The purpose of the Vestal Virgins' service was to preserve the city's sacred fire, which represented the vitality of the city of Rome—as long as the fire burned, Rome would survive. Vestal Virgins were prohibited from marrying during their three-decade period of service, and they faced death if they violated their vows of chastity. Instead of bestowing their fertility upon a man for the purpose of his generational continuity, the Vestal Virgins were seen to dedicate their valuable female fecundity to the ongoing vitality of Rome.

In compensation for having to give up what were thought to be women's fundamental life desires, to marry and have children, Vestal Virgins were accorded some measure of social independence. Unlike other women, they did not need to have a male guardian, and they also had some economic autonomy. From a modern feminist perspective, a Vestal Virgin's giving up of an expected life with a man, functioning as wife and mother, granted her much greater independence than her married sisters. To the ancient Romans, these "privileges" a Vestal Virgin had were economically necessary to support her in her old age, since she would not have the expected familial means of support available to most women.

Other Rites

As a result of Roman conquests of Egypt and the Near East, the religions of these civilizations greatly impacted Roman beliefs. As noted, since Hellenistic contact, Greeks and Romans adopted the worship of Isis, whose like-minded focus on motherhood the Romans valued. The emphasis on morality in Isis' worship characterized two other religions imported from the Near East. Roman matrons adopted Jewish women's practices, and Christianity, an offshoot of Judaism originating in Judaea in the first century C.E., appealed to women throughout the empire, some of whom were among its earliest martyrs.

Sharply differentiated from these morally oriented religious practices was the worship of Anatolian Kybele introduced to the Romans as Cybele. Her Roman rites elaborated her connection with her mortal consort Attis, whose self-castration in the goddess's honor served as a model for her mortal devotees. Cybele's ecstatic rites, whose practices included fasting, feasting, and bathing in the blood of a bull or goat, continued till late antiquity.

The polytheistic nature of ancient religions permitted this syncretic mixing of beliefs, which often tolerated diverse views with little problem. People

Figure 2.5 Detail of goddess, Xeste 3, upper floor, wall painting. Akrotiri, Thera (Santorini), Greece, ca. 1700–1500 B.C.E. Drawing by Paul Rehak, reproduced by the kind permission of John Younger and the University of Texas Press.

recognized that other cultures had their own gods and customs, which they sometimes equated with their own. When rites were outlawed, it was usually for nonreligious reasons, such as the Roman banning of Dionysian rites for promoting licentious orgies or Christian practices for subverting state interests. In this environment, Roman women had the privilege of worshipping a spectrum of powerful goddesses that represented the breadth of ancient Mediterranean beliefs.

Figure 2.6 Kore with Dorian peplos, marble. ca. 530 B.C.E. Nimatallah/Art Resource, NY, Acropolis Museum, Athens, Greece.

Three

A Woman's Life in Ancient Cultures

LIFE STAGES FROM BIRTH TO DEATH

Ancient family structures were predominantly patriarchal. Nevertheless, after the religious realm, the domestic sphere gave women sources of power and identity. Other family members often shared the household, such as the father's parents and any siblings without their own household. A woman's kin were less likely to reside in her husband's household, unless they had no male relatives to care for them, or the wife's wealth and status prevailed. Isolated instances of matrilineal descent and inheritance patterns emerge sporadically in the ancient record.

Women's lives were typically divided into infancy-childhood, adolescence, adulthood, and old age. Puberty, childbirth, and menopause served as visible biological markers for three of women's transitions, while the social institution of marriage commonly signaled a woman's entry into recognized social adulthood. To ancient peoples individuals were not considered sufficient within themselves, but their identity and purpose in life were subsumed within their role in the family, and the role of the household in the larger community. Thus, woman's role in the family was central to her identity.

Infancy through Girlhood

Outside Egypt, the birth of a girl was greeted less enthusiastically than that of a boy, and a female infant was believed to cause greater pollution to the mother than a male infant. Infant mortality was high, perhaps 25–35 percent dying in the first year of life. In the Babylonian flood story, the gods decree miscarriages, stillborn births, and infant deaths in order to limit population. Late Roman records indicate that half of all children died by the age of 10, while demographic studies of Roman Egypt estimate a woman would have had to bear five or six children just to maintain population levels. Reducing the birth rate by one child would have halved the population within a century.

Because the first years of life were so precarious, mothers and nurses used amulets, prayers, offerings, and incantations to ward off childhood diseases and severe injuries. The ancient Mesopotamians believed Inanna blessed a healthy baby with joy and sweetness, to everyone's delight. Conversely, the prevalence of childhood mortality may have prompted the widespread beliefs in a bogeywoman, like the Mesopotamian demon Lamashtu, who suddenly snatched children to their death.

The high death rate of infants and young children underlay the great cultural emphasis on fertility, successful childbirth, and rearing a healthy child into adulthood. Nevertheless all these ancient cultures practiced infanticide because of deformity or to control family size. Mesopotamian texts speak of people rescuing an infant from a dog's mouth. Female infanticide was far more prevalent. Girls were thought to drain family resources since at marriage they took away part of their natal family's wealth in the form of a dowry. The common practice of infanticide suggests that the infant was not considered a child until it proved to be viable and had been formally accepted into the family, typically by the father.

If the father, who frequently could determine alone whether an infant lived or died, decided to raise a girl, she was not ritually introduced into the father's paternal clan rolls like her brothers. In Sparta, exceptionally, a council of female elders may have determined the fate of a female infant. In ancient Rome, families with more than one daughter did not give them individual names but identified them by appending the number of their birth order to the feminine form of their father's family name, such as Julia Prima, Julia Secunda, and so on. Despite these inequities in treatment, daughters who were raised were loved and cherished, and they played important roles in kin and civic relations.

Some documents offer formal advice for raising the infant. In a letter which Myia, the daughter of Pythagoras and Theano (see chapter 8), wrote to Phyllis, she applies the Pythagorean principle of *harmonia*, "balance," to her approach to infant care.

It is best to put the newborn to sleep when it has been suitably filled with milk, for then rest is sweet to the young, and such nourishment is easy to digest ... Don't continually give the child baths. A practice of infrequent baths, at a mild temperature, is better. In addition, the air should have a suitable balance of heat and cold ... the house should not be too drafty or too closed in ... and the bedclothes should be not rough but falling agreeably on the skin. In all these things nature yearns for what is fitting, not what is extravagant.[1]

Mothers typically nursed infants to age two or three, and they carried their babies in their arms or in a sling. Greek vase paintings show babies sitting on potties, and those not yet toilet trained wore diapers, aprons, or nothing. All children played with toys—wooden and clay animals, balls, and spinning tops were popular everywhere. Greek girls played a game similar to jacks with animal knucklebones. The favorite girls' toys were dolls and miniature replicas of adult female tools, such as cooking or weaving implements.

Parents loved their children and showered them with affection, fondly embracing and kissing them. Grandparents' greatest joy was to bounce their

Figure 3.1 Nefertiti, Akhenaten, and princesses Meretaten, Meketaten, and Ankhesenpaaten, painted limestone relief. Amarna, Egypt. 18th Dynasty, ca. 1345 B.C.E. Bildarchiv Preussischer Kulturbesitz / Art Resource, NY, Ägyptisches Museum, Staatliche Museen zu Berlin, Berlin, Germany.

grandchildren on their knees. Among Inanna's powers was kissing a baby's lips, perhaps to protect the infant with her divine breath. An Egyptian plaque depicts a tender family tableau: the pharaoh Akhenaten and queen Nefertiti seated on their thrones with their three daughters—Ankhesenpaaten on Nefertiti's shoulder, Meketaten on her lap, while the king holds Meretaten (Figure 3.1).

All children were raised by their mothers to the age of five or six. Except in Egypt, the food rations for girls were often lower than for boys. Unlike their brothers, who frequently enjoyed some education or social pursuits, girls remained at home, learning from an early age the adult skills they would need to know. Aristocratic girls often received tutoring at home, becoming literate and gaining political, business, or intellectual knowledge. Again, exceptionally, elite Spartan girls may have received a formal education that paralleled the boys', learning Spartan lore and values through choral songs and dances.

Menarche, Puberty, Menstruation

Ancient texts rarely mention menstruation, since women did not preserve in writing their customs at menarche and for monthly periods. Menarche commonly occurred at about age 13 to 15. Isis and Artemis were connected with menstrual blood. The red cloths sometimes adorning Isis' images may have represented sanitary napkins, and Egyptian laundry texts refer to menstrual cloths. Other than the Greek rites of transition, we do not know if families formally celebrated their daughters' developing puberty. It is likely that the female kin held private, family celebrations during which they recognized the girl's maturation and welcomed her into their circle of fertile women.

Ancient peoples regarded a woman's monthly bleeding with awe. A woman's ability to bleed without injury and the association of her monthly periods with fertility rendered menstruation mysterious to men, which generated concepts of pollution. Eating certain foods or carrying out some activities during menstrual periods were taboo, but women were not isolated or forbidden contact with men. Some societies considered a woman unclean during her period and for some time after, and that she needed to undergo a purification, typically a bath, to cleanse away her polluted state. Menstrual blood could have far-reaching effects—a menstruating wife or daughter could legitimately excuse a worker at Deir el-Medina, Egypt, from work.

These attitudes that attributed concepts of impurity to menstruating women and the customs that developed from them dramatize how patriarchal ideologies distorted women's basic biological functions, essential for their fundamental societal role, into the key instrument for demonizing her. At the same time that the menses were seen as polluting, Greek medical theorists considered them a type of purification which cleansed the excess liquid women accumulated in their bodies.

Egyptian texts do not call women unclean or claim that they need postmenstrual purification, but they call the bleeding itself a purification. One Egyptian text eagerly looks forward to a girl's upcoming first purification. Illuminating is an indigenous American view that treats menstruation, called moontime, as a woman's most sacred time, when she is at the height of her medicinal powers. Her menstrual flow is regarded as spiritually and physically purifying the woman. Traditionally, the Yurok society of California was organized around women's monthly cycles, which set the rhythm for all societal activities. From this perspective, the work pattern of the Egyptian laborer may have analogously been shaped by his wife's and daughter's menstrual cycles.

Marriage

Throughout most of antiquity, girls were married shortly after menarche. Sparta notably advocated that girls marry at a more mature age of 18. In a work entitled *Oeconomicus*, "Household Management," the fourth-century B.C.E. Athenian male writer Xenophon recommends that a girl be completely untutored and ignorant of the world. She should be married right after menarche to a much older man who would then instruct her in all she needs to know in order to manage his household. Xenophon may have made these recommendations in jest, but the reality probably differed. Even if they were inexperienced sexually, girls probably received extensive preparation for their adult, married lives, if only from observing the activities of their female relatives and increasingly helping them as they grew.

Marriage completely changed a girl's life, as she left her natal family to live in her husband's or his family's home. The latter situation was more severe since it often required the young bride to serve her mother-in-law, a relationship notoriously fraught with tensions. Her wedding night was also reputedly the girl's first heterosexual sexual experience, whose effect on the girl no doubt varied with her preparation and the age and care of her spouse. While stories often portrayed a girl's marriage as a wrenching experience, it was at the same time, and maybe for that very reason, celebrated as the most joyous day in a girl's life.

Because marriage was not a religious concern in most ancient cultures, there was not any religious sanction for marriage, but weddings publicly marked the community's recognition of the couple's new status as husband and wife. This new status entailed the couple's readiness to establish a household together, to bear and raise children, and to perform their respective civic and religious obligations. In many ancient cultures, men were required to get married and start a household, and in some cases even have sired children, before they could participate in the civic life of their community. Likewise, marriage and childbirth signified women's attainment of complete adulthood.

For the upper class, marriage secured the financial obligations between the two families contracting their son's and daughter's union. The lower social classes did not generally contract formal marriages, but cohabited for necessity, convenience, social propriety, and affection. Roman marriage customs in the late republic illustrate the potential complexity of marital negotiations. A Roman woman could get married with *manu*, in which her husband gained control over her, or without *manu*, where her father retained his guardianship. In both, a woman continued worshipping her natal family gods. In a marriage without *manu*, a woman remained within her family clan, which highlighted her status as daughter within her natal patriline. Without *manu*, a woman's natal male kin served to monitor her husband's treatment of her, and with her guardian residing in another household, she would have had some greater independence than one whose husband held authority over her. But a woman could negate the force of a marriage with *manu* by absenting herself from her husband every year for three nights in a row. Such a legal escape clause might also have acted as a check on her husband's authority over her, which he might easily lose.

Roman law forbade slaves from marrying legally. Slave unions were informally recognized as cohabitation that carried no legal authority—children were considered illegitimate and the woman could not be accused of adultery. However, slaves referred to one another as husband and wife in grave epitaphs, which shows that they regarded these unions as valid marriages.

Childbirth and Adoption

One might debate the question of whether "biology is destiny," but in ancient civilizations biology determined much of women's productive activities. After marriage, childbirth marked the next major shift in a woman's life. Bearing children was a woman's primary function in life and one that was expected of all women of all classes. In a society concerned with the survival of the mother through childbirth, the survival of the infant to childhood, and of the child into adulthood, having children and becoming a mother held fundamental cultural importance. Most women probably embraced marriage and motherhood as fulfilling their essential familial and community roles and as bestowing upon them their cultural identity as women.

Healthy children were the longed-for outcome of marriage. Childlessness was typically blamed on the wife, providing the husband with grounds for divorce. A Roman husband's eulogy known as the Laudatio Turiae, "the Praise of Turia," proclaims that he remained married to his wife even though she did not bear him any children, that he was outraged when she suggested divorce or other surrogacy, and that he had no need of children when he had such happiness with his wife. While rare, this sentiment shows that beneath the formal societal laws and customs, a couple's love for one another could profoundly shape their decisions.

Becoming a mother literally meant a woman's life. If divorced for childlessness and returned to her natal family, a woman might be maintained by brothers or other male relatives in a lowered status as a servant to the matron of that household rather than managing her own domain. If a woman had no family members willing to take her in, she would have to find employment, be sold into slavery, or starve. A woman divorced for childlessness probably had difficulty finding another husband. Those who managed to marry a second time and became pregnant redeemed their positions. Egyptians and Mesopotamians practiced surrogacy: a woman was hired, or a slave woman bought, to bear a child for a childless couple to adopt as their own—the situation the Bible describes for Abraham, Sarah, and their Egyptian slave woman Hagar. One Egyptian saying warns a man against abandoning his wife who has not conceived a child.

Men who were childless readily adopted sons to carry on their paternal line. Girls were rarely adopted; a girl's male relative might adopt her upon the death of her father, to act as her guardian in order to provide her a dowry and marriage arrangements. Exposed female infants might be rescued from death to be raised as a slave, often a prostitute. Both Mesopotamian and Egyptian women could adopt children. In a Middle Babylonian text a woman, possibly an older widow, adopts a girl to care for her in her old age. One set of Egyptian documents describes the husband of a childless couple adopting his wife, Rennefer, as his daughter so she could inherit his property. Years later as a widow, Rennefer adopts her brother and three children, two girls and a boy, borne by a slave woman she and her husband had bought to be a surrogate mother. Despite the surrogate arrangement, because their mother was a slave, Rennefer first freed the children before she adopted them.

Mother and Matron

Once a woman had successfully given birth, she completed her status as an adult woman—a wife and mother. This status endowed her with standing

in her family and among other women, and it granted her the right to participate in religious and civic activities.

As wives and mothers, women's lives revolved around childrearing, and
feeding and clothing their families. The nursing mother was a characteristic representation, which may also have carried magico-religious meanings.
Besides the ideal portrayals, such as Isis and Horus, from the earliest periods
Egyptian queens represented themselves as nursing their offspring. Although
royal Egyptian women rarely breastfed their infants, this portrayal stressed
their essential role in bearing and nourishing the heir to the throne.

The biblical commandment to honor one's mother and father well illustrates ancient Egyptian and Mesopotamian ideas about the esteem one owes
one's mother. An Egyptian New Kingdom scribal instruction emphatically
exhorts the son to his moral obligations. A woman devotes herself to raising
a child and cheerfully performing all tasks, however unpleasant they appear.
In turn, the adult child should demonstrate his appreciation of all his mother
endured to bring him to life and to adulthood by treating her respectfully in
her older age.

Besides caring for the children, women ran the household. This included
preparing food, keeping the house clean, fulfilling household rituals, and
conducting or supervising all cloth production. Women also gathered wood
or other fuel and water, chores usually relegated to servants and slaves.
Watering places figure significantly throughout Mesopotamian, biblical, and
Greek literature. A Greek vase painting depicts women collecting water at
an elaborate community fountain (Figure 3.2). The pairs of women on each
side leaving with the pitchers standing on their heads suggest the communal
nature of this activity, which other vase paintings reinforce by showing the
women engaged in lively conversation as they come to and from their water
collection. Moreover, this, like many other vase paintings, depicts the intri-
cacy of women's weaving, offering an insight into the appearance of their
dress that perishable cloth does not allow.

As mothers and matrons, adult women had some social rights. In general,
the home was the woman's domain, the arena in which she had some say while
her husband dominated in more public, civic activities. A fifteenth-century
B.C.E. Egyptian text directs a man to leave the home to his wife and not to
interfere with her authority there. In Egypt the title Mistress of the Household
may have carried social import, possibly comparable to a man's official role in
Egypt's administrative bureaucracy. Numerous representations of the Mistress
of the Household, both on funerary stelae and as small wooden statuettes, such
as that of Tiya from Medinet el-Ghurab (Figure 3.3), reveal the importance the
Egyptians accorded women for their extraordinary work in raising children and
managing all the domestic work successfully. Another Egyptian saying calls
anyone who wrongs the mistress of the home a fool whose lot will be cursed.

In all ancient societies wealthier women freed themselves from domestic
tasks by supervising the servants and slaves who performed them. Women
of more modest resources had to do all the household work themselves, with
perhaps the aid of some servants and other family members. Whether legally

Figure 3.2 Women at fountain, black-figure hydria. ca. 520 B.C.E. HIP / Art Resource, NY, The British Museum, London, Great Britain.

free or enslaved, the lives of most women centered on performance of similar tasks, often side by side.

Men in many of these ancient cultures could set up a second household with a concubine, which often received legal recognition as long as it did not interfere with the wife's abode. A concubine might be of any social class, and she was probably grateful to have a household. But her status was lower than that of a wife, and the children she bore might not be accepted as legitimate players in the society's official positions.

It is doubtful that many women could have chosen not to marry or bear children, or that they would have received cultural validation if they did not fulfill their expected cultural roles. Some ancient Egyptian evidence indicates unmarried women residing on their own, but their status is unclear—some interpreters suggest temple personnel, others that they were concubines. Egyptian census data for a soldier named Hori record that he had five unmarried sisters living in his home, three of whom his son still supported years later. Without any more information it is impossible to know why so many daughters in one family remained unmarried, and whether it was by their choice. General evidence suggests this was not the preferred situation.

Figure 3.3 Tiya, Mistress of the Household, painted wood. Medinet el-Ghurab. ca. 1360–50 B.C.E. The Metropolitan Museum of Art, Rogers Fund, 1941 (41.2.10). Photograph, all rights reserved, The Metropolitan Museum of Art, New York.

Status of Adult Women

In ancient Greece and Rome, women were never considered legal adults, but were under a man's authority throughout their lives. Her father was typically a girl's guardian, and, with some exceptions, after marriage a woman's husband held this authority. This legal restriction often meant that women could not engage in business on their own, initiate lawsuits or answer to one in court, or make their own marital arrangements or other decisions about their lives. Ancient Athens, often promoted as the fount of Western ideals of democracy, was also the most restrictive in its subjection of women to male authority, known as *kyria*. Legislation of the first Roman emperor Augustus exempted elite women who had borne three sons and freedwomen who had borne four sons from certain taxes and from the restrictions of male guardianship.

The earliest Mesopotamian evidence and that for Minoan and Etruscan women shows they enjoyed a status comparable to men's. In dramatic contrast to the male guardianship imposed on adult Greek and Roman women, ancient Egyptian women interacted with men, did not wear veils, wore clothing suitable for the climate, and, within the hierarchical, patriarchal parameters of the society's institutions, were apparently able to make decisions about their own lives.

In the last three centuries B.C.E., the Greek and Roman conquests of Egypt led to greater interactions among the three cultures. The more egalitarian status of Egyptian women ameliorated the status of colonial women compared to their counterparts back home. However, the influences moved in both directions, and elite Egyptian women began emulating the customs of the Greek and Roman colonialists, even asking to be assigned a male guardian when they had never required one before.

Adultery

Ancient laws of adultery targeted women and dealt harshly with female adultery. Each society told moralistic tales of the disasters incurred by the actions of wanton, adulterous wives. Marriage laws aimed to insure the husband's biological line, which could only be guaranteed by the wife's strict sexual marital fidelity. A wife's adultery was typically cause for immediate divorce, even if the man did not wish it. A woman had to forfeit any dowry or other material goods she brought to the marriage, items which she or her family received back in the much rarer cases of the husband's fault for divorce. In some societies, the penalties for a woman's adultery could mean her ostracism from the community, enslavement, or even death, penalties which the man also incurred in some circumstances.

In an interesting twist, an Egyptian letter describes the actions villagers at Deir el-Medina took in defense of a wife whose husband was having an affair with an unmarried woman. Only the arrival of the police stopped the villagers from assaulting the single woman and her family, but they forced the man to get a divorce. The incident suggests that at least in some periods and places, and perhaps more often than we know, the community undertook to protect the marriages of its inhabitants, which included protecting the wife as well as the husband from the damaging consequences of their spouse's marital infidelity.

Not surprisingly, despite legal strictures and cultural reprisals, adultery occurred. In the late republic and early empire, several aristocratic Roman women were involved in highly public sexual scandals, and the emperor Augustus exiled his own daughter Julia for not abiding by his moral decrees. In contrast, the fourth-century B.C.E. Greek writer Xenophon states that the Spartans had no concept of adultery. An unmarried Spartan man might make arrangements to sire children through another man's wife, with the result that a woman would manage two households. Contemporary scholar Sarah Pomeroy doubts that the strong-willed Spartan woman would have been excluded from the negotiations for such arrangements, which she calls "husband-doubling."[2] The Spartan situation may be a genuine rare case of polyandry, which probably developed in order to deal with a shortage of women and the need to produce sons for the many citizen households. But the consequences substantially increased women's economic and domestic powers.

For cultures highly concerned with curtailing women's sexual activity, ancient Greek and Roman texts regularly portrayed married women as quasi-independent sexual beings who freely consorted with their lovers virtually under their husband's noses. These dramatic portrayals are strikingly open in showing women as flagrantly flaunting society's expectations of their sexual fidelity in order to pursue their own sexual desires.

Notably the greatest heroine in ancient Greek mythology was Helen, notorious for her extramarital sexual liaisons. Helen was renowned for abandoning her husband, child, and home to accompany her Trojan lover, Paris. One strain of Greek literature, especially Athenian drama, strongly condemned Helen as an adulteress and home destroyer, but another portrayed her positively. The earliest Greek poem, Homer's *Iliad*, describes Helen with awe. When she approaches the male Trojan elders on the city parapet, King Priam exclaims,

We cannot blame the Trojans or well-armored Greeks
for suffering pains a long time on account of this woman—
her face looks strangely like an immortal goddess.[3]

Although Priam continues by saying that it would be better if she returned home, none of the Trojans demands her expulsion, and the king treats his beloved daughter-in-law gently.

Likewise, in a poem extolling the power of love, the female poet Sappho held Helen up as the human exemplar of Aphrodite's divine power of erotic desire. While Athenian tragedies vilified Helen, Athenian wedding ceramics portrayed her as the ideal bride who embodied the same qualities of beauty and sexuality that the goddess Helen represented in Spartan ritual.

Despite the severe social and legal penalties against female adultery, Helen's story persisted. An illuminating parallel emerges in the Laguna Pueblo tales about their deity Yellow Woman, whose extramarital affairs result in significant cultural benefits. In a fundamental cultural tale, Yellow Woman is married to the infertile Spirit of Winter. As she forages for food, she encounters the fertile Spirit of Summer, whom she brings home. Their intercourse produces life-sustaining vegetation. Yellow Woman's father ritually welcomes the Summer Spirit, and the entire community celebrates her for the abundance the two generate, while her apparent adultery goes by without notice. Other stories result in the people's receiving buffalo meat and other valued resources from Yellow Woman's liaisons.

Yellow Woman's and Helen's sexual activities have an inherent cultural appeal because they illuminate basic ideas about fertility, reproduction, and community benefice. The Laguna tales portray the positive dimensions of these extramarital liaisons overtly, while the Greek ones depict Helen's sexual activity ambivalently. Interestingly, some cultural practices reinforce the positive views. Part of the wedding vows in ancient India compelled the bride to admit to adultery regardless of whether she ever had sex. Ancient Greek sources on Spartan women's marital practices articulate the ideas underlying this custom, for they state that adultery heightens sexual desire which thereby engenders more vigorous offspring. Although the condemnation of Helen's adultery ultimately prevailed, beneath the veneer of sexual restrictions lingered a perception of women as fully active sexual beings, whose multiple lovers represented the elemental vitality of female sexual energy and procreativity.

Because Helen's ritual and mythological home was in Sparta, the stories of Helen's many lovers might reflect Spartan women's greater latitude for extramarital affairs. Laguna scholar Paula Gunn Allen offers a valuable insight into Yellow Woman's connection with social mores. To a people deeply concerned with moral behavior, Yellow Woman's mythic actions do not prescribe actual women's conduct. Rather, the symbolic value of Yellow Woman's sexual multiplicity transmits notions of their own powers that the Laguna women employ in socially approved ways.[4]

The literature and the divine images present concepts of appreciated female sexual dynamics that deliver a double message. They affirm the valued place of female sexuality in the society, providing positive models for women's fundamental societal contributions. At the same time, these empowering images of female sexuality emerge in profound tension with the society's moral restrictions, which resulted in castigating the women who embodied these ideals. The portrayals of Helen from ancient Greek culture to the modern West have straddled these two poles, the stunningly beautiful icon of female eroticism on the one hand and the vilified adulteress on the other.

Sexuality

All these ancient cultures recognized women as sexual beings. Respectable wives were to exercise their sexuality only within approved parameters—in marriage and ritual. Husbands were expected to please their wives sexually. Mesopotamian texts speak of a husband's delight in his wife's heated sexual desire. Female sexuality was regarded in both positive ways—sexuality as leading to fertility—and negative—unregulated female sexuality portrayed as destroying masculinity, families, and communities. It is because women were seen as powerful sexual beings that these ancient cultures felt compelled to control women's sexuality rigidly so that men could be assured of the biological paternity of their sons.

In order to assure female sexual inviolability, girls were closely guarded to prevent any contact with males before marriage, and married women were not allowed extramarital affairs. In contrast, as long as they fulfilled their obligations to produce sons for the paternal line, men were permitted any sexual outlet they desired. In most ancient cultures, those defined as the free, citizen, usually upper-class men could engage in sexual conduct with any man or woman of lower or slave status. He would, however, incur serious legal and civic penalties if he seduced an upper-class woman. By reinforcing the sexually restrictive status of elite women, the law underscored the sexual implications of class divisions as women and men of lower classes were legitimate sexual prey to any upper-class male.

In a passage of Homer's *Odyssey,* the goddess Kalypso protests the society's sexual double standard. She accuses the male gods of jealously depriving goddesses of their mortal male lovers, while the gods enjoy as many female lovers as they wish.[5] As a goddess Kalypso can voice what a mortal female character could not. The passage may thus reflect actual women's feelings about their society's conflicting attitudes to women's and men's sexual activity.

Because cultural thinking rooted sexuality in concepts of the sacred, some ancient rituals encouraged sexual activity in culturally sanctioned forms. We have seen that ancient Egyptian, Mesopotamian, and Greek fertility rites entailed sexual intercourse in ritual contexts that aimed at promoting both human and agricultural fertility. These rituals acknowledged the elemental power of female sexuality. Besides their sacred and fertility-enhancing purposes, these rituals may also have granted married women sanctioned occasions for ventilating the frustrations of their subordinate social positions, providing them with welcome sexual variety from the customary sexual restrictions on their lives.

An episode in the Mesopotamian hero tale, *The Epic of Gilgamesh,* interestingly connects female sexuality with the formation of human culture. In the tale, Shamhat, a temple priestess of Ishtar, is called in to bring the man of the wild, Enkidu, from a state of unsocialized, animal-like nature to the status of civilized man. A full week of sexuality is the first step in this acculturation process, during which time Enkidu acquires human language and experiences human intimacy, which stirs a longing for human companionship. Shamhat completes Enkidu's socialization by teaching him to eat the foods of civilization—bread and wine—to clothe himself, to bathe and to use oils and fragrances. Like the sweep of the goddess' powers in the "Hymn to Ishtar" (see chapter 1), this episode reveals the pivotal role the Mesopotamians believed female sexuality played in the development of civilization.

Some free women of lower classes and slave women held ideals of premarital virginity and of marital fidelity in emulation of aristocratic ideals, as evidenced by tombs of Roman freed couples which express deep feelings about their marital bond. But maintaining these ideals must have been difficult for women whose class status by definition made them sexually available to men, and it may be that non-elite women felt freer to engage in multiple sexual affairs. Prostitutes obviously had far greater sexual experience than elite wives. Although prostitution was often imposed on women and girls due to enslavement, debt, or the threat of starvation, some texts suggest that at least some sex workers enjoyed their trade and that they received pleasure as well as a livelihood from their sexual congress. Biting Roman satirical texts claim that elite women played out their voracious sexual appetites by working as prostitutes at night in the cheapest brothels.

Marriage institutions highly regulated elite women's heterosexual relations. However, ancient Egyptian and Roman love poems rarely celebrated marital sex, but delighted instead in illicit affairs, both pre- and extramarital (see chapter 9). Greek and Roman comedies portrayed women as sex-starved, as avid users of dildoes for self-gratification, and as enthusiastically carrying on adulterous affairs. Whether reflecting actual behavior or women's and men's fantasies about women's sexuality, these poetic and comedic images show that women's sexual activity did not conform entirely to cultural prescriptions. Moreover, even with their husbands within marriage, women may have had options other than only reproductive sex. Anal intercourse, practiced for the purpose of birth control, may also have served as a pleasurable form of sexual activity without risk of pregnancy.

Ancient Greek and Roman texts distinctively treated with open delight a subject glossed over in many cultures—homosexual desire and relations, in particular, female homosexuality. Greek love poetry by both women and men portrays homoerotic attractions and homosexual activity as pleasurable (see chapter 9). In his *Symposium,* the fourth-century philosopher Plato defines male homoeroticism as the highest type of love, and the only kind that can lead to intellectual and spiritual enlightenment. Zeus' abduction of the male youth Ganymede formed a popular subject in Greek literature and art. The prominent display of this abduction in the exterior sculpture of the Archaic temple of Athena on Athens' Acropolis demonstrates the significance the story held for an ancient Greek audience. This open treatment of homosexuality shows that the ancient Greeks, like many other cultures, did not divide sexuality into categories of hetero- or homosexual depending on the sex of one's partner. As seen, marriage and procreation were expected of everyone, but as sexual beings, the Greeks regarded both women and men as expressing their sexual desires in multiple ways.

Against this background, female homosexual activity appears as one point in a spectrum of possible sexual expression. A fifth-century terra-cotta sculpture portrays a rare scene of two women together in intimate affection in a possibly homoerotic moment (Figure 3.4). Ancient evidence indicates primarily the pedagogic function of ancient Greek homoerotic relations, which are more clearly delineated for the relationship between an older youth or man and a younger male. A few scattered references suggest that women probably continued their homosexual friendships into adulthood, which may have provided them continuing opportunities for sexual expression throughout their lives.

Chastity

By the second century C.E., a growing emphasis on women's chastity rather than fertility emerges in diverse sources. Ancient tales claim that the reason the gods imposed war and disease on human beings was to reduce overpopulation. Nevertheless, as we have seen, earlier cultural emphasis consistently focused on the necessity of fertility to keep communities going. But in the vast population shifts of the Hellenistic and Roman empires, women may no longer have felt it necessary to fulfill their reproductive potential. From a patriarchal standpoint, a woman's wish to avoid having children necessarily meant that she would remain virginal and celibate, someone who would never engage in sexual intercourse. These shifts in thinking coincided

Figure 3.4 Two women, terracotta. Possibly from Myrina, Asia Minor, ca. 100 B.C.E. The British Museum/Art Resource, NY, London, Great Britain.

with the rise of Christianity, where sexual chastity formed a fundamental theological precept.

Widows

Since women married young typically to an older man, even with the high rate of mortality in childbirth, wives often outlived their husbands. From the earliest period, Mesopotamian laws provided for widows, including her rights to her dead husband's property, her residence, and what properties she might keep if she remarried. Husbands often specifically provided for their wives' care in the case of their death to insure they would not become destitute. In a reversal of the common expectation that sons will be responsible for their elder parents' care, especially their widowed mothers, Old Babylonian marriage contracts stipulate that a daughter or her husband will support the wife's widowed mother. These clauses may reflect closer personal bonds between Mesopotamian mothers and daughters. They also indicate that women had the financial resources, and the legal and civic standing, that enabled them to fulfill this responsibility. These clauses show that then as now it was best to spell out contractually the financial obligations of both partners entering into the marriage.

A young widow often remarried; an older widow would make a less attractive marriage partner, since she would be unlikely to bear sons for her new husband. Elite older widows in Egypt, Mesopotamia, and Rome preferred their independence. Often inheriting from their husbands, these wealthy women took advantage of their abundant circumstances to engage in business or other professional affairs. A Middle Assyrian law proclaims that if a woman's husband and father-in-law are dead and if she has no sons, she may go wherever she pleases. The second-century B.C.E. Roman widow Cornelia famously rejected the marriage offer of Ptolemy VIII of Egypt to concentrate on raising the 12 children she had borne to her first husband, thereby also fulfilling the Roman ideal of a *univira*.

Widows of lower classes were not so fortunate, as they had to fend for themselves and their children. Care for widows and orphans forms a running motif throughout Egyptian and Mesopotamian laws and moral texts, which warn against taking advantage of the widow, a woman vulnerable without a man's protection. A king displays his compassion by the care he bestows upon widows. Mesopotamian temples, which served as a kind of social service agency, took care of unwanted infants, the infirm, widows, and the old, all groups who had no other sources of support. Widows furnished clothing to the temple in exchange for their care.

Old Age

Women's lives were hard, and they rarely lived into their forties. Yet some women survived their childbearing years to experience menopause and old age. Mesopotamian evidence suggests that elder women were in better health than elder men and may have outlived them. Then as now women dyed their gray hair, henna and juniper being long used in Egypt and Mesopotamia for this purpose. Ancient peoples held ambivalent views about old age. They deplored the physical, mental, and psychological debilities accompanying old age. The Mesopotamians encouraged older people to drink more wine since alcohol provided a welcome palliative to the emotional and physical ailments of age. On the other hand, surviving the numerous vagaries of life to reach old age was considered a reward for a virtuous life. The greatest gift of old age was the opportunity to know one's grandchildren. While most faculties diminished with age, wisdom increased. Elder women were regarded as sages, sometimes holding formal or informal positions within their communities.

Age did not mark an end to work as most women as well as men had to continue to contribute to their own and to their family's sustenance as long as they could. A devastating bane of old age was dependency on one's children. The many exhortations to children to tend to their aged parents well illustrate the tension this dependency caused. Without children or other family members to care for one, old age could quickly lead to destitution and starvation. As noted, Mesopotamian temples offered the old some support.

Death

Women were believed to experience the same kinds of transitions into the next world as men, and basic funerary rites were generally the same for both. Differences emerged in the grandeur of the funerals, with men commemorated by greater displays, tombs, and monuments. By the same token, women's elaborate funerary rites signified their high social status.

Women prepared the dead for burial (except for the Egyptian upper class, where professional embalmers performed these activities). This included washing the body, dressing it, and wrapping it in its burial shrouds. Women were the primary mourners, their cries and dirges intended to express the sorrow of the living and to aid the dead on their journey into the next world. Assuming the roles of Isis and Nephthys, women played a major part in Egyptian funerary rites. The Greeks sanctified women's essential funerary role by proclaiming it to be a wife's honored duty to perform the final rites for her husband.

Funerary monuments from ancient Greece, Rome, and Greco-Roman Egypt reveal love for the dead woman. Those who died before puberty or marriage were mourned for dying before they reached their prime. Often called brides of Hades, death rather than marriage became their crowning state. Many grave markers mourned the loss of women who died in childbirth, sometimes with the infant, sometimes leaving a motherless newborn. These women, along with those who lived through many childbirths and a lifelong marriage, often received great praise from their husbands for their faithfulness, industriousness, and excellent mothering of their children. Even if these are idealized remembrances, they reflect the love and affection men held for their mothers, wives, daughters, and sisters. These commemorations, which required an expenditure of funds and personal energy, materially demonstrate the loved and valued places women held within their families, as illustrated in Figure 10.5, the funerary monument of Aththaia from the Roman imperial period, second century C.E.

WOMEN AT HOME

Domestic Space

The physical space in which most women spent their lives was modest. The two Egyptian specially built workmen's villages of Amarna and Deir el-Medina, fifteenth century B.C.E., provide rare glimpses into the home space of an average Egyptian worker. These village row houses measured about 16 by 30 feet at Amarna and 16 by 50 feet at Deir el-Medina. The thick mud-brick walls served as excellent insulators in summer and winter, while bundles of reed sealed with mud provided watertight roofs.

These houses included a front reception area, a larger central living room, two back rooms used as a bedroom and a storage room, a courtyard where the cooking occurred, and frequently an additional underground storage area. Exterior back stairs led to the flat roof, where many household activities took place through much of the year. A limestone mortar for pounding grain with a pestle was sunk into the floor of the central room, and some were outfitted with a milling device to grind the broken grain. The permanent fixture of these implements demonstrates their importance in women's household chores. When they could not be conducted outdoors domestic activities took place in the central and back rooms. Lamps were plentiful, filled with oil and wicks to provide light in all the rooms. Although the back part of the house was sometimes referred to as the women's quarters, women do not seem to have been confined to that area, but to have had freedom of movement indoors and out.

Food animals like sheep or goats lived in the courtyard and in the house, and any indoor cooking areas had vents for the smoke. Whenever possible, kitchens were outdoors and detached from the main house, some with covered connecting passageways. Similar beehive-shaped ovens for baking bread or firing clay have been found in cultures worldwide. Egyptian ones had a flat top on which other items might be heated while the bread was baking. Where wood was scarce, dried dung made an efficient, long-lasting, and surprisingly odor-free cooking fuel. Oven remains at Amarna show residue of sheep dung mixed with straw.

Ancient homes did not have indoor toilets. People availed themselves of the outdoors or of chamber pots when needed inside. Egyptians lived near the Nile, where they conducted their bathing and laundering. All refuse was thrown out, including human waste. For rural dwellers in the hot, dry Egyptian climate, this was not usually a problem since items decomposed fairly quickly. Women employed insect repellents composed of various substances and sweet-smelling incenses made from frankincense, myrrh, and other spices to mask and fumigate odors within the house. Pets, notably cats, helped control rodent infestation.

Large, extended families inhabited the household. Middle Kingdom census and ration documents provide a personal demographic profile of two households. Census rolls record that the household of a soldier named Hori, which was considerably larger than those in the later workmen's villages, included his wife, infant son, mother, and five female relations, probably unmarried dependent sisters—eight adults in all. Years later after Hori's death, his son Sneferu continued to live there with his grandmother, mother, and three unmarried aunts. Other documents show that a small landowner named Heqanakht received rations for his wife, mother, their personal maids, three other women—possibly daughters or daughters-in-law—six men—probably Heqanakht's sons—and the family of at least one of the sons. Whether these 14 adults plus children lived in the same house is not known.

Rural dwellers could readily expand the basic house shape by adding on rooms as needed. Smaller urban residences were crowded closer together in the more limited city space, and later Roman urban centers teemed with apartment houses. Built with contingent walls, without sanitation or running water, and inhabited by large families, urban homes were darker, dirtier, smellier, and noisier, and the streets were not much better as all refuse was thrown into the street.

The homes of the wealthy provided greater comforts. Many featured rooms built around a central courtyard, which was embellished into gardens with fountains, shade trees, and aromatic plants, and surrounded by porticoes. Some were two or three stories high with windows high in the walls. Some Egyptian homes had limestone-lined bathrooms in which the bather stood in a stone basin fitted with a waterproof outlet and enclosed by a screen. A servant standing behind the screen poured water over the bather. Some also had a small toilet room next to the bathroom that consisted of a modern-looking wooden toilet seat placed on two brick pillars and set over a bowl of sand that was periodically replaced. A small pool in the floor of the atrium, entry room, of Roman homes collected rain water from an opening in the roof. Pipes led from this collecting pool to kitchen and bath areas, and an overfill pipe drained away excess water. The Romans also had extensive urban water systems with pipes that delivered water to public buildings, the homes of the rich, and to the general populace.

Many wealthy homes contained separate structures for servants' quarters and household industries, including grain storage, baking, beer brewing, weaving, craft production, and carpentry. Many enclosed their compound by a mud-brick wall with a single guarded entrance to the street. Whether because of Egyptian influence on later domestic architecture, or because it provides a convenient design for the temperate Mediterranean climates, this basic ground plan characterized the homes of wealthy Hellenistic Greeks and Romans.

Frequently a male protective deity watched over homes; both wealthy and modest. Egyptians painted images of the god Bes, a squat, protective male deity, on the front of their dwellings, less frequently Isis or her son Horus. Ithyphallic, "with erect penis," representations of the god Hermes watched over the entryways to Athenian homes, as did an ithyphallic Priapus for Roman abodes. Wall niches in the front room of Egyptian and Roman houses held images of gods or ancestors where offerings could be left. To signify the gods' acceptance, Romans painted snakes taking the offering left on the altar.

Paintings on plaster decorated the walls of many homes. Dancing scenes animated the front rooms of two houses at Amarna. In one, a group of Bes figures dances toward the pregnant goddess Taweret (Figure 3.5), while the other portrays a procession of women dancing. Paintings that depict a great variety of scenes—architectural façades, gardens, idyllic country landscapes, mythological subjects, and portraits—adorned the walls of Roman homes. Two Pompeian female portraits, one with her husband, portray the women in the same pose (Figure 3.6). In their left hands they hold a writing tablet by their chests, and they touch a pen to their lips with their right. In Pompeii, where women were actively engaged in commerce and some public affairs, these writing implements might have signified their professional position.

Figure 3.5 Egyptian pregnant hippopot-
amus goddess Taweret. Werner Forman /
Art Resource, NY, Egyptian Museum,
Cairo, Egypt.

Like their walls, the floors of Hellenistic and Roman houses were richly decorated in mosaic tile. One entryway warns the visitor with a large black-and-white silhouette of a chained growling dog above the words *Cave Canem,* "Beware the Dog." An earth-toned mosaic portrait of the Greek poet Sappho in the floor of a late Roman villa in Sparta depicts her gazing out past the viewer with a faraway intensity, suggesting a state of divine rapture. The mosaic portrait demonstrates the continued importance of this female poet a thousand years after her life. The inclusion of Sappho's portrait with those of male poets around a central image of several Muses may also indicate that the room was used for creative endeavors and that women as well as men engaged in the intellectual pursuits there.

A strong demarcation between women's and men's living spaces emerged in Athenian living patterns, with the men's rooms in front and downstairs and the women's rooms in the back and upstairs. Texts probably present an idealized image of elite women confined to the women's quarters and venturing out only for religious festivals. Only wealthy women who had slaves and servants to collect water, go shopping, and conduct other needed public activities could have afforded to be so restricted in their movements. If

Figure 3.6 Woman with writing materials, wall painting. Pompeii. Erich Lessing / Art Resource, NY, Museo Archeologico Nazionale, Naples, Italy.

valid, this situation demonstrates that women of the elite class do not always benefit from their status, but that their privileges might constrict them in ways not imposed on women of lower socioeconomic classes.

Personal Grooming and Hygiene

Personal cleanliness and grooming figured importantly in ancient women's lives. To the Mesopotamians, having clean clothes and water to bathe in were two of the blessings of mortal life. Egyptians bathed regularly in the Nile. Mycenaean and Hellenistic excavations have unearthed bathtubs very similar in shape to modern free-standing tubs, while Romans visited public baths, which either had separate sections for women and men, or separate days for each. One Greek vase painting shows two women around a small tub with sponge and towels. Egyptians used harsh, nonlathering substances like natron (sodium carbonate), soda, and ashes for cleaning themselves. Both women and men oiled their skin generously after bathing to ease the harshness of the cleansing agents and to protect their skin from the mostly hot, dry, and sandy desert climate. The Greeks mixed sodium carbonate, which they called *nitron*, with oil to form a soap, and they lavished on olive oil after bathing.

Egyptians cleaned their teeth with a toothpaste made from plant roots. To sweeten their breath, women chewed little balls of myrrh, frankincense, rush-nut, and cinnamon. The ever-present abrasive desert sand wore away tooth enamel and caused many dental problems. However, without sugar in their diets, inhabitants of other environments did not face some of the problems of cavities and tooth decay plaguing many moderns.

Ancient peoples, including men, extensively depilated their body hair for hygienic as well as cosmetic reasons. Egyptian women's tombs contain metal tweezers, knives, and razors to shave and pluck unwanted hair, and whetstones to keep the implements sharp. Greek women removed their pubic hair by plucking and singeing with hot coals, and according to one Greek account Etruscan women and men removed all body hair with pitch. For festive occasions, Egyptians wore perfumed wax cones on their heads, as illustrated in Figure 5.5.

Women's rooms and graves of all cultures and periods contained jars for cosmetics, oils, and perfumes—and mirrors, everywhere made in the same basic oval or round shape with a handle. Bronze Etruscan mirror frames were intricately carved with romantic and erotic scenes that displayed the sensual openness of Etruscan women's lives. Egyptian and Greek women held mirrors by handles sensuously shaped like a young naked woman holding fruit or flowers in her hands (Figure 3.7). The mirror's convex shape displayed the woman's face, hair, neck, and upper chest in the disc above the naked girl. Since the mirrors did not stand on their own but had to be held, this tactile contact intensified the intimate connection that the sensuous, erotic images carved on the mirror must have left upon the women who handled them daily. An Etruscan-found painting on the inside of a drinking cup, mid-fourth century B.C.E., shows three nude women at their toilette, the woman at the left retrieving something from a basket whose lid she holds up, the woman in the middle gazing at her face in a mirror, and the woman on the right perhaps assisting her (Figure 10.1).

Cosmetics had hygienic as well as beautifying purposes. Besides the aesthetic appeal, from predynastic times, Egyptian women and men painted their upper and lower eyelids to protect against sun glare and eye infection. The inscriptions on the four linked wooden ointment containers from the eighteenth dynasty (Figure 3.8) well represent this range of beautifying and hygienic purposes. The three legible inscriptions identify their contents as "excellent kohl" for make-up, "open vision," an eye solution, and "repels blood" to check bleeding. Over time women switched from a green kohl made from malachite to a galena-based dark gray kohl. In one fashion trend women combined the two colors, applying green at the brows and corners of the eyes and gray on the lids and lashes. Rouge was made from red ochre, which was mixed with oil to form a lip gloss. Egyptian women tattooed their bodies, but this practice was increasingly associated with the lower social classes, as prostitutes decorated their bodies extensively with tattoos.

Figure 3.7 Mirror handle as young girl, bronze. Argolid, Greece. ca. 530 B.C.E. By permission of the Staatliche Antikensammlung und Glyptothek, München, Germany.

Mycenaean and Greek women used white lead as a face paint and vermilion for cheek and lip color. Instead of a therapeutic benefit, Greek women poisoned their bodies with this toxic application. Later Greek and Roman moralists condemned facial makeup as a cheap bodily adornment that masked a woman's true beauty and that was suitable only for prostitutes. The frequency, and stridency, of these exhortations shows that few followed them, but that most women of all classes preferred to wear makeup.

Finally, women and men of all cultures and periods greatly attended to their hair. Hairstyle often signified differences in age, gender, or social status, and indicated whether one was in mourning. Women developed elaborate coiffures. Minoan wall paintings portray both women and men with intricate braids, still seen in later Greek *korai* statues. Early Greek poetry commonly describes a young woman as "the girl with the pretty braids." Just as in modern times, ancient fashion trends can be tracked by surveying women's changing hairstyles.

Figure 3.8 Linked ointment containers, wood. Egyptian New Kingdom, 18th dynasty, ca. 1570–1290 B.C.E. The British Museum/Art Resource, NY, London, Great Britain.

Through all periods and cultures women have adorned themselves with jewelry of all types—earrings, necklaces, bracelets, rings, and so on—as can be seen on many of the female figures illustrated throughout this book. These might sometimes be fashioned into quite elaborate designs, as illustrated by Figure 0.3, a gold earring that depicts the winged Greek goddess Nike, "Victory," with a tall, intricate headdress, driving a two-horse chariot. Possibly with ritual meaning, a late Egyptian gold earring from the Meroitic Period features a double image of the goddess Hathor each wearing her horned headdress above a panel of five rosettes from which hang four studded balls with blossoms dangling from each (Figure 10.3).

Four

Health and Medicine

BACKGROUND

Sources on Ancient Medicine

Like most ancient writings, medical documents reflect androcentric views. Scholars call the Egyptian and Mesopotamian documents of the mid-second millennium B.C.E. magico-medical texts since they embed medical advice within religious and magical dimensions of healing practices, the emphasis clearly on the latter. The differing approaches of Greek and Roman healing practices reflect the profound changes in ways of thinking that developed from the Greek "scientific revolution" (see chapter 8). Although still distinct from modern treatments, the Greeks increasingly based their diagnoses on observable and testable physical phenomena rather than on supernatural explanations. However, the medical documents rarely record the women's experiential knowledge.

The Greek medical texts begin with the writings of the early fourth-century Greek physician, Hippokrates of Cos, often called the "father of medicine"—Western doctors still swear by a modern version of the Hippocratic Oath. Hippokrates left an enduring medical legacy by advocating that the doctor conduct himself according to strict moral standards of behavior and not try to seduce the young women or men of the household. Hippokrates observed that doctors needed to recognize that women's diseases differed from men's if they were to treat women's illnesses properly. He also acknowledged that doctors must listen to what a woman has to say of her ailments, since they would laugh at any male physician who would claim to know more than they do about their own bodies.

Five hundred years later in the second century C.E., three Anatolian Greek physicians expanded Hippokrates' ideas—Aretaeus of Cappadocia, Galen of Pergamon, and Soranos of Ephesos. Galen's works remained highly influential in the Latin West, particularly his concept of the four humors whose imbalances caused illness. Of especial importance both in the Greek East and with translations into the Latin West were the writings of Soranos, whose *Gynaecology* is the most comprehensive account of the functioning of the female body from Greco-Roman antiquity. Significantly, Soranos criticized the fantastic, self-serving medical approaches of other Greek and Roman physicians. In contrast, Soranos' texts present more enlightened discussions of the female body, and they display the greatest influence of women's own experiential knowledge.

Ancient Healing Practices—General Overview

Staying healthy, avoiding diseases, and recovering from illnesses, injuries, or infections would have been daunting in times that knew little about antiseptics or antibiotics. Even maladies that modern peoples consider temporary bouts of ill health, like diarrhea, the "common cold," flu epidemics, or cuts, could be devastating to people without an effective means of combating them. On the other hand, weak infants and children died, while those that survived developed crucial immunities to help them withstand at least some of life's health hazards.

Diagnoses were based on the patient's descriptions of their ailments and on observing one or more factors—temperature, skin color, hair or nail texture, condition of the eyes, mouth, tongue, saliva, stool, urine, and any other observable factors such as bleeding, coughing, mucus, rashes, and so on. Medical practices in these ancient Mediterranean cultures effectively employed diet, fasting, medicinal herbs and drugs, ointments, salves, poultices, cupping, bloodletting, and surgery to treat various conditions and injuries. Surgical tools very similar in shape and function to modern ones have been found in all these ancient societies. Diet was generally recognized as an important component for good health as were the ill effects of overindulging in food or alcoholic beverages, risks only the wealthy needed to worry about. The medical writings acknowledged that women deprived of food were in poorer health and encountered more problems with their menses and pregnancies than if they ate sufficiently. Likewise the notion of exercise, popularized in the Latin phrase *mens sana in corpore sano*, "a healthy mind in a healthy body," was something only the elite would have to concern themselves with as most people's lives were filled with extensive physical labor.

Dreams and snakes comprised significant elements of ancient healing practices. Healing sanctuaries often had dormitories where patients slept with the expectation that their dreams would reveal their diagnoses and treatments. The caduceus of two snakes wound around a staff still symbolizes the field of medicine in the West. Exactly how snakes were employed for healing purposes is not known—their venom was probably extracted and applied to therapeutic purposes.

In Greek and Roman medical practices, coprotherapy, use of feces or urine for medical treatment, was administered only to women and continued until the sixth century C.E. The underlying rationale of its use reflected Greek notions of pollution and purification. Since women were seen as being dirty, polluting creatures, substances that were also considered dirty, especially excrement, served as ideal homeopathic vehicles for spiritual and therapeutic cleansing.

When considering these varied medical practices, it is important to keep in mind the placebo effect. Although Western medicine can point to real advances, like antibiotics to treat infections, our medical system works for the same reasons as those of other cultures—belief by the people of the culture in the efficacy of the healing practices, whether performed by shaman or physician. Ancient healing practices were closely interlaced with religious and magic beliefs, and overseen by a healing deity. Isis was the Egyptian goddess of medicine, and Gula the healing goddess for the Mesopotamians. Hygieia, "Health," had her own sanctuaries and was often depicted together with the principal Greek god of medicine, Asklepios. The secular orientation of modern Western medical and research practices tends to obscure the significance of spiritual belief in healing. Modern research shows that people with a belief in divine spirits that can assist in their healing fare better and exhibit higher rates of recovery. Consequently, ancient peoples' deep belief in the gods and in the spiritual dimension of their healing would have formed key elements in their medical practices.

Women and Healing Practices—Overview

Addressing all aspects of women's reproductive activities, ancient medical texts depict concerns in both normal and complicated circumstances with menstruation, conception, pregnancy, prenatal care, miscarriage, abortion, labor, delivery, postpartum and neonatal care, lactation, and menopause. Until the rise of male medical professionals, women often served as the primary healers and pharmacologists, possessing experiential knowledge they would have acquired from their family caretaking and plant-gathering activities. The few female physicians ancient texts mention mostly treated other women.

One story describes a woman who underwent medical training dressed as a man. Before women in labor trusted her to treat them, she had to expose herself to prove she was a woman. But since as a woman she was not allowed to receive a medical education, she was later charged with unlawfully practicing medicine. The Athenian women defended her, telling their husbands they were condemning to death the very person who had given them life. In the story, the law was changed to permit free women to study medicine—in reality, however, these were few.

This tale does reflect the difficulties a male physician faced in treating female patients, who only spoke with great reluctance to a male doctor. A male physician typically asked his female patient to examine herself, or, if she was young and unknowledgeable, to have an older experienced woman examine her and inform the doctor of her condition. These procedures preserved the woman's modesty, and they suggest that at least some women were keen observers who could accurately report on the conditions they examined.

Demonstrating their pharmacological knowledge, women were the ones skilled in working with roots and plants, to fashion spells and potions for good or ill, activities that resulted in the ambivalent positions women occupied in their cultural ideologies. Admired for employing their pharmaceutical expertise beneficially, women were feared for their ability to use these substances maleficently. In time, women working with herbs were demonized, denounced as witches and practitioners of evil. The story of Medea was notorious in the Greek tradition, a foreign woman frighteningly powerful in her knowledge of drugs and magic, who brought death and destruction to anyone who crossed her or just happened to stand in her way. First presented with terrifying power in Euripides's fifth-century play *Medea*, throughout the Western literary tradition the character Medea has epitomized women's destructive knowledge and potential that are beyond men's ability to understand or control. From ancient Rome to modern Europe to contemporary film, Medea has remained a fascinating subject to dramatists, writers, and artists.

GYNECOLOGIES

The Female Body

Lack of understanding about female organs compounded the ancients' general ignorance of how the human body functioned. Medical practitioners recognized the cervix and uterus, but they seem unaware of the other female organs. From his anatomical dissections, the third-century B.C.E. researcher Herophilos discovered the ovaries, which he called twins on analogy with the common Greek term for the male testes. Herophilos also discovered the Fallopian tubes which he thought were connected to the bladder.

In general, the male body was deemed the ideal, the female body falling away from that ideal to varying degrees. The Hippocratics uniquely thought that women's bodies had beneficial additional parts, the womb and a lower mouth, secondary routes for blood or fluids to exit the body, which gave women an advantage over men in surviving acute fevers. At the other extreme, Aristotle considered the female body a mutilated version of the male, and that what rendered her body female was its inability to concoct semen out of blood. Herophilos proposed rather that women's bodies presented a reverse image to men's, arguing that women had reproductive organs inside their bodies that were analogous to men's external organs.

Galen combined these latter two theories, agreeing with Herophilos that women's internal reproductive system corresponded precisely to the male's external reproductive organs. Galen argued further that the very fact that woman's system was internal was what made her less perfect than the male, for her inability to project these inner parts outward demonstrated her innate weakness. He concluded, however, that the creator would not have made half the human race imperfect unless there was some greater advantage to such mutilation.

Whatever qualities theorists attributed to their male physical norm, by definition the female body comprised its aberrant opposite. To Aristotle and Galen men were hot and women cold. Holding the contrary view, the Hippocratics elaborated male and female physical differences—men's bodies were cool, dry, firm, and compact while women's were hot, wet, loose, and porous. Because of their warmth and porousness women's bodies accumulated excess liquid that was released periodically as menses or other bodily excretions. Men's bodies, being more compact, did not thus accumulate liquids, which they, in any case, might dissipate more readily because of their greater physical activity.

Ancient medical theorists held some insights about women's bodies we still find valid today. Greek physicians pointed out that women's lives spent indoors with little exposure to the sun and fresh air, and with less physical activity than men's, were contributing factors to women's ill health. Once again, their jobs often required slaves and women of the lower classes at least to be more active and to conduct more of their activities outdoors.

The most bizarre theory about a woman's body to emerge in ancient medical texts, one which persisted across cultures for well over fifteen hundred years, was the notion of the wandering womb. These ideas first appeared in the Egyptian Ebers medical papyrus of the mid-second millennium B.C.E. and were further advanced in the theories of later Greek and Roman medical writers. The belief was that the uterus did not have a fixed place in the body, but that it wandered around, sometimes rising toward the throat, other times descending, which might cause vaginal prolapse. The common treatment was fumigation with appropriate smells, an ancient form of concentrated aromatherapy. If they thought the womb had risen, sweet-smelling suppositories were inserted into the vagina to attract the womb downward and foul-smelling substances were applied to the nose or placed in the mouth to repel it away. They employed the opposite therapy if they believed the womb had fallen.

Accompanying this notion of the wandering womb was the idea that women had an open passageway in their bodies which connected the womb to her mouth and vagina. It was along this passageway that the womb might travel through the body, or the passageway itself might be blocked, preventing conception or causing a difficult birth. Remedies similar to those for the errant womb were prescribed for these duct blockages, which comprised the most frequent explanation for female ailments. In one test, used by both Egyptians and Hippocratics, a strongly scented object like garlic was placed in the woman's vagina overnight. If the smell could be perceived from her mouth the next morning, it demonstrated that this internal passageway was free of any obstructions, and that she was fertile and able to conceive.

The concept of the wandering womb accorded well with Greek perceptions of women that likened unmarried, adolescent girls to wild animals who were properly tamed by marriage. The Hippocratic texts most commonly prescribed sexual intercourse and pregnancy for most female maladies, for they believed that pregnancy weighted the womb down to its proper place. As the means by which a woman fulfilled her procreative purpose, pregnancy catalyzed a woman's body into achieving its perfected form. Heterosexual intercourse initiated the movement of a woman's body to its proper balance, while pregnancy and childbirth were believed to complete this natural process.

Because the Greek word for the womb was *hysteron*, "what lies behind," anything connected to the womb was *hysterika*. Since for Hippokrates all women's diseases stemmed from the womb, all female disorders were *hysterika*, which referred organically to ailments derived from the womb. However, in modern Europe, Hippocratic texts have been read as describing what eighteenth- through twentieth-century European researchers have called *hysteria*, usually a female condition, though it has occasionally been applied to men. The modern European interpretations have attributed emotional, mental, and psychological disorders to the Hippocratic medical explanation.

This adaptation of the ancient Greek term that referred physically to the womb to a modern emphasis on behavioral dimensions has been read back into the Hippocratic texts as though they were describing the same conditions a nineteenth-century observer might see. Recent unmasking of these misreadings reminds us once again how diligently we must aim to understand ancient evidence within its own cultural milieu. It also demonstrates another continuity in the history of Western medicine, as modern psychiatrists have prescribed the same treatments of marriage, heterosexual intercourse, and pregnancy as cures for the conditions they label women's hysteria.

The ancient medical texts do not refer to the clitoris. The first-century B.C.E. Greek writer of geography, Strabo, claims that Egyptians like Jews—whom he regarded as Egyptian in origin—circumcised the males and excised the females. Strabo may well be right about circumcision among Egyptian males. But there is no record of clitorectomies among Jews, nor do ancient mummies support Strabo's claim for female excision by ancient Egyptian women. It is striking that this rare allusion in ancient texts to the clitoris does so through the lens of its forcible removal, if only in the author's imagination.

We do not know if women spoke of their bodies in the same terms as the medical texts or whether these ideas only crystallized male notions. It is noteworthy that Soranos challenged the prevailing medical views about the wandering womb and the use of aromatic fumigations to treat it. Opposing these ideas, Soranos prescribed what may best be called intense tender loving care mixed with local medical therapies. He first recommends making the woman comfortable, rubbing her with oils, washing her down, and keeping her warm. Then over several days he prescribes cupping, bleeding, suppositories, hip baths, and certain foods to relieve the woman's symptoms. Soranos' female-centered approach to gynecology—his concern for the woman, soothing her, and keeping her warmly wrapped—may reflect women's medical care for one another that this one male physician incorporated into his practice.

Menstruation

Unusual among ancient medical texts, Soranos' *Gynaecology* provides a clear account of the many physiological changes a woman experiences at menarche, during her monthly periods, and at menopause. In contrast to many theorists who advanced their therapies as universally applicable, Soranos recognized that each woman will undergo her menstrual cycles differently, some with lighter flows, some with greater, some for fewer or more days, some preferring to rest, others to carry on with moderate activities. Soranos thought rest was preferable, and he advised against bathing, especially on the first day of blood flow. Nor did Soranos think that menstruation was necessary to a woman's good health, but instead he considered it to be harmful, except when needed for conception.

In his discussion of menstruation Aristotle claims that a menstruating woman would cause a clean mirror to turn bloody dark. His explanation for this occurrence is that since the eyes are filled with blood vessels, a woman's menses affect the eyes as they do other body parts. The changed condition of the eyes in turn disturbs the air which then mars the surface of the mirror.

The Greeks used *vitex agnus castus* (also called chastetree) for a variety of medicinal, ritual, and utilitarian purposes. Artemis was integrally associated with this tree in several ritual contexts that also deepened her connection to girls' menses. The tree's fibers were strong enough to make ropes and wickerwork, and its leaves were used in perfumes and as an anti-inflammatory. Athenian women of the fifth century sat on *agnus castus* branches during the major fall rites for Demeter, the Thesmophoria. A Spartan coming-of-age ritual for Artemis recorded in Roman times describes adolescent boys being whipped with *agnus castus* branches till they bled. This rite may have aimed at simulating the experience of female bleeding.

By far the most prevalent uses for the *agnus castus* plant was to treat a range of female conditions—as it still is today—and extraordinarily, it seems to have dual effects. The Hippocratic texts describe its use as an astringent to staunch severe blood flow and to encourage conception, both of which reveal the retentive properties of the plant—to stem the blood and to hold the seed. It was also used for expulsive purposes: as an abortifacient, to bring on labor, and to expel the afterbirth. It is likely that women used it more liberally than the Hippocratic texts indicate.

The ancients were aware that menstruation was connected to conception—a woman could not conceive until she had started menstruating, and missed periods signified she was probably pregnant. Likewise, the ancients observed that if a girl had not started menstruating or if she had long intervals in between her periods, she would probably have trouble conceiving or carrying a baby to term. Given the poor diets of many ancient women, and given that many endured lives of intense physical labor, the actual intervals between periods may have been long, and some women may have experienced little menstrual bleeding in their lives. The Hippocratic physicians interpreted such menstrual irregularities as internal blockages of the normal blood flow, which might be forced out of other orifices, such as the mouth, nose, or anus. More likely, however, the blood accumulated, causing feelings of numbness or suffocation, which in extreme cases incited adolescent girls to suicide by drowning or hanging. The Hippocratics recommended that the girl be immediately married and mate with her husband, because they believed that heterosexual intercourse would open the blockages that were preventing normal menstruation. Biblical texts condemned the idea of a man having sexual intercourse with his wife when she was menstruating, but the Hippocratics prescribed it as a therapy to prevent future amenorrhea.

Intercourse

Reinforcing societal attitudes, the Hippocratics believed that women who had regular heterosexual intercourse with their husbands were healthier than women who did not. They saw dual advantages to intercourse—it kept the womb moistened, preventing it from drying out and contracting, which would cause severe pain. They also believed that intercourse heated the blood, rendering it more fluid, which thereby facilitated the passage of the menses, whose blockage caused illness. As often, the second-century C.E. physician Soranos opposed the general medical belief that heterosexual intercourse, pregnancy, and childbirth led to an amelioration of a woman's physical condition. Far from treating female ailments, Soranos held that these experiences contributed to women's ill health.

On the contrary, he advocated lifelong virginity as a healthier lifestyle for both women and men. Soranos' sharp departure from the conventional beliefs of Greek and Roman doctors probably reflects the changing views of the early centuries C.E. when concepts of sexual chastity were increasingly promoted first in the worship of Isis and then in the rapidly expanding new Christian communities. Medical theories, evolving alongside other changing cultural ideas, valorized these changes by furnishing them with a presumed authoritative rationale.

In *On the Generating Seed and the Nature of the Child,* Hippokrates, like an early Kinsey, describes the sensations both men and women experienced during intercourse. He contends that when the vagina is rubbed during intercourse it disturbs the womb which produces pleasure and heat throughout a woman's body. A woman releases moisture into the womb and externally too if the womb is open wide. A woman experiences pleasure from the beginning of intercourse, which reaches its peak when the man ejaculates, the excitement of both ending at the same time. Hippokrates claims a woman receives less pleasure from intercourse than a man, although hers lasts longer. The sudden rush of a man's ejaculation gives him a greater, more intense surge of pleasurable sensations. Hippokrates' theories contrast with mythological views that claimed women enjoyed greater sexual pleasure than men. A popular tale related that the blind seer Teiresias was chosen by the god Zeus to resolve an argument with his wife, Hera. Zeus claimed women enjoyed sex more, and Hera claimed that men received the greater enjoyment. Teiresias received this dubious honor because another story tells of his unique experience to have lived life as both a man and a woman. Because Teiresias agreed with Zeus that women enjoyed sex more, Hera struck him blind for which Zeus then compensated by bestowing on him the gift of prophecy. A tale replete with complex layers of gender identity, this mythological example augments the medical descriptions that present in a positive way the pleasure women derive from sex.

In his recommendations for the ideal circumstances for intercourse, Soranos considers the well-being of the woman and of the future child. Using an agricultural analogy that compares a woman's body to the soil a farmer prepares before sowing his crop, which needs to be properly sifted and readied for the reception of the man's seed, Soranos advises massaging a woman's abdominal region to promote evacuation of solid and liquid waste before intercourse. He then recommends that the woman have a light meal. If she engages in intercourse on an empty stomach, her hunger will interfere with her sexual desire, but she should not overindulge in food or drink, which would make her sluggish and dampen the fertilizing potency of coitus.

Soranos also stated that a woman should be sober during intercourse because drunkenness could cause strange hallucinations in her soul that would then get passed on to the fetus. It is noteworthy that Soranos acknowledged that women have souls and that some of their spirit essence is transmitted to the offspring, both ideas in stark contrast to Aristotle's contentions.

Conception

The ancients recognized that intercourse was necessary for conception, and that semen was an essential element. Creation stories teem with human-like reproduction of the gods, and sacred marriage and fertility rites encouraged sexuality in order to promote fertility. A common image of fertilization is the agricultural one of planting the male seed into fertile female ground, which the Greeks interpreted to mean that the male seed animates the female raw material. Narrowing the conventional Greek view, Aristotle claimed that the woman contributed nothing to the creation of the child, since her body merely furnished the matter for development of the male-generated fetus.

The Hippocratics advanced the contrasting idea that both sexes contributed seed which mixed, acquired breath, and then developed as the new embryo. Theorizing about genetics, Hippokrates held that both women and men produced both strong and weak sperm. If both contributed strong sperm the offspring would be male, if weak sperm, female. If one parent contributed strong sperm while the other provided weak, then the one that prevailed would determine the sex of the child.

The ancients connected certain foods with fertility. Egyptians recommended that those wishing to conceive eat lettuce—Egyptian lettuce was tall and straight and produced a milky-white liquid when pressed, which was associated with the male god of fertility. Women hoping to conceive ate pomegranates, which were associated with female fertility throughout the Mediterranean. In one test for fertility, Egyptian texts advised a woman to sit on a mixture of date flour and beer. The concoction would cause a fertile woman to vomit, the number of retches indicating the number of future pregnancies she would have.

Soranos presented some typical Greek views to determine whether a woman could conceive judging by her external appearance. If she exhibited mannish, compact, and overly sturdy characteristics, or appeared their opposite, too flabby and moist, she would unlikely be able to bear children on the premise that the uterus would mimic the body's general qualities. If the uterus were too hard, it would not be able to accept the male seed, or if too loose, it could not hold it. Moreover, the position of the uterus could prevent fertilization if it tilted away from or lay too far back in the vagina.

If a woman did not conceive, she would employ numerous devices to promote fertility, beginning with prayers, spells, or other magical means. The numerous offerings that beseech the gods or ancestors to help an infertile woman to conceive testify to how seriously ancient peoples regarded infertility. One significant obstacle to conception was the ancient belief that a woman's most fertile time was immediately after her menstrual cycle when her womb was thought to be most open and therefore more likely to accept the man's seed. Of course, this was not the only time of month couples engaged in intercourse. But for husbands who copulated with their wives only minimally each month for the sole purpose of reproduction, their figuring on the days following their wife's menstrual cycle as the target fertility days would not usually produce the desired offspring.

Conversely, women who thought they were practicing contraceptive sex by waiting another week or so before having intercourse actually increased their chance of conception. Here Judaic practice may have been more successful, since Judaic law stipulated that a couple should avoid intercourse for two weeks from the beginning of the wife's period. Following her postmenstrual purification, she and her husband were to come together as though for the first time as husband and wife. The two-week mark sets their renewed mating around the time of month we now understand ovulation to occur, when a woman is most likely to conceive.

Contraception and Abortion

Although most efforts were directed at conception and the successful birth of a healthy child, women employed methods to prevent conception and abortions to terminate unwanted pregnancies. Infanticide was probably regarded as a type of late abortion, since it could be several weeks or months before an infant was considered viable. Soranos distinguished between the two and considered contraception to be safer than abortion. In earlier periods there was little if any opposition to either contraception or abortion on moral or religious grounds. A man's desire for legitimate offspring might lead him to intercede for personal and familial reasons, if he were even aware of the contraceptive or abortive attempts of his wife. Likewise, the state might intervene if it believed such prevention of childbirth contributed to a population decline, as was the case in early imperial Rome, which declared abortions illegal for a brief time. In one clause of the Hippocratic oath, the physician claims he will not administer abortifacients, but elsewhere the Hippocratic writings do prescribe abortion-inducing treatments.

Moral considerations entered the medical texts at some point. Soranos claimed that some physicians refused to administer abortifacients because the practice of medicine required them to preserve what nature had created. Others prescribed abortive remedies with discrimination, not, they claimed, to abort fetuses because of adultery or the woman's desire to keep a youthful figure, but only if there were some problem endangering the life of the mother or of the embryo.

Attempts to prevent pregnancy often entailed use of herbs or magical practices, with varied effectiveness. Egyptian women inserted vaginal suppositories of different substances, including a mixture of ground acacia tips, which contain gum arabic, a substance that chemically interacts with sperm to retard conception. They also used honey and crocodile dung, presumably dried out and placed inside cotton pouches, which may have effectively served to block the sperm and possibly even acted as a spermicide.

Soranos presented several contraceptive remedies, including smearing the cervix before intercourse with various substances, some of which may have served as effective blocks—olive oil, honey, cedar or balsam resin, on their own or together with white lead, alum, or galbanum mixed with wine. He also suggested a lock of fine wool at the orifice of the uterus and several vaginal suppositories comprised of a vast array of substances with constricting properties that would cause the os to shut down and not admit the semen. Many of these recipes contain ground pomegranate peel, which in modern laboratory experiments resulted in lowered fertility in rats and guinea pigs. Although the ancient conditions of its use differed radically from a controlled laboratory environment with measured, highly concentrated doses, the frequent inclusion of ground pomegranate peel in contraceptive suppositories suggests that it yielded the expected outcome.

Among his other contraceptive techniques Soranos advised a type of *coitus interruptus*, recommended only in one other known Hippocratic text, the woman to hold her breath and pull back a little just before the man ejaculates. She should then immediately rise, squat down, induce sneezing, wipe all round her vagina, and drink cold water. Interestingly, both texts attribute the responsibility for pulling away before ejaculation to the woman. How common this method was in antiquity we cannot know, but it does receive some scattered references. In his attempt to seduce a young woman in one of his poems, a seventh-century male Greek poet claims he will use *coitus interruptus*, clearly implying that he will take the more expected male initiative of pulling out before ejaculation.

Other commonly practiced means of contraception included anal intercourse in numerous sexual interactions—wives in marriage, and mistresses, temple priestesses, and prostitutes. Finally, for contraceptive purposes women may have deliberately drawn out breastfeeding, which tends to suppress the menses and functions as a woman's natural means of contraception.

Women employed various abortifacients to induce abortion, including pennyroyal, rue, *vitex*, and willow bark. One Hippocratic text recommends that a woman jump up and down vigorously, kicking her buttocks with her heels. Soranos provides a rationale for this treatment by stating that in order to separate the embryo a woman needs to exercise strenuously. Soranos recommended numerous therapies that should be repeated until one achieved the desired results. To soften the inner lining of the uterus, for two to three days a woman should take lengthy baths, eat little food, drink no wine, and use softening vaginal suppositories. The woman should be bled heavily which was believed to cause miscarriages. Finally, walking and leaping energetically, being shaken violently by farm animals, carrying heavy objects beyond her strength, and use of diuretics should cause the embryo to disengage and be expelled. After an abortion Soranos advised treating the vaginal region as though for inflammation, and he strongly warned against using toxic substances or sharp objects that could seriously injure the mother.

These extensive lists of contraceptive and abortive methods show that women of all ages and cultures, as well as desiring fertility, have always sought a means to stop their reproductive potential, and that they have liberally availed themselves of opportunities to prevent conception and to abort the embryo. Decisions to kill the newborn infant seem to have rested generally with the father, but women probably largely determined if they were going to take contraceptive or abortive measures. Soranos' exhaustive discussion of these counter-reproductive methods displays, as he does elsewhere, his primary concern for the woman, and that she should be aware of the most effective and least injurious remedies.

Pregnancy

The ancients were aware of the typical term of pregnancy. Egyptian women readily calculated their due date figuring from the presumed time of conception, a knowledge that Hippokrates claimed experienced Greek women knew. The Egyptians devised several tests for detecting pregnancy, including taking the pulse, examining the breasts, and checking the eyes and skin color, all of which undergo changes with pregnancy. One test entailed the woman urinating daily on grains of barley and emmer wheat, which would reveal what we today identify as the changing levels of hormones in a pregnant woman. They believed that if the barley sprouted first, she would have a boy, but if the wheat sprouted first, it would be a girl. If neither sprouted she was not pregnant.

Greek doctors also used various tests to detect pregnancy. They claimed a woman would know immediately upon conception if she were pregnant, Aristotle asserting that a pregnant woman had a certain feeling in her groin, and that a woman was able to feel her womb close upon becoming pregnant. One test was to give the woman a mixture of honey and water to drink. If she became colicky she was pregnant.

The idea of a closed womb arose in a different way in ancient Egypt where pregnant figurines probably used as amulets for protection during pregnancy do not depict the genitals, which were marked on figures of nonpregnant naked women. These images with "closed genitals" symbolized protection of the womb against miscarriage and other complications since they portray the vaginal opening as safely closed throughout the pregnancy until its proper time for opening at delivery. One figurine has a tampon inserted into her vagina, probably to prevent bleeding and miscarriage. Some interpreters suggest that the so-called Isis knot used as a protective amulet may represent the tampon the goddess used when she was pregnant with Horus and which therefore may have been an actual item used by pregnant women.

Next to childbirth, pregnancy took its toll on women's health. Several factors of ancient life exacerbated any inherent dangers arising from women's reproductive activities. Many pregnant women were still girls with poor diets and generally unhealthy lifestyles, which resulted in delayed maturation and more vulnerable physical condition. Many became pregnant right at menarche so that their just-developing pubescence left their bodies ill prepared to deal with the demands pregnancy and childbirth exacted on a woman's body. Several Greek writers argued that for the health of the mother and baby all girls should follow the Spartan example, where girls were nourished equally with boys, had regular outdoor exercise, and where they were not expected to marry until age 18.

Women prayed, made offerings, and wore amulets to protect themselves during pregnancy and childbirth. Amulets were often carved with apotropaic, "evil-averting," images, such as the Mesopotamian demonic underworld god Pazuzu who protected the fetus against another demonic underworld god Lamashtu, who was believed to kill unborn babies by touching the mother's stomach seven times. Egyptian women invoked Taweret, a female deity in the shape of a pregnant hippopotamus standing erect on her hind legs, her belly protruding in front (Figure 3.5). Taweret had the legs of a lion, the tail of a crocodile, and narrow, pendulous human breasts. She carried a knife to cut the umbilical cord in her right hand which rested upon the ankh life symbol.

Egyptian women also wore amulets of the dwarf god of sexuality Bes for protection. Like the unattractive Bes, Taweret's monstrous appearance probably had an apotropaic purpose. Walls of Egyptian houses were painted with images of Taweret and Bes, and many contained statues, offering tables and basins dedicated to the pregnant goddess. Models of the birthing room also adorned Egyptian homes, no doubt to insure a successful birth. The prevalence of these birth deities and images reflects their consuming importance to an ancient married couple and may indicate the prominence of female rituals in domestic rites.

Hippocratic texts list several factors that might cause miscarriages. If the womb were too smooth, lax, or open, or had lacerations, it would not be able to hold the embryo. Another woman could check a woman's uterus when she was not pregnant to determine if it was smooth. If women with these uterine problems were cared for, they might give birth normally. Other conditions producing miscarriages included a woman's ill health, picking up overly heavy objects, leaping into the air, going with too little or too much food, excessive drinking, fainting, becoming frightened, shouting violently, or being beaten. I have deliberately placed this last item, which Soranos lists much earlier in his series in an apparent equivalence to all the other factors, at the end to emphasize this abusive feature of ancient women's lives, which many texts simply take for granted.

Childbirth

Childbirth presented the greatest risks to a woman's life, and various literary texts regard women's travail in childbirth as equivalent to the pains and perils a man faces in battle. In Euripides' play of the same name, the heroine Medea proclaims that she would rather stand behind a shield in battle three times than give birth once. Prayers for protection and offerings in gratitude for a successful birth figured prominently in ancient women's lives. Female deities of childbirth were invoked for their protection. Egyptian spells called upon either Hathor or Isis. In order to assure a successful delivery, one spell identifies Hathor as the laboring woman: "Hathor, the Lady of Dendera is [the] one who is giving birth!"[1]

An early second-millennium Egyptian story relates that four goddesses—Isis, Nephthys, Meshkenet, and Hekat—assisted the queen Rudjedet when she miraculously gave birth to triplets. The actions of the goddesses must represent the actions the midwife and her attendants routinely took to help the mother safely deliver the infant—Isis as midwife stood in front of the woman chanting, Nephthys supported her from behind, Hekat took some action to speed the delivery, and Meshkenet greeted the newborn. Besides the midwife, most of the attending women were probably family members, as only a wealthy woman would be able to hire more than one person to assist in her labor and delivery. Poor women may not have even had a midwife's help; many probably delivered alone or with the aid of female relatives.

Two different Mesopotamian myths recited at the birth ended with incantations to facilitate a successful labor and delivery. One Mesopotamian myth called "The Cow of Sin [the Moon god]" relates the difficult labor being experienced by the Moon god's wife, who is in the shape of a cow. The myth ends with the chant: "Just as Maid-of-the-Moon-God [Inanna] gave birth easily, so may the maid having a difficult delivery give birth."[2] As with the Egyptian birth spells, the woman giving birth is identified with the reigning birth goddess, whose own successful labor augurs well for the mortal woman. The verbal power of singing these tales and chants was believed to help the mother in labor, like belly dancing, which also originated in the ancient Near East as a sympathetic magico-religious dance intended to aid the woman in labor. By evolving into a chant designed to aid the woman, the Mesopotamian myths set the actual birth taking place in the mythic context of the creation of the first human beings, thereby sacralizing the birth of the newborn.

The powerful portrayal of a possibly divine female figure giving birth from the Neolithic village at Çatal Höyük (Figure 1.2) shows that society's valuing of women's fundamental activity of giving birth. Together with other visual and literary portrayals, this image of a woman seated on a birthing throne reveals that ancient practices of childbirth took nature and gravity into account—women gave birth in a kneeling or squatting position or seated upon a birthing stool. As referred to in Egyptian texts, a small Egyptian clay plaque illustrates a woman giving birth while squatting upon two large bricks, the baby's head protruding downward between her legs (Figure 4.1). Soranos extensively described the shape of a birthing stool in order to give the woman maximum support and facilitate the birth of the baby.

[Provide] a birthing stool so that the mother may be arranged on it ... a wide space in a crescent shape must be cut out in it [of a size appropriate] ... to prevent the woman from being pulled down beyond her thighs because the opening is too great, and on the contrary to prevent her from having her vagina pressured by it being too narrow (which is a greater problem).[3]

Midwives play important roles in all texts. The midwife's expertise ranged from those adept at normal labor and delivery to those who could

Figure 4.1 Woman giving birth, votive plaque. Egyptian, Greco-Roman period, ca. 332 B.C.E.–305 C.E. The British Museum/Art Resource, NY, London, Great Britain.

also treat prenatal, postnatal, and other female conditions and complications. Although midwives' experiential knowledge was probably vast,
because midwifery dealt with women's health care issues, it received
little attention in men's medical documents or respect from male medical
professionals.

Soranos gave detailed instructions to the midwife, first to wash her hands
with hot oil and have her fingernails cut, then to manipulate the cervix so
it is facing down, rub it with oil, and prepare for the baby to emerge. At the
same time that he instructed the midwife on what to do if the woman's water
does not break and if she needs to induce labor, he attended to the care of the
woman giving birth, detailing the items needed to ease her pains during labor
and delivery and to facilitate her recovery after the birth. He advised having on hand warm water, soft cloths for both mother and baby, and various
herbs for their aromatic and recuperative properties to help the mother.
He recommended that three women, not necessarily health practitioners,
be ready who can gently calm the woman's fears—two should stand at her
sides, and one behind her to support her in her labor pains. Finally, Soranos
instructed the midwives on how they should position themselves modestly
below and opposite the mother, maintaining contact with the mother's face,
so she can reassure her that the labor is going well.

It is unusual for Soranos, a male physician, to be providing such detailed
knowledge of childbirth. He may well have attended normal births, as some
doctors did. Once again, he may also be transmitting what he learned from
midwives in this traditionally women's field of expertise. Soranos' attention
to the moral probity of the midwife as she was performing her duties was
rooted in the high moral conduct demanded of Hippocratic physicians. His
may be sound advice to a male medical practitioner attempting to take on
the role of midwife—one did make this attempt, but women did not trust
him to assist them. It is unlikely that most midwives were even aware of
Soranos' remarks. Midwives certainly were familiar with the female body,
and it is unlikely that women in cultures used to sensual and sexual interactions in various women's fertility festivals practiced the kind of false modesty
Soranos advised.

His advice, however, reflects the changes in perceptions of women's
roles in the early centuries of the common era, especially once Christian
ideas began to prevail. These new developments aimed to cut off any hint
of female sexuality that might arise in any situation. Even how women
helped one another in traditionally women's-only environments now came
to be monitored and regulated by men. Altogether it is clear that women
and health workers put considerable effort into making the woman in labor
comfortable and supported, and to ease her pregnancy and birth as much
as possible. This support ranges from the ritual and mythic associations to
the physical forms of comfort provided the woman in labor and the new
mother.

Hippocratic texts suggest that as a rule Greek physicians did not attend
births, but were called in for complications. Texts speak of manipulating the

embryo if it is breech, and prescribing astringent compresses and suppositories to stem the flow of blood. Some texts also suggest therapies to bring on the afterbirth, whose absence they believed threatened future fertility. Greek medical theorists thought that the lochia was comprised of excess menstrual blood the fetus did not use. Hence, the texts regard symptoms of lochial displacement as similar to those caused by blockages of the menses. One remedy to encourage the afterbirth was to grind up a turtle liver, which had been removed while the turtle was alive, and serve it in human breast milk.

After a successful birth, thank offerings were dedicated to the goddesses of childbirth. The Greek goddess Artemis was primarily associated with the presexual young, and births were not to take place in her sanctuaries because they would pollute the holiness of her shrines (the same held true of deaths). At the same time, Artemis was a goddess of childbirth and afterbirth, invoked by women in labor, and she received both thank offerings by women after a successful birth as well as the garments of women who died in childbirth. Egyptian women remained confined for 14 days after giving birth, which gave the mother time to heal and recuperate while protecting both mother and child from infection.

Death in childbirth threatened women's lives throughout antiquity. Hippocratic texts identify the symptoms of puerperal fever as insomnia, hallucinations, cold sweating around the head, cold extremities, and irregular breathing. Greek and Roman epitaphs reveal the poignancy of women's deaths in childbirth. One imperial Roman epitaph reads

Sacred to the gods of the dead.
Rusticeia Matrona lived 25 years.
The cause of my death was childbirth and malignant fate.
But stop crying, beloved spouse, and take care of our son with love. For my spirit is now with the stars in the heavens.[4]

Another reads:

Daphne, bride of Hermes, I've been freed; even though the master wanted to free Hermes first. Fate made me first, fate took me first. All that I bore, the tears I so often shed I leave to my husband, since I just had a baby, though the master did not want me to. Now who will feed him? Who will take care of him for the rest of his life? The Styx snatched me away to the gods.
She lived a pious woman for 25 years.[5]

Reflecting equivalence in gender roles, a Spartan woman who died in childbirth received the same funerary honors as a warrior who died in battle.

Lactation

The Hippocratics thought that breast milk was menstrual fluid that had been diverted from the womb and refined into milk. Egyptian paintings suggest soothing, private bowers where the mother could nurse her child, beautifully exemplified in the late New Kingdom drawing of a woman nursing her infant while seated on a stool amid hanging vines (Figure 4.2). Soranos believed breastfeeding exhausted a woman's body, and he recommended a wet nurse to help the mother recover from childbirth and get ready for the next pregnancy. While the Greek moralist Plutarch advocated that the mother breastfeed her own child, he too suggested a wet nurse if the mother was unable to nurse or if the couple wanted another child right away. Elite women in all these cultures regularly employed wet nurses, while poorer women would have been grateful to find a woman willing to nurse her baby if she was unable to lactate. As with other irregularities, therapies of teas, suppositories, and topical massaging with special ointments were aimed at releasing the blockage and encouraging the milk to flow.

Soranos prefaced his exhaustive description of the ideal wet nurse by claiming first that it was best for the mother to nurse her own child, since that way she developed the closest bonds to the infant. Because he considered breastfeeding to be extremely draining of a woman's body, he recognized that for their health and extended well-being, many women would prefer to hire a wet nurse. Soranos provided his detailed advice on wet nurses only after giving a nod, perhaps, to the strain of social thought that emphasized the strengthened mother-infant bonds formed when the mother nursed her own child. Such sentiments are evident in the late second-millennium B.C.E. Egyptian "Instructions of Any," which lists a mother's breastfeeding as one of the many tasks she carried out for her child.

In his *Gynaecology,* Soranos detailed the physical qualities a wet nurse should have for the healthy nursing of the infant. She should be a woman between 20 and 40 years old who has given birth at least two or three times. According to Soranos, women who have given birth to just one child were inexperienced in childrearing and had breasts that were still infantile in development, while women who had borne and nursed multiple children were wrinkled and did not produce the best milk. Moreover, for the best quality milk Soranos stated that the wet nurse should be healthy, large, of good constitution and color. Her breasts should be medium size, loose, soft, and unwrinkled, and the nipples of just the right size and density to enable a smooth, but not overabundant flow of milk.

Soranos then added behavioral criteria to the physical, which he regarded as directly influencing the woman's ability to produce quality breast milk. The wet nurse should abstain from any form of immoderate and wild behavior, including sexual intercourse, drinking, and similar lewd and pleasurable activities. Besides the moral dimension of these bans, Soranos claimed these activities dampened the wet nurse's affection for the infant. They further lessened or suppressed entirely the flow of milk, since these activities stimulated menstrual flow or even conception, which thereby spoiled the milk.

The effects of drunkenness compounded these as they tainted both the woman's spirit as well as her breast milk. In her inebriation the wet nurse might leave the infant unattended or harm him. Medically Soranos believed that wine's effect on breast milk could cause conditions in the infant ranging from sluggishness to more severe convulsions or coma. He contradicted those

Figure 4.2 Woman nursing an infant, painted limestone ostracon. Deir el-Medina, Thebes, Egypt, later New Kingdom, ca. 1300–1100 B.C.E. The British Museum/Art Resource, NY, London, Great Britain.

who claimed that only a woman who had given birth to and was suckling a male child should nurse a male infant, and likewise for a female infant, but claimed that there was no difference in the milk a mother produced contingent to the sex of the child she had borne or was nursing.

Menopause

Soranos gave a brief, rare attention to the subject of menopause, where once again he seeks to ease this biological change for the woman, which he regards as the reverse of menarche. He advised that women take care that menopause not occur suddenly: "for even if the body is changed for the better, the sudden disruption causes discomfort," since the body reacts to new conditions, "like an unfamiliar illness." Soranos recommended that women use the same remedies that first induced menstrual flow in their youth as a way to extend their periods for a more gradual cessation. He asserted that menopause improves a woman's body, thereby reinforcing his view that menstruation drains a woman physically.

It is refreshing that Soranos' brief discussion of menopause, the closing words on this chapter's final topic, regarded menopause as a natural, beneficial change in a woman's life. Although Aristotle's unverifiable, female-debasing theories predominated in the Western tradition, Soranos' concern throughout for care of the woman and his more intelligent medical accounts offer a more enlightened picture of ancient Greek and Roman women's medical issues.

Figure 4.3 Women pressing flowers to make perfume, sarcophagus relief. Egypt, 18th dynasty, ca. 17th c. B.C.E. Erich Lessing/Art Resource, NY, Louvre, Paris, France.

Five

From Home to Market—The Economic Bases of Women's Lives

In every society, women have worked. Their basic tasks have been remarkably similar across cultures and time—childbearing and rearing, food acquisition and preparation, textile manufacture, and preparation of the dead. In pre-state societies, women engaged in many of these activities collectively, which the society recognized as fundamental to the continuity of the group. Hence, women were highly valued, held important positions, and saw their activities prized, while they themselves received honor and esteem for their indispensable contributions to the society.

While pre-state societies distinguished between women's and men's spheres of activity, these were generally regarded as complementary realms, where everyone's work was valued. The high status accorded women's activities in pre-state societies eroded with the development of centralized state organizations, whose patriarchal social institutions increasingly circumscribed women's economic participation. The domestic sphere was no longer only the foundational locus of women's activities, but it came to signify the restricted roles permitted to women.

DOMESTIC-BASED ECONOMIC ACTIVITIES

Women's economic activities, which were carried out almost entirely in the domestic sphere, formed the mainstay of the society. With the development of hierarchically organized states that paid men for their work in civic administration or in building the state's infrastructure, women's domestic work was left uncompensated. At the same time, the three areas of women's unpaid domestic activities—child care, food preparation, and textile production—evolved into forms of employment that drew upon their female-defined tasks.

These primary areas of female paid work were often low-paying and were as likely to be filled by slaves. Roman imperial funerary inscriptions identify slaves and freedwomen of the royal household performing the same domestic tasks. Enterprising women were able to turn their domestic-based activities into lucrative occupations. Moreover, those who had the good fortune to perform these tasks for the royal family or other high-status individuals might be well compensated, and they could take advantage of these opportunities to advance both their own station and that of their families.

Child Care

As previous chapters have shown, women's childbearing and rearing activities served as a central focus of their lives. It also provided women their principal form of employment, including the jobs of midwife, wet nurse, nurse, nanny, and governess. Because these jobs centered on children, the women fulfilling them generally received respect for their roles, even when the jobs were carried out by slaves, and they offered women a familiar and generally safe work environment. Moreover, the latter three positions of nurse, nanny, and governess often gave single women the added comfort and protection of being part of their employer's extended family, which provided them with a home life they might not otherwise have had.

Midwives

Midwives learned their practice by apprenticing to elder female relatives who were midwives. Some documents describe midwives purchasing a young girl to train into the field. Even an adolescent girl might contract to train and work with a midwife, and eventually establish her own practice. Midwives could expect decent pay for their critical assistance in childbirth. Elite women and possibly even those of moderate means could afford a midwife, but poor women probably could not, unless some midwives offered their services *pro bono,* "for free," or *pro parvo,* "for a little." Literary references to midwives assume they are women who have borne children themselves. Mesopotamian and Greek literary allusions favor postmenopausal women, and some Greek sources even identify adolescent unmarried girls, who would presumably not yet have given birth, as suitable midwives. In accord with Hippocratic medical tradition the Greco-Roman physician Soranos emphasized the need for the midwife to be of high moral character.

Soranos's advice accords with a line of Greek thought that viewed every aspect of the child's development as requiring models of moderation. Recall that Soranos also recommended the woman's spiritual, physical, and emotional purification before intercourse so that she might exert the best possible influence upon the conception of the fetus. This expectation of the high moral standards of the child care worker increased with the growth of the child as those responsible for the child's physical, conceptual, and educational development would have exercised a greater role in shaping the child's character.

Wet Nurse

Once the baby was born, wet nurses were regularly employed. Ancient Egyptian documents show the exalted position a wet nurse might achieve. Probably herself the wife or mother of a high official, the wet nurse to the future king held an esteemed position that accrued lifelong honor to herself and her family. In addition, close bonds would have developed between her own offspring, especially if male, and the heir designate, further strengthening her family's ties with the royals. Documents from the workmen's village at Deir el-Medina mention the hire of wet nurses, but it is not known if they were hired because the mother died or could not produce milk, or whether the lower classes tried to emulate the practices of the elite. It is possible that if women at Deir el-Medina worked at paying jobs, they would have had both the resources and the desire to hire a wet nurse so they could continue their paid employment.

Wet nursing is the most frequent occupation listed for freedwomen in ancient Athenian inscriptions. In the "Homeric Hymn to Demeter," when the goddess Demeter takes on mortal form, she appears as an old woman who might be hired to nurse an infant. A late third-century C.E. letter from a Greek man living in Egypt offers to pay for a wet nurse since he does not wish his daughter to breastfeed. Two contracts from Alexandria, Egypt, in 13 B.C.E. spell out the financial and behavioral terms of the wet nurse's employ. In both cases the Greek or Roman employer hires a woman of Persian heritage to serve as wet nurse for an infant they have rescued from exposure and whom they wish to raise as a slave, one of the two infants identified as a girl.

While the financial terms of the two contracts differ somewhat, the other provisions are quite similar. One contract negotiated for a Roman male specifies that the wet nurse is to be paid 8 drachmas a month for 18 months along with olive oil, and that she has received a 9-month advance on her wages. If at 9 months she has satisfactorily been fulfilling her duties, she will receive the remainder of her wages. The second contract made for a Greek woman employs the wet nurse for 16 months at 10 drachmas of silver per month plus specified quantities of oil. The wet nurse is given a 3-month advance at which point upon a satisfactory evaluation she will receive her outstanding wages.

Both contracts entailed similar requirements and conditions of employment. Both women nursed the infant in their own homes and were to bring the child to be inspected by its owner three or four times a month. Both contracts specified that the wet nurse be responsible in her conduct, and that she not do anything that would spoil her breast milk, including sleeping with her husband, becoming pregnant, or nursing another infant. Both also specified the severe penalties the wet nurse would incur if she violated the contract, which included having to pay back any wages she had received, forfeiting outstanding wages, and paying damages, expenses, and hefty fines. Both women together with the named husband of one were liable to prosecution if they failed to fulfill their contractual obligations. Another contract from the second century C.E. acknowledges the receipt by a slave owner for the wages and expenses incurred during the two years his slave worked as a wet nurse for another's daughter. The owner further stipulated that he had no complaints and would bring no actions regarding this or related matters.

By the Greek and Roman periods women's preferences for wet nurses angered male moralists, who stressed that in order to carry out properly her maternal duties a mother should nurse her own infant. Epitaphs underscored a mother's virtue by stating that she breastfed her own children. The second-century c.e. Roman philosopher Favorinus claimed that only an unnatural mother would abandon at birth a baby she had nourished in her womb for nine months. To those who argued that it made no difference who nursed the baby, Favorinus responded that from the beginning the mother's milk, which he believed was "tinged with the father's seed," had a direct effect on the baby, so that feeding an infant with a stranger's milk was a corruption of the newborn's nobility of body and mind. Exacerbating this situation, in Favorinus's view, many women hired wet nurses solely for having breast milk without any consideration of their chastity, sobriety, and moral character. Initially these debates about the moral rightness of hiring wet nurses seem to have remained within male intellectual circles with little relevance to actual women's lives.

Earlier in the letter Myia wrote to Phyllis on infant care, she advised her friend on the qualities to look for in a wet nurse—some of the same conduct that the Alexandrian contracts stipulated. Myia's letter does not question the appropriateness of hiring a wet nurse to breastfeed the infant. Rather, she assumes the normalcy of this practice and counsels her friend on the qualities a wet nurse should have. In her letter Myia enumerated several traits to avoid—the wet nurse should not be temperamental, talkative, prone to sleepiness, uncontrolled in her appetite for food or drink, or a foreigner. Instead, she should be modest, orderly, and Greek. She should avoid sleeping with her husband since her primary task was to nourish the infant, which set the foundation for the child's life. Because of their presumed probity and experience, Spartan wet nurses were highly esteemed and in high demand.

Soranos addressed at length a wet nurse's ideal moral conduct. She should first of all be affectionate to the infant and carry out her duties promptly, in an orderly fashion, and with good feelings. Since the infant imitates the nurse's disposition, her sullenness or anger would adversely affect the child, who instead responds sweetly to favorable treatment. For these reasons Soranos counseled against hiring a wet nurse given to superstition or ecstatic ceremonies who might thereby lead the infant astray through faulty reasoning. He too advocated that the wet nurse be Greek so that the baby becomes accustomed to the best speech. Finally, in a recommendation surely only the wealthy could afford, Soranos suggested the mother employ several wet nurses since it would be traumatic for the infant if his accustomed wet nurse were to become ill or die and he might suffer an adverse reaction to new milk.

Nurses and Governesses

Some wet nurses, especially if unmarried, may have continued to serve as the child's nurse as it grew. Whether the same woman or a new hire, elite women employed nurses, nannies, and governesses to conduct the active work of raising their children. These women carried out all child-rearing tasks from feeding, diapering, bathing, and crooning to the baby to playing with, disciplining, and educating the child as she grew. These women in particular were to exhibit the highest standards of moral behavior since they were intimately engaged in forming the child's moral character and intellectual development. Even if slaves, these women tended to be more highly educated, especially the governesses, and to be highly respected as well—at least by the adults employing them.

One letter to her father the king, by a princess presumably married to a lesser king in another city, reveals the petulance of royal offspring. She complains to her father that she does not like the governess he has sent, that she has sent her back, and that she wants her father to send another one who will be more to her liking. On the other hand, childhood nurses might form close bonds with their charges. Some Egyptian tomb paintings and funerary stelae include nurses in their family portraits, and letters home ask after the health of the nurse. Homer's *Odyssey* shows the continued closeness the mature hero still shares with the old nurse of his infancy, Eurykleia.

Often deriving from child care was the work of the household servant and the lady's maid. The latter may have nursed the infant, raised the child, and then continued to function as the woman's personal servant once she was grown and had married. These domestic servants enjoyed a status often approaching that of family member. They were permanent household employees whose pay came in the form of a secure livelihood with their basic necessities met and their employer's largesse, in addition to any direct compensation they may have received.

Food Preparation

Food in the Economy

After child care, food preparation and textile manufacture were the two other major areas of women's domestic responsibility that generated paid labor. They differed, however, from child care derived employment since both food and textile production could be turned into cottage industries. An enterprising matron could produce surplus items which she could then sell or exchange in community or international markets.

Food was the foundation of the economy as it was of life. Ancient diets typically centered on two staples, bread and drink, supplemented by other foods. Women produced these staples, and myths illustrate that women's associations with these essentials were deeply embedded in the cultural psyche. Women engaged in all aspects of food acquisition, preparation and selling for the variety of edibles ancient peoples consumed. Rural women—who were the majority, but about whom we have least documentary evidence—were actively involved in food acquisition through agriculture, herding, and gathering. Egyptian wall paintings show women laboring in the fields with men, though possibly at different tasks. Other paintings show elite women gathering wild plants while the men fish and hunt fowl (Figure 5.1).

Figure 5.1 Marsh Scene, Tomb of Menna. Thebes, Egypt. 18th Dyn, ca. 1420–11 B.C.E. Courtesy of the Oriental Institute of the University of Chicago.

The painting shows women and slaves gathering riverine plants. A naked girl kneeling in the boat pulls plants up with her hands. Mesopotamian documents list women's agricultural activities—removing clods from furrows, cutting thorns, or digging the irrigation system. Women winnowed, carried and removed grain, and worked on tugboats transporting the grain.

Women regularly gleaned the fields, that is, collected whatever grain was left by the harvesters. Ancient Judaic law required landowners to leave a tithe, tenth, of their field to be gleaned by the poor. The biblical book of *Ruth* uses Ruth's gleaning of her kinsman Boas's fields as the setting for their romantic encounter. In reality, such work may have exposed women in unwelcome ways to men's attention, possibly making them vulnerable to attack. In another harsh reality, Egyptian, Mesopotamian, and biblical documents and myths advise storing grain for up to seven years to withstand times of drought—which were sometimes prolonged and devastating.

Grains ground from cultivated native grasses of barley, millet, oats, and wheat formed the principal food staple—bread. Grinding the grain was typically women's work, in both city and country. A mid-third millennium Egyptian painted wood tomb model shows a woman on her knees grinding grain using a broad pestle in an elongated, duck-shaped concave mortar (Figure 5.2). Her eyes-forward gaze may suggest the meditative nature of this repetitive activity. As a corollary to bread preparation, in Egypt and Mesopotamia women were the beer and winemakers. Beer or wine formed a liquid staple to the ancient diet, that only rarely included water to drink, and that did not have tea or coffee. Another Old Kingdom Egyptian tomb model shows a woman with the same far-off gaze mashing barley bread in a large urn to make beer (Figure 5.6).

Virtually a second food staple was legumes—peas, chickpeas, fava beans, lentils—and pulses—the edible seeds of leguminous plants, all of which

Figure 5.2 Woman grinding grain, painted wood. Egyptian Old Kingdom, 5th dynasty, ca. 2565–2420 B.C.E. Nimatallah/Art Resource, NY, Museo Archeologico, Florence, Italy.

women prepared in a variety of tasty dishes. Women gathered wild edible plants and cultivated home gardens, which supplied various fruits and vegetables eaten fresh in season and preserved. Women grew at home or gathered in the countryside garlic, leeks, mushrooms, onions, herbs, and spices, which added flavor to the diet. (Many also had medicinal uses.) Fruits formed sweeteners for cakes, often made from sesame seeds. Figs grew throughout the Mediterranean region; grapes and pomegranates spanned from Mesopotamia to Italy. Dates were prevalent in Egypt and Mesopotamia. A second-millennium B.C.E. Mesopotamian cylinder seal depicts women harvesting dates. The presence of the crescent moon in the scene suggests that the women are working in the cool of the night and perhaps in accord with the phases of the moon. In Greece and Italy, olive oil was a dietary essential and played a key economic role; women frequently worked as the oil pressers. Sesame oil was also produced, and salt was a prized condiment, both for preservation and for flavoring.

Ancient women engaged in some animal husbandry—herding, hunting, and trapping small animals. Biblical stories tell of female herders, usually the daughters of the household, and a late Egyptian inscription identifies a female employed as a shepherdess. Women engaged in hunting small game like rabbits. A female speaker in a New Kingdom Egyptian poem talks of the string of birds she is bringing home to her mother. Most people, even in urban environments, were able to keep a few fowl—chickens, ducks, and geese—and small domesticated animals—pigs, sheep, and goats. These provided eggs, cheese, and yogurt, but apparently not milk.

Seafood supplied the principal protein for coastal or riverine dwellers, where most ancient peoples resided. Egyptians readily picked up dead or dying fish the Nile's inundation left along the riverbanks. Meat, a rarer treat, was usually eaten on festivals or other special occasions. Small animals were most commonly domesticated, especially in rocky, mountainous regions such as Greece that offered little hospitable terrain for cattle raising, and where pastoral herding or pig raising more readily supplemented rural farms. Even where cattle-grazing predominated, such as Egypt and the open pasturelands of Anatolia, the Near East, and Italy, only the wealthy could afford cattle ranching while most people had much rarer access to beef. Despite women's familiarity with animal preparation, almost universally ancient cultures recognized men as the animal procurers and butchers.

Except in Egypt, women received smaller food rations than men, and girls smaller portions than boys. In some places this inequitable distribution extended to giving a mother nursing a female infant lower rations than one nursing a male baby. This inequity in rations confirms that women probably ate less than men. In households where food was scarce and provisions carefully allocated to last the month or season, all people starved some and women starved the most.

Only royalty and the wealthy could afford imported foods and spices. A dinner plate in a second-dynasty Egyptian royal tomb of an elderly woman includes bread, porridge, roast or cooked fish, pigeon, quail, kidneys and beef, cheese, fresh berries, stewed figs, honey cakes, and wine. The first-century C.E. Roman writer, Petronius, in his *Satyricon,* satirizes Rome's nouveau riche and their extravagant, decadent tastes, as the wealthy freedman Trimalchio parades out trays of exotic foods that his cook has fashioned into sumptuous culinary creations.

The most basic economic activity derived from food acquisition was selling or trading surplus foods in open markets. Egyptian women controlled whatever surplus they grew and whatever they obtained for it. It is universally recognized that whoever controls their own economic resources generally has significant command over their own lives. This apparent economic autonomy furnished Egyptian women with the material base for their relatively equitable gender status in Egyptian society. Selling food and other items at community markets provided rural peasants with a basic source of income, where a woman might sell together with her husband or on her own. If she were an unmarried widow or divorcée, small-market trade might be a woman's only means of support and only barrier from total destitution. From independent market vendors to small grocers, shop signs from ancient Rome portray women as shopkeepers, which they may have owned or managed (Figure 5.3).

Prepared foods next provided numerous commercial opportunities. Women's work making bread and beer readily developed into bakery and brewery cottage industries. Remains of commercial bakeries have been found throughout the ancient world, and bread was among the first food commodi-

Figure 5.3 Woman greengrocer, marble relief. Rome, ca. 2nd c. C.E. Museo Ostiense, Ostia, Italy. Scala/Art Resource, NY.

ties traded for external economic exchange. Women formed the principal labor force for grinding the grain, forming the dough, and baking the bread, and they may have run their own home-based industries. But men held official titles of baker or brewer and usually ran the commercial bakeries and breweries, overseeing and benefiting from the women's productive activities.

In Egypt bread and beer functioned as the basic currency of exchange, the means by which the state paid its workers. The minimum daily ration to feed a husband, wife, and children was 10 loaves of bread and two jugs of beer. Estate owners and those of higher rank received up to several hundred loaves, which they distributed among their families and large numbers of estate workers. The often bloody spectacles produced in the amphitheaters throughout the Roman Empire offered frequent occasions to distribute bread and other foods. These "bread and circuses" figured significantly in keeping the often large, unemployed masses in Rome both amusingly occupied and fed, thus forestalling any potential riots.

Another cottage industry developed to provide hot meals. Urban dwellers appreciated hot lunches, which were often prepared at home and sold on the streets from a cart or from one's own back or shoulder packs—the ancient equivalent to New York's street hot dog vendors. The next step, comparable to today's pizza, gyro, or hamburger stands, was sidewalk eateries, remains of which line the major business streets in the ruins of Pompeii, itself an ancient international trade center. A marble top with round holes into which pots of food were placed fits over a space for fuel to keep the food warm. Women cooked the food, helped by men, and among Pompeii's businesswomen, some must also have owned these sidewalk diners.

The Cultural Meaning of Food and Drink

Besides being prized as a basic necessity of life, food and drink were highly appreciated for their sensuous qualities—appealing to the taste and associated with erotic pleasures. Apples were almost universally offered as love tokens, and pomegranates were widely associated with the vulva.

The tall Egyptian and Mesopotamian lettuce, which emitted a milky white liquid, served as a metaphor for an erection, while for the Greeks figs could represent either female or male genitalia. Beer and wine were particularly regarded as gifts of the gods, as their mind- and body-relaxing properties were much appreciated by hard-working ancient people. One of the epithets of Egyptian Hathor was the Drunken Goddess, and the Romans called the god of wine Dionysos Liber, "Liberator."

Stories illustrate bread's fundamental role in ancient peoples' perception of the world. Eating bread distinguished civilized peoples from those whom agriculturally based societies deemed uncivilized. Both bread and beer or winemaking were the products of human cultivation of wild grain and fruits, which together symbolized civilized life for many societies. The Greeks often invoked Demeter and Dionysos together as symbolic of civilized society.

A passage in the Gilgamesh epic describes another function bread may have served. In order to prove to the hero Gilgamesh that he has slept for a week, a matron bakes a loaf of bread each day, whose different stages of hardness and moldiness indicate the time elapsed. Since women baked the bread and handled the food remains, one can speculate that they devised a rudimentary counting system and calendar like the ingenious solution in this tale.

Social customs resolved the problem of what to do with the great quantity of meat available when a large animal is killed, meat which does not keep well without refrigeration in hot climates. Egyptian, Etruscan, and Roman elite were noted for their dinner parties, which offered a network of meal exchange that shared meat with other families who could depend on the reciprocity of meal giving. Presumably people of all classes shared this custom, as it still prevails throughout these regions today. For the Greeks, who invested the killing of an animal with religious significance, a sacrifice entailed the ritual slaughter of the animal and offering the aromatic smoke of a thighbone wrapped in burning fat as a dedication to the gods. The meat was then consumed by the congregants—either roasted or boiled and eaten on the spot or distributed in portions to be cooked at home.

Many stories portray the fundamental social significance of meal-sharing as a key component of hospitality. Biblical and Greek tales describe hosts feeding their guests and sometimes allowing them to bathe before inquiring their name or purpose. Good characters of all social classes in Homer's *Odyssey* practice hospitality, regarded as a law overseen by the chief god Zeus, while the lack of hospitable manners marks the uncivilized. Offering hospitality was intimately linked with women's activities. Women prepared and served all the food; in Genesis, for example, Abraham instructs Sarah to feed the disguised angels who have just arrived as strangers. Current practices in societies that share similar customs of hospitality and meal sharing confirm what ancient allusions suggest—women took great pride in preparing tasty meals and in being able to feed their families and guests.

Women's provision of beer was seen as equivalent to her supplying bread for sustenance. Both beer and wine were prized for their relaxing, euphoric effects that helped ease the hardships of daily life—the Mesopotamians regarded wine as an anodyne for the pains and depression of old age. As with bread, myths portrayed women's intrinsic association with these liquid necessities. In Gilgamesh's quest for immortality, he meets the divine tavern owner and beer maker, Siduri, who impresses upon the hero that he cannot attain the life of physical immortality that he seeks. Siduri elaborates the joys of mortal life he should cherish:

As for you, Gilgamesh, fill your belly with good things;
day and night, night and day, dance and be merry, feast and rejoice.
Let your clothes be fresh, bathe yourself in water,
cherish the little child that holds your hand,
and make your wife happy in your embrace;
for this too is the lot of man.[1]

The sage female tavern owner reminds the hero of the delightful advantages of civilization, all of which women provide—food, clothing, dancing, sex, children, joy, and love. As seen, both Egyptian and Mesopotamian rituals presented women and men with opportunities for much feasting, drinking, sexuality, and merriment, all in expression of the joys of life that goddesses provided and that mortal women embodied.

Greek and Roman attitudes toward women drinking reflect these cultures' different ideologies, which regarded wine as a man's drink. In the "Homeric Hymn to Demeter," the goddess proclaims that she is forbidden to drink wine, which is understood to be the drink of Dionysos, but she instead drinks a mixture of water, barley-meal—Demeter's grain—and pennyroyal.[2] However, ancient comedies satirized women equally for their dual lusts for alcohol and sex.

We can surmise that women may well have fantasized about and longed for the very things that might provide some welcome relief from the hardships of their daily lives. Perhaps in reaction to Etruscan women openly feasting with their men, among the earliest Roman laws was the provision that a man catching his wife with alcohol on her breath could be grounds for divorce. Once again, features that earlier Egyptian and Mesopotamian cultures had prized as aspects of women's essential cultural roles became transformed by late antiquity to signify women's unruliness. These activities, far from illustrating the great gifts of the mother goddess, now functioned to stigmatize women for not containing their sexual and mind-liberating desires within patriarchal limits of female behavior.

Textile Manufacture

The third staple of women's activities was cloth manufacture, which entailed spinning and weaving flax, cotton, linen, or wool fibers, dyeing when appropriate, and making the needed clothing, bedding, and table, floor, wall, and window coverings. All these stages of textile production consumed women's lives. Since Neolithic times, loom weights by the thousands have been found in women's burials, home work areas, and textile factories. In order to meet the constant demand for new cloth, textile production comprised a major industry. Wealthy homes might well have their own fabric manufacturing plants that employed scores or even hundreds of workers, for both household and commercial purposes.

Late third to early second millennia B.C.E. Mesopotamian records indicate about 12,000 weavers in one city and 13,200 in another. Some of these women worked in commercial weaving factories attached to palaces, temples, or wealthy estates. The city of Ur outsourced weaving work to surrounding villages, which enabled women to produce commercial textiles while working at home. Supervisors were typically men; one estimate suggests one overseer for 220 weavers. Ancient Egyptian evidence indicates men too may have woven, though to what extent is not known. Curiously, among the many scenes depicted in Egyptian tomb paintings, very few illustrate weaving.

In contrast, Greek vase paintings depict various stages of women's cloth production, and Greek literature portrays elite women and goddesses as always engaged in either spinning or weaving. A sixth-century painting that encircles its oil flask depicts pairs of women engaged in all aspects of cloth production. The side of this vase shown here depicts two women working the ancient upright loom, one separating the weft strands while the other pushes through a large shuttle with the all-important loom weights visibly fulfilling their function of pulling the weft threads down (Figure 5.4). Flanking this central image are two more women, their backs turned to the women weaving. The one on the left is spinning long strands of yarn faced by a woman carding the wool, while the figure on the right is folding the finished cloth together with another woman. Like the scene of the women gathering water at the public fountain (Figure 3.2), the pairs of women working together suggest again the communal nature of some women's work.

Even if aristocratic women did not actively participate in textile manufacture, that the literary and visual evidence portrays them as well as female divinities performing these tasks shows what powerful symbols spinning and weaving represented. These ancient media images of women always working at their spindles or looms promoted the cultural ideals of elite women's industriousness and proper fulfillment of their matronly roles. At the same time these portrayals may reflect the actual work entailed in cloth production, since it takes five spinners to keep one weaver supplied with yarn. Women may well have used every spare moment to spin the thread from the raw fiber. Since cloth is perishable, vase paintings often provide an inkling of the artistry of women's weaving skill.

Surplus cloth provided a major item for economic exchange outside the household. Egyptian women could sell their own weavings and keep the proceeds from these sales. In other cultures men often controlled the sale of cloth in external markets. Women performed the work and their immediate supervisors may have been women, but men more typically owned the larger plants and conducted the higher levels of business transactions. Because of weaving's essential function in the household and as an item of trade, women's skill in weaving was highly valued. In *The Odyssey* Penelope's superior weaving talents are publicly and repeatedly acknowledged, a prized gift from the goddess Athena, who oversaw women's artistry in the craft of weaving.

Figure 5.4 Greek vase said to be found in Attica. Attic, black-figure, VI, ca. 560 B.C. Attributed to Amasis Painter. Image © The Metropolitan Museum of Art.

As in indigenous American cultures, Greek women's weavings were prized as ceremonial offerings and in gift-giving exchanges. As seen, the rites for many female deities entailed the annual weaving of a new robe for the cultic statue of the goddess in her temple. To illustrate the significance of weavings in women's gift-giving, in *The Odyssey* Helen presents Odysseus's son with one of her own fine weavings as a departure gift. While women no doubt took pride in their ability to feed their families, the product of their weaving skills furnished a more durable sign of their creative and economic talents.

The first appearance of Helen in *The Iliad* reveals another aspect of weaving in ancient Greece, its function as a metaphor for the creation of poetry. In her first appearance Helen rises from the "great, purple, folded robe" into which she is weaving the story of the Trojan War battles to go tell the Trojan elders the names of the principal Greek combatants.[3] This scene portrays Helen, whom Greek literature often associates with the creation of poetry, as transferring her creativity from the mute modality of the plastic art of weaving to the oral modality of verbal expression.

This idea of weaving as a metaphor for female creativity combined with Greek male suspicion of women so that women's weaving came to signify deceit. The *Odyssey* passage that first and most highly praises Penelope for her weaving talents uses the image of weaving as both a literal and figurative deceit.[4] Through the ruse of weaving a shroud for her father-in-law which she unravels each night, Penelope puts off marriage to her unwelcome suitors for four years. The poem underscores Penelope's interlaced talents at weaving and cunning by portraying her as successfully deceiving the suitors through her weaving. Contemporary semantic idioms continue to reflect these metaphorical aspects of women's craft of weaving—we regularly speak of spinning a yarn, weaving a tale, or weaving a snare.

Postproduction textile work included laundering, and commercial launderers provided another source of paid employment for women and men. In Pompeii, the profession of fullers, those who shrink and thicken wool and which was comprised mostly of men, developed into a discrete industry at times separate from the weaving factories. Women also worked as seamstresses and dressmakers, manufacturing not only the basic fabrics but the finished clothing as well. Some women are identified as weaving in gold, no doubt a specialized skill.

Mourners

Like the other female-related endeavors, women's responsibility in preparing the dead for burial also generated some paid employment. The most common paid funerary work for women throughout these Mediterranean cultures was as mourners (see Figure 2.2). The addition of even a few women to a man's funerary cortege demonstrated his importance, and people of wealth might hire dozens of female mourners to show their exalted status in this world and to help escort them to the next.

OTHER ECONOMIC ACTIVITIES

Lower and Middle Economic Classes

At all times in all cultures women of lower and middle economic classes worked at numerous occupations. It is not always possible in the records to distinguish between a slave worker, whose compensation would get paid to her owner, from a free person trying to eke out a living for herself and her family. Besides all the child, food, and textile associated forms of employment, women worked in trade, personal adornment, medicine, entertainment, prostitution, crafts, and more. Some job titles identify women as: barber, brick maker and layer, construction worker, horse tender, ibis feeder, reader, and scribe.

Some women in ancient Egypt were listed as "sealer," the person in charge of sealing and guarding property in the absence of locks. Although men were typically the sealers within the state bureaucracy, these female sealers may have worked within the home. Near the end of the Hellenistic period an epitaph of an Athenian woman who worked at the royal court in Alexandria, Egypt, identifies her as raised to be a foreign storeroom attendant to watch over the king's wealthy possessions.

Mesopotamian documents show that slaves were trained as scribes to accompany princesses who were married to foreign rulers. These personal scribes insured that the royal woman could correspond home without having to use male scribal intermediaries. Mesopotamian and Egyptian records occasionally refer to a female scribe in circumstances that suggest she was paid for her work. As with many of these positions, she probably did not work for the state or with men, but used her scribal skills for female clients.

In Mesopotamian and biblical sources, perfume-making was an important women's occupation. The relief carving on an eighteenth dynasty Egyptian sarcophagus (Figure 4.3) depicts women pressing flowers in a large urn to make perfume, while a woman on the left approaches with a platter of more flowers. Perfumes were prized for personal hygiene and enhancement and because they fulfilled ritual needs. Greek and Roman inscriptions also list women as perfume sellers, and women of all cultures were involved in cosmetics. Their manufacture was often an extension of women's herbal knowledge, as some, like henna and kohl, were also believed to have medicinal properties. Women sold cosmetics and they helped other women to apply theirs. Women also worked as hairdressers, especially to the aristocratic families of imperial Egypt, Mesopotamia, and Rome.

Athenian inscriptions list women as vendors of cloaks, frankincense, herbs, honey, olive oil, salt, sesame seeds, shoes, and unguents. This list must represent a sampling of the merchandise women offered for sale, and it shows that women sold whatever items they might gather, produce, make themselves, or obtain from others for profitable resale.

Third-millennium Mesopotamian seals depict women as potters. In historical Greek times, once artists started signing their works, only men's names appear as the potters, vase painters, and sculptors. One vase painting includes a woman among several studio artists, and another seems to depict a woman painting a man's portrait. A famous mosaic panorama of Alexander the Great defeating the Persian king Darius II at the Issos River was reputed to emulate the original picture painted by a woman named Helena. In the first century C.E. the Roman naturalist Pliny the Elder names several female Greek painters dating back to the Archaic period.

Until the rise of male medical professions, women served as the primary healers and pharmacologists. Although women were generally excluded from formal medical training, sources from all these ancient cultures suggest some women did receive a more professional medical education and worked as physicians.

At least some Mesopotamian and Egyptian musicians and dancers held religious or courtly offices, and may not have been considered hired employees. But throughout most ancient cultures, women worked as various types of entertainers, including acrobats, actresses, dancers, musicians, and singers. These occupations of varying status might also be filled by slaves or prostitutes. Egyptian tomb paintings portray female musicians entertaining at home and at banquets. A painting from the tomb of Horemhab from the late fifteenth century shows women of different ages with varied stringed and reed instruments very likely performing at a public festival (Figure 5.5). From both Egypt in the mid-second millennium B.C.E. (as illustrated in Figure 10.4) and Tarentum, southern Italy, almost a millennium later, survive illustrations of female acrobats. Greek records individually name female singers, dancers, and flute and lyre players, while numerous Roman inscriptions name female actresses, musicians, and gladiators.

Besides brewing the beer and wine, women also ran the taverns. While the literature depicts divine tavern owners and beer makers like Siduri as wise and respected, actual bars in Mesopotamia as elsewhere were frequented by men and prostitutes, and female bar owners and workers occupied the lower socioeconomic strata. Inscriptions from Pompeii indicate women worked as bar waitresses and may have been tavern owners. Many female tavern workers were also slaves and prostitutes.

Whether it is in fact the oldest profession, references to prostitutes appear in the earliest levels of Mesopotamian literature. These references show different degrees of sexual service, from the lowest level sex worker under the bridge to the temple priestess of Ishtar, who presumably received some respect for her sexual activity on behalf of the goddess. The English word

Figure 5.5 Women musicians, wall painting. Tomb of Horemhab, Thebes, Egypt, ca. 1420–1411 B.C.E. Erich Lessing/Art Resource, NY, France.

"fornicate" derives from the Latin word for "arch," *fornix,* the places where the poorest women engaged with men for sex. Women ran brothels as well as working in them. Pompeii's brothels were filled with graphic sexual wall paintings and inscriptions referring to the prostitutes who plied their trade in their dark, squalid rooms.

Ancient Greeks distinguished between prostitutes, who sold only sex, in brothels or on the streets, and *hetairai,* often well-educated and cultured "companions" to men, who provided various forms of musical and intellectual entertainment, as well as sexuality. A *hetaira* might be completely supported with her own home by a man, from which she might reach for the coveted status of a respectable female citizen. A famous fourth-century Athenian court case, "Against Neaira," by the orator Demosthenes, relates the attempts of the former *hetaira* Neaira to pass herself and her daughter off as legitimate Athenian citizen women. Since Demosthenes' speech only represents his client's prosecution, we do not know if the charges were justified or how this case was decided.

Paintings on drinking cups often show *hetairai* at a symposium, a men's drinking party, which might include entertainment and discussion, such as portrayed in Plato's *Symposium.* One cup exterior shows two *hetairai* at a symposium playing a cup-toss game known as *kottabos,* another depicts a *hetaira* playing a flute, while a third portrays a man and woman reaching out to each other in mutual gestures inviting sexuality. One cup interior reveals a *hetaira* holding the head of her besotted companion while he is visibly retching, a less pleasant duty she might have to fulfill. Painted inside the cup, the image may also be a reminder to the drinker of what awaits him should he over-imbibe.

Another sign of women's general parity with men in Egyptian society is that they, like the men, were subject to the state system of labor conscription known as corvée whereby all Egyptians had to work for the state on public building projects for subsistence wages. The rich often bought their way out of such service, which then fell upon the poor to fulfill. Women frequently provided the domestic labor support for the men's building projects, such as supplying clothing for the male corvée workers. In further evidence of equal treatment, women who tried to avoid their corvée obligations faced the same harsh punishment as the men.

Slave Women

As noted, slave women performed all women's tasks. Most worked in child care, domestic duties, and weaving. Considered property themselves, their owners benefited from the value of their labor by not having to pay them beyond supplying their minimal requirements of food, clothing, and shelter. Before large-scale state societies needed slaves to satisfy their massive labor requirements, slaves were regarded as extensions of the family, without legal rights to be sure, but often treated like other family members. Except for the very poor most ancient households maintained at least one or two slaves, which may explain why we generally do not hear of women hired to clean houses as a domestic maid. This work was apparently carried out by the matron, her children, and the house slaves.

The expanding ancient kingdoms developed large slave institutions to benefit from the great numbers of conquered peoples. Captive educated Greek women worked as doctors and teachers to elite Roman families. Other Roman documents record slave women working at the same tasks alongside other women. Although the wages a slave woman earned were typically paid to her owner, some slave women amassed enough of their pay to manumit themselves.

Elite Women

In all cultures, elite women had far more resources at their disposal that enabled them, if they so chose and if their situations permitted, to engage in higher levels of business practices than their less economically fortunate sisters. In ancient Egypt, Mesopotamia, and Rome, elite women held positions as estate managers, overseeing agricultural production, storage, and distribution, as well as the production and sale of any household industry, including textiles, oil, beer or winemaking, crafts manufacture, and so forth. In the royal residences, women supervised the women's quarters, managing all the staff and activities conducted there. Wealthy women might own businesses, engage in trade, lend money, and invest in their community's infrastructure.

Documents from the earlier periods of Egypt and Mesopotamia show women having full legal and economic equality with men for any commercial activity. Old Kingdom Egyptian records indicate that women regularly held administrative positions within the palace, sometimes even overseeing the work of men. However, by the Middle Kingdom, early second millennium, women's names were no longer listed in these positions. Third- and early second-millennia documents from several Mesopotamian cities, including Mari and Ebla, show women actively engaged in their city's economic life at all levels. Wives of Old Assyrian merchants were regularly involved in large-scale business dealings, representing their husbands in commercial and legal negotiations. However, these records do not indicate how much of the money the women handled they were able to keep and dispose of as they wished. Despite the various social restrictions imposed on Roman women, those of the elite class seemed to engage in commercial ventures with apparent autonomy.

Women generally had freer use of inheritances for their own purposes. Female-friendly inheritance laws in ancient Egypt, Mesopotamia, Sparta, and Rome resulted in some women acquiring great wealth. Mesopotamian women could have themselves adopted as sons by childless individuals, part of the transaction including the transference of real estate to the adoptee. Documents list several women as acquiring large estate holdings through such land adoption contracts. These women might then manage the land and its products, or engage in real-estate exchange. Spartan women were notorious for using their wealth for conspicuous display, especially in racing horses at the Olympic games. The fourth-century B.C.E. Spartan Kyniska proudly proclaimed on stone that she was the only Greek woman ever to have won an Olympic winner's crown. The Voconian Law passed in Rome in 169 B.C.E. barred men in the highest property class from bequeathing more than half their property to their daughter, both to restrict the daughter's accumulation of wealth and to keep the property within the patriline.

In the late third and mid-first centuries B.C.E. the senate in the Roman Republic enacted legislation requiring wealthy women to contribute to the state coffers from their personal wealth. The first of these was the Oppian Law, which was passed at the beginning of the second Punic War. In the two years before the law's enactment, the Romans had suffered two devastating defeats in northern Italy under the Carthaginian general Hannibal, which decimated the male Roman population, so that almost every woman mourned the loss of a close male relative. At the same time women benefited financially from these dire circumstances. Under Roman laws of intestate succession, daughters inherited equally with their brothers, and if their brothers were also killed, they would inherit all. Consequently, some women benefited liberally from this windfall. With so much of the male population deceased, tax revenues fell and Rome was unable to meet its financial obligations. These circumstances led to the passage in 215 B.C.E. of the Oppian Law, which limited the amount of gold a woman could possess to half an ounce and prohibited women from extravagant displays of wealth. Over the next few years, the Roman state confiscated any financial windfall many women had received, and it continued to tax women as well as men, including women's dowries and other personal possessions, in order to maintain its revenue base.

The second Roman law that imposed a tax upon wealthy women's property was also enacted during a time of political crisis, this time, however, one of civil not external strife. Both laws show that those women in some cultures who may have amassed wealth, especially through inheritance, were for these same reasons subject to taxation by the state, sometimes at rates more onerous than imposed on men. These two particular Roman laws taxing women's property offered Roman women occasions to protest publicly against what they saw as unfair taxation, their actions to be discussed in the next chapter.

Illustrative of the active commercial dealings of Roman women was the position of Eumachia, a wealthy businesswoman of Pompeii whose family manufactured bricks. Eumachia was a patroness of the guild of fullers, one of fewer than 5 percent of women who served as a patroness of a men's labor guild. Eumachia financed the construction of several public buildings, colonnades, and crypts, including an elaborate tomb for herself. An inscription proclaims Eumachia's beneficence in paying for the large public building in Pompeii's Forum, the center of the city's commercial, legal, and religious activities, which she dedicated in her own name and that of her son in honor of the goddesses Concordia, "Harmony," and Augustan Piety. In recognition of Eumachia's munificence, the fullers erected her statue inside the building.

Figure 5.6 Woman mashing barley bread to make beer, painted wood. Egyptian Old Kingdom, 5th dynasty, ca. 2565–2420 B.C.E. Scala/Art Resource, NY, Museo Archeologico, Florence, Italy.

Whether of the elite, middle, poor, or slave class, women of all times and all cultures have worked at the entire spectrum of occupations. Although circumstances forced many into menial or demeaning jobs, others at all economic levels have been able to turn their situations to their own best advantage. Whether high or low on the economic scale, women have always been economically resourceful for themselves, their children, and their families. Moreover, recognizing the advantage of economic independence, women everywhere attempted to eke out whatever benefits they could for themselves in their economic situations. This pursuit of economic advantage in whatever way possible at all levels of the society concretely shows women's resilience and initiative, and it provides a solid material underpinning to the ritual and personal dimensions of women's lives we have so far seen.

Six

From Matrons to Female Kings—Women Who Ruled from Home and from the Throne

Women have led many modern nations, but the idea of a woman ruler still seems exceptional to many people. In ancient and modern patriarchal states men have proclaimed male rulership to be a natural and moral norm. These societies have regarded women's ascendance to ruling power as unusual if not unnatural. To the ancient Egyptians a female ruler went against the established order of the universe, *maat.* In his *Politics,* the Greek philosopher Aristotle theoretically validated such thinking by claiming that women were by nature unfit to rule. A Chinese saying succinctly sums up this view by stating that a woman ruling would be like "a hen crowing at dawn." Notable exceptions to the rarity of women's rule are the preferences for female rulers that emerged in the developing ancient Japanese state, in the African nations of Kush and western Africa, and possibly in the Bronze Age Minoan culture on Crete.

INDIGENOUS MODELS OF WOMEN'S PUBLIC DECISION MAKING

Western researchers expect evidence of women rulers to prove that they have commanded full reigning power. However, without necessarily holding the title of ruler women have exercised significant authority in their society's governance. In other societal configurations, where spheres of activity can have shapes and patterns of interaction radically different from familiar Western ones, women have enacted decisive leadership roles behind the scenes rather than in the spotlight.

Indigenous American societies provide valuable models for viewing women's community decision-making roles, since the decisions of the elder women characteristically direct the society's functioning, while men visibly execute the women's directives. These political dynamics have been well documented for the nations of the Iroquois Confederacy, and they are evident in many other indigenous nations in the Americas and globally.

A poem by contemporary Cherokee poet Norman H. Russell, entitled "Two Circles," illustrates this point.

there are two circles
the men make a circle in the center
around the large fire
behind them the women make a circle
in the cold shadows

the men speak much wisdom
they make all the laws
they make all the decisions
then they look behind them to the women

if the women shake their heads
the men must begin again.[1]

Many indigenous societies provide models of a dual governing structure in which men fulfill public leadership roles while the ultimate governing authority rests with the women who direct the course of the men's deliberations and actions. Other societies organized concepts of dual gender governance in other ways. The ancient nations of Japan and West Africa had dual sex governance systems in which each gender handled their own affairs, and in some the women adjudicated the conflicts that arose between the two. These examples show some of the ways women have influenced public decision making. In particular, women might significantly shape policy behind the publicly visible rulers, and their voices from the wings may have carried greater weight than official documents record.

NONROYAL WOMEN'S INFLUENCE ON GOVERNANCE

Greece: Elis, Athens, and Sparta—the Elusive Female Citizen

Ancient Greek women did not formally participate in civic governance, but several literary references explore the idea of women's political leadership. One source claims that after the ruling tyrant of Pisa near Olympia had died, the Pisans and the neighboring Eleans chose 16 women from the local communities to resolve their disputes and establish peace. Later this Council of 16 Matrons of Elis oversaw the weaving of the goddess's robe and the adolescent games for Hera, which paralleled the Olympic games for Zeus, but no other documents record their political activity.

The idea of women as effective peacemakers and even political leaders captivated two Athenian male writers—the comic playwright Aristophanes and the philosopher Plato. Besides two plays that fantasize women assuming leadership of Athens' male democratic system, Aristophanes' comedy *Lysistrata*, produced in 411 B.C.E. and highly popular today, suggests ways real women may have influenced community decision making. The play hinges on the fantastic premise of a women's sex strike to stop the war—fantastic because the men, who had ready access to other sexual partners, were already away.

Nevertheless in the play Lysistrata organizes all Greek women into successful political action. Lysistrata demonstrates women's awareness of public matters, twice remarking that women question their husbands about their acts in the assembly, chastising them for injudicious decisions. A half century later, the orator Demosthenes warns jurors to consider their verdict carefully because their wives will question their husbands' decisions when they come home.

Aristophanes' play underscores women's governing ability. The women take over Athena's temple, the Parthenon, where the city treasury is kept, in order to cut off funding for the war. Lysistrata affirms that just as the women manage household matters, including budgets—using the metaphors of cleaning and carding wool for cleaning up city politics—so they have the experience to run the city's affairs. The Chorus of elder women bases their right to speak and act publicly on two other female-specific activities—the many female transition rites they performed growing up (see chapter 2), and the high cost they pay by bearing the sons that become war's cannon fodder. Finally, in her last appearance, Lysistrata grounds her actions in men's prerogatives by citing the lessons she learned from her father as authorizing her public voice.

Intermixed with the comic humor, Aristophanes presents compelling reasons for listening to women's views on public policies that rest on women's domestic tasks, their ritual roles, and their place in the larger civic community. He suggests that women are capable of leadership roles and that they might well execute these roles better than men. Possibly in some cases Athenian women were able to shape public policy in these ways.

Aristophanes may have based the character Lysistrata, whose name means "releaser of armies," on two outspoken Athenian women. First was a contemporary priestess of Athena Polias, "of the City," Lysimakhe, whose name means "releaser of battle." As a public figure, the mortal representative of the city's patron goddess Athena, the priestess Lysimakhe may have had or assumed greater authority to speak out on public matters. More notorious in her day was the Miletos-born Aspasia, who lived with the fifth-century leader of Athens, Perikles, after he divorced his Athenian wife in 445 B.C.E. Diverse sources claim that Aspasia, whom leading Athenian figures consulted for her moral and political advice, greatly influenced Perikles' policies, including possibly inducing him to start the Peloponnesian War.

Aspasia's position may also have influenced the philosopher Plato's portrayal of women's ruling potential in his utopian dialogue, *The Republic*, in which the character Sokrates proposes that among the ruling class, whom he calls the guardians, women would fill the same leadership roles as men. Sokrates asserts that there is no difference between women and men as regards their ability to govern, and if one educated the guardian women the same as the men, they would be able to rule equally well in his ideal state.

Neither Aristophanes' comic fantasies nor Plato's intellectual utopia described women's actual roles. Indeed, Plato eliminated women's ruling potential by consigning them to their traditional domestic roles in his final work, *The Laws*. But these diverse treatments show that both popular and intellectual circles entertained the idea of women's governance, and women may well have contributed to the debate. In the other major Greek *polis*, Sparta, women possibly had a greater role in decision making. It is note-worthy that the feminine form of a politically engaged citizen, *politis*, was not used for Athenian women, but was used of Spartan women, which may indicate something about their public role. It is also notable that most of the utopian social features Sokrates advocates in Plato's *Republic*, especially those pertaining to women's roles, derive from Spartan practices.

Ironically, the source most hostile to Spartan women provides key insights into their possible decision-making role. In his *Politics* Aristotle asks what difference it makes if Spartan "women rule or if the rulers are ruled by women," implying that Spartan women substantially influenced men's public decisions, perhaps even exercising command from the wings. To Aristotle the Spartan *polis* failed to establish its authority over its women, whom Aristotle brands as licentious, out of control, and the cause of civic disorder. He coined a new term for his view of Spartan women's conduct—a *gynaikokratia*, "rule by women," on the same analogy as *dêmokratia*, "rule by the people." In a popular saying, an Athenian woman asks a Spartan woman why they are the only Greek women to rule their men, to which the Spartan woman responds, "Because we are the only ones who give birth to men." As in matriarchal indigenous cultures, Spartan women situated the source of their community-wide activism in their essential, central roles as mothers.

Aristotle's remarks tantalize us with women's governing potential, but they do not reveal Spartan women's actual decision-making authority. Ancient evidence describes a completely male governing system, where women held no formal leadership roles. At the same time, in contrast to the nega-tive images of Athenian women speaking up at home on matters of public policy, sources suggest Spartan women and even girls were esteemed for their outspokenness. Herodotos tells a story of the king's daughter, Gorgo, who receives praise for the sage advice she gives her father during negotia-tions with a foreign emissary.

Another of Aristotle's critiques suggests the possible political structure in which Spartan women may have actively shaped their city's policies. Aristotle claims that Spartan women refused to abide by the laws of Lycurgus, the revered legendary Spartan lawgiver, all of whose provisions addressed only men's concerns and paid no attention to the women. The Lycurgan laws probably recorded the men's customs while the women continued to follow their own ways, which had not been committed to writing.

What Aristotle regarded as the women's willfulness in flouting the Lycurgan law suggests rather the operation of a dual sex governance system, with the women in charge of the girls' education and of female matters parallel to the men's oversight of male concerns. Like their royal counterparts everywhere, women in Sparta's two ruling houses contributed to the image of the public activity of Spartan women, who occasionally took actions that brought them to public prominence, and they too suffered the consequences of failed political decisions.

Rome—Elite Women Take Action

In his detailed account of early Rome, the Roman historian Livy relates numerous legends of women who took actions that shaped the development of Roman political institutions. Two tales epitomize the legendary images of women. The first emphasizes female chastity in the face of sexual assault as the faithfully married Lucretia commits suicide rather than be raped by an abusive Etruscan king. Turning her personal tragedy into a public protest, Lucretia summons her father and husband to witness her suicide, first explaining the reason for it. In Rome's legendary early history, Lucretia's act catalyzes the overthrow of the monarchy and establishment of the Roman Republic. In this tale, Lucretia, her male kin with their political supporters, and the force of legend literally transformed her personal act into a momentous political event. Whatever reality underlies this tale, it reveals a feature typical of Rome's legendary history—women's actions, whether alone or in groups, shaped national political affairs.

The other legendary tale describes the Sabine women. In Livy's version, after their requests for brides were rebuffed by the neighboring Sabines, the early Romans invited the Sabines to a festival at which the Roman men deceitfully abducted the young Sabine women. Once they had the women in their control, Livy claims the Roman men treated them respectfully, convinced them of their honorable intent, and persuaded the women to marry them and become the mothers of the Roman nation. When the women's fathers came to rescue their female relatives, now married and pregnant, the women interceded and successfully convinced their male kin to establish an alliance with the Romans and live in peace. Thus began the city of Rome.

The reality behind this story was no doubt considerably more violent than this self-serving historical account. Nevertheless, all these stories show women actively shaping public events at the very heart of Roman history. Like these legendary tales, there were several occasions when Roman women publicly demonstrated their political views, individually and in groups. One intervention by women early in the Roman Republic was invoked for centuries as an example of women's positive civic influence. In 491 B.C.E., backed by Roman women, the aged mother Veturia and wife Volumnia of the exiled leader Coriolanus successfully dissuaded him from attacking Rome.

One striking example of Roman women demonstrating for their rights occurred in 195 B.C.E., to demand the repeal of the 20-year-old Oppian Law. Besides the tax burden, the law banned women, but not men, from extravagant displays, both of mourning and of wealth—women were forbidden from wearing purple or from riding in carriages within a mile of Rome and any Roman town, except for religious festivals.

Several factors contributed to the women's public protest. Several years before, when Hannibal offered 8,000 Roman prisoners for ransom, the women openly entreated the senators to ransom their kinsmen. Moreover, during wartime without close male kin to serve as their guardians—men who had deep familial reasons for careful oversight of their female relatives—a probably distant state-appointed guardian would have left women freer to act independently. Ironically, while these circumstances granted them some greater autonomy, women also became vulnerable to exploitation, which the state's confiscation of women's inheritance windfall superbly illustrates.

All these factors culminated in women's open demonstrations outside and within the Senate for repeal of the Oppian Law. Livy presents senators' arguments for and against the law's repeal. Arguing against repeal was the conservative consul Cato, who claimed women had to remain under male control in order to keep them respectable. He threatened that if the men allowed the women to become equal to them, the women would soon turn into the men's masters with no check on their unbridled extravagance. Speaking in support of the women's demand for repeal was Valerius, who recalled several women's actions that benefited Rome—the Sabine women, the appeal to Coriolanus, and the Roman women's recent actions during the Carthaginian crisis. Valerius recognized the necessity for women to display their wealth since they were denied all other means of public recognition. Whether due to the arguments of Valerius or of others, the women achieved their goal, and the law was repealed.

These women's actions were recalled as times of great sacrifice and nobility by another woman, Hortensia, in a speech she gave in the Roman Forum in 42 B.C.E., just two years after the assassination of Julius Caesar. In yet another time of war, which, as Hortensia notes in her speech, is the common state of affairs—for "When have there not been wars?" she asks—1,400 women were being taxed to pay the expenses of the three Roman leaders known as triumvirs. Unlike the situation 150 years earlier, the current danger was not from an external enemy, but a crisis due to civil war. The women being taxed were the female relatives of men condemned to exile or death for their opposing political views, which motivated the women to protest the law's unfairness.

In her speech, which was acclaimed in antiquity, though only a Greek version 200 years later exists, Hortensia argued several key points. Since their men had been taken, confiscating their property would leave them destitute. If they themselves had done wrong to the state, then they should be punished, but if not, why should they have to suffer these penalties? Finally, she argued that like the women during the second Punic War, they too would generously contribute for the defense of Rome, but they refused to finance civil strife.

The women holding an open demonstration in the Forum angered the triumvirs, who berated them for refusing to contribute money when the men had to serve in the army, and the officials forcefully pushed the women out of the tribunal. The people, however, outraged by this treatment, supported the women so that the next day the triumvirs lowered the number of women subject to the tax to 400 and imposed a tax on all men of a certain wealth status.

Most outstanding of influential Roman women was Cornelia, daughter of the general famed for having conquered Hannibal, and mother of 12 children for her husband Tiberius Gracchus, three of whom survived to adulthood. Cornelia pushed her sons, both of whom became tribunes, the highest elected representatives of the people, to more aggressive political actions, and she was rumored to have killed her daughter's husband because he opposed her son's policies. Though herself not of royalty, Cornelia may have conducted herself as the regal heir to the great Roman conqueror, and her actions evoke those royal women took on behalf of their sons.

ROYAL WOMEN'S AUTHORITY BEHIND THE THRONE

In monarchical realms access to the ruler was typically restricted to the royal family and their close retainers. Royal women everywhere, by virtue of their exalted rank and class status, enjoyed extraordinary levels of influence on their son's, husband's, and at times father's reigns. Both legends and historical accounts from all dynastic societies portray the ambitious maneuverings of royal women. Greek tales tell of the powerful Mycenaean queens, Helen and Klytaimestra, while later documents reveal the politically active roles taken by women of the ruling houses of Egypt, Mesopotamia, Sparta, the Hellenistic Greek kingdoms, and Rome. Although a few royal women formally exercised ruling authority, they mostly enjoyed two positions that afforded them the greatest opportunity to wield substantial influence behind the throne. One was as queen, the king's wife, but even greater authority usually rested in the highly important role of queen mother.

Queen Mothers

In ancient Egypt, the queen mother held a formal title and ceremonial duties. The queen mother was closely identified with Hathor, Isis, or Mut as mother of the king, and she probably played a considerable role in determining the selection of the next king. Often exercising greater power than any other individual in the ruling hierarchy, sometimes including the king himself, the queen mother might well rule as her son's regent while he was a minor, and then maintain a strong influence throughout the king's lifetime.

Ancient Mesopotamia records several influential queen mothers, beginning with Abi-Simti, wife of Shulgi, the Third Dynasty ruler of Ur, 2094–47 B.C.E. Fortuitously, extensive correspondence reveals the considerable authority exercised by Addu-duri, mother of the powerful king of the northwestern city of Mari, Zimri-Lim, 1779–45 B.C.E. Characteristic of the official roles King Zimri-Lim entrusted to all his female relatives, Addu-duri handled wide areas of responsibility, including the general functioning of the palace and temples, and she may have served as governor of Mari.

Contemporary letters show that Addu-duri was in charge of palace supplies and slaves. In one letter Zimri-Lim advises her to deal harshly with runaway slaves to prevent the frequency of escapes. In another letter palace servants appeal to her to intercede on behalf of an aged male slave who had served the palace since his youth, but who was callously being given away as a gift to someone else. Gifts intended for the king were sent to Addu-duri who as palace administrator formally received these tributes on the king's behalf. Two of the king's letters instruct her to make ceremonial weapons out of several silver jugs that a vassal king had sent.

Addu-duri also managed such temple matters as sacrifices, supplying objects for cultic use, and conveying the temple prophecies to the king. Addu-duri formally investigated legal claims in property and money disputes, and her position obliged her, like other high officials and vassal kings, to contribute to the palace stores of grain, a tax on the wealth she derived from her royal appointment. It is significant that only after her death did the king's wife Shibtu become prominent in many of these same offices.

After another millennium the names of several queen mothers emerge from the Assyrian period. In the late ninth century B.C.E. lived Sammuramat, known as Semiramis to the Greeks, and wrongly credited by them with creating the Hanging Gardens of Babylon, one of the seven wonders of the ancient world. Sammuramat maintained her active regency even after her son, Adad-nirari III, came to power. Possibly commemorating her introduction of the worship of the Babylonian god Nabu, two inscribed statues at the entrance of a new temple to the god are dedicated for the life of both the king and his mother. Moreover, Sammuramat often made dedications in her own name, which she placed before that of her son. Just over a century later Naqi'a-Zakutu, the favorite wife of the Assyrian king Sennacherib, 704–681 B.C.E., twice exerted her influence over the selection of the next king. She first secured her son Esarhaddon's succession to the throne (680–69), even though he was the youngest of Sennacherib's sons. Later, she played a key role in the ascendancy of her grandson Ashurbanipal, 668–27 B.C.E., despite his also having an older brother.

The power exercised by the queen mother, whether or not officially recognized, demonstrates the ambition of powerful women in male-controlled governing systems. Notoriously, queen mothers have readily used violence and intrigue to insure their sons' succession. Olympias, mother of Alexander the Great, reputedly murdered her husband, Philip II of Macedon, and others so that Alexander could ascend to the throne. Agrippina, mother of the Roman emperor Nero, similarly murdered off any opposition to her son. The bond between a king and his mother often meant the king could trust and confide in his mother where he might harbor suspicion of others. Kings of Ugarit regularly informed their mothers on affairs of state, and they sometimes deployed their mothers on diplomatic missions abroad. The queen mother might serve as a trusted counselor and stand-in during the king's absence, as Addu-duri did for Zimri-Lim, and as Olympias effectively ruled the Macedonian palace while her son Alexander was off on his imperial conquests.

King's Wife

Though usually not as powerful as the queen mother, the influence the wife of a king may have had upon his rule was due to many factors, among which were certainly the personalities of the king and queen and the circumstances of their rule. Some queens greatly influenced their husbands' rule and left their mark in the historical record.

Mesopotamia

Shibtu, the wife of Zimri-Lim, exercised even greater powers than her mother-in-law Addu-duri. Numerous letters between Shibtu and her natal family on the one hand, and between Shibtu and her husband while he was away on his many campaigns on the other, offer rare glimpses into royal family communications. Besides revealing continuing affection with her natal family, King Yarim-Lim and Queen Gashera of Aleppo, Syria, Shibtu's letters inquire about her land in Aleppo and voice her opinion on other matters, indicating that she maintained some influence with her natal kin and city.

In their letters to one another, Shibtu and Zimri-Lim inquire into each other's health, and assure the other of their own well-being and that of their city or endeavors. Although Shibtu expressed some anxiety when one of Zimri-lim's campaigns did not go well, generally these letters did not record personal feelings, but the details of official governing correspondence. The letters show that Shibtu had general oversight of the palace, the temples, the workshops, the city of Mari, and its environs, functioning as the king's deputy during his absence. She was overseer of important male officials and administrators, an unusual position for a woman, and she transmitted their needs and concerns to the king.

Shibtu likewise oversaw the women of the palace and the workshops. Her correspondence with her husband shows that a key result, if not purpose, of warfare was the conquest not only of land, but especially of people—men blinded to do the necessary menial labor, women primarily to work as weavers. Among his various conquests Zimri-lim sent Shibtu a number of women with instructions to assign them to work in the textile factories, except for 30 who may have been intended for the king's harem but were later dedicated to the temple of the god they had previously served.

Egypt

Powerful Egyptian wives of kings arose throughout the dynastic record. The fourth dynasty tomb of Queen Meresankh, mid-third millennium B.C.E., depicts this early queen in various independent activities, including scenes with her mother, Queen Hetepheres. In one they are boating together in the marshes. A striking statuary portrait imitates the formal composition of royal couples, but instead of the pharaoh and his queen, this one shows the queen and her mother (Figure 6.1). Early Egyptian royal female burials reinforce the impression these images give. The extravagance of these burials, which at times exceeded those of men, indicates the high status some royal women attained in the earliest periods of Egyptian history. However, nothing reveals their actual roles.

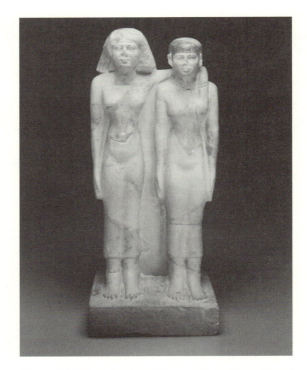

Figure 6.1 Pair statuette of Queens Hetepheres II and Meresankh III, limestone. Egyptian, Old Kingdom, Dynasty 4, reign of Menkaure, ca. 2490–72 B.C.E. Find spot: Egypt, Giza, Tomb G 7530-G7540. 59.3 x 26.5 cm (23-3/8" x 10-7/16"). Photograph © Museum of Fine Arts, Boston. Harvard University—Boston Museum of Fine Arts Expedition 30.1456.

Better documented are two memorable New Kingdom wives of kings. The first was Queen Tiye, principal wife of Amenhotep III, early fourteenth century B.C.E. (Figure 6.2), who, unusually for someone not of royal descent, succeeded in becoming the pharaoh's principal wife. She achieved a comparably rare honor for her nonroyal parents, who were memorialized on monuments and buried in the Valley of the Kings. Accompanying her husband throughout his reign, Tiye was the first wife of an Egyptian king to be regularly portrayed in art, texts, and scarabs alongside the king. She was the first queen to incorporate the horns and disc of the goddess Hathor into her headgear, which may reflect an increasing emphasis on the solar and divine aspects of queenship that paralleled an analogous emphasis on the solar and divine aspects of kingship during her husband's reign.

Figure 6.2 Queen Tiye, head, yew wood. Medinet el-Ghurab, Egypt. 1347–45 B.C.E. Bildarchiv Preussischer Kulturbesitz / Art Resource, NY, Ägyptisches Museum, Staatliche Museen zu Berlin, Berlin, Germany.

In contrast to customary portraits of the pharaoh larger than his queen, in one colossal monument Tiye's statue is equal in size to the pharaoh's. Another tomb painting portrays her sitting on a throne illustrated with images of Tiye as a female sphinx trampling her female enemies. This decorative scene transformed the iconography that typically commemorated male rulers' conquests to show Tiye in a heroic male exploit, with all figures from the sphinx to the conquered foe represented as female. Finally, the extent of Tiye's influence may emerge in the fact that she was the mother of the next pharaoh, who challenged millennia of Egyptian tradition to become the heretic king, Akhenaten.

Perhaps the best-known prominent wife of a king was the principal wife of Tiye's son, Amenhotep IV, Nefertiti, who expanded her mother-in-law's powerful role. The many images of Nefertiti well illustrate the meaning of her name, "A Beautiful Woman Has Come." Nefertiti's husband established a new religion founded on belief in a monotheistic sun god Aten. He changed his own name to Akhenaten, "Spirit of the Aten," and he built a new capital at Amarna, which enabled him to install his own priesthood at some distance from the traditional sanctuaries. Nefertiti participated visibly and enthusiastically in her husband's new religious program, with numerous relief carvings demonstrating her importance.

A touching family portrait (Figure 3.1) shows Akhenaten, Nefertiti, and their three daughters: Ankhesenpaaten on Nefertiti's shoulder and Meketaten on her lap, while the king holds Meretaten. This portrait well illustrates the fashions and art conventions of this period: unisex clothing, less-rigid art forms, and less-rigid gender distinctions that portrayed men and women androgynously. Several plaques portray Nefertiti's crucial role in performing public ritual. These images underscored Nefertiti's importance, showing her as actively and publicly co-ruling with her husband. Visual images portrayed her with the insignia of a king, although she never received official recognition for this capacity. Besides a famous painted limestone bust, images of Nefertiti abounded, reflecting her popularity as a subject in the Amarna royal art workshops. After the death of her daughter Meketaten at age 13 in childbirth, Nefertiti fades from public view.

We know little about Nefertari, principal wife of Ramses II, thirteenth century B.C.E. Ramses featured her on the temple for Hathor he built at Abu Simbel, and her splendidly painted tomb reflects her importance. She herself sent greetings to the Hittite queen Pudukhepa, a rare example of women's correspondence. A painted relief of Nefertari at a board game like chess (Figure 6.3) offers an even rarer glimpse into women's recreational activities.

Greece and Rome

About a thousand years later a few powerful kings' wives stand out in the ruling dynasties of Macedonia, Ptolemaic Egypt, and Rome. Four Ptolemaic Greek queens in Egypt, Arsinoë I and II and Berenike I and II, third century B.C.E., were married to the first two Ptolemies to rule Egypt. All four aggressively secured their positions by murdering their rivals. They held important public ritual roles, had festivals inaugurated in their honor, were benefactors of major public works, were deified according to Egyptian custom, and were celebrated in Hellenistic and Roman poetry. After marrying her full brother Ptolemy II, Arsinoë II significantly expanded her own role, and she is credited with improving Egypt's military and political affairs and expanding Egyptian sea power. Her brother built the Egyptian city of Philadelphia for her, which he named in her honor, "Sister" or "Brother-Loving"—a very different meaning of sibling love than attributed to the name by the founders of Philadelphia, Pennsylvania.

Finally, some wives of Roman emperors achieved outstanding influence. Notable was Livia, the third wife of the first Roman emperor Augustus. Like her powerful predecessors, Livia promoted public works, advanced her favorites at court, and interceded for those seeking the emperor's audience. Augustus reputedly took notes on her advice that he studied later, and Livia met with ambassadors and envoys on his behalf. Although he was not Augustus' biological heir, Livia succeeded in advancing her elder son

Figure 6.3 Nefertari playing senet, painted stucco relief. Valley of the Queens, Thebes, Egypt. 19th Dynasty,
1279–12 B.C.E. By permission of The Getty Conservation
Institute. Copyright © The J. Paul Getty Trust 1992. All
rights reserved.

Tiberius to the privileged status of heir to Augustus' rule. A powerful king's
wife, Livia thus insured a continued influential status as queen mother.

Livia's influence emerged not only through the actions she took but also
through the images projected of her. Augustus deployed various visual media to
project his idealized picture of Rome's rulers as a model Roman family. Consequently, in statuary and on commemorative gems, cameos, and coins, Livia was
portrayed as the ideal Roman matron, a fertile and loving Roman mother and
grandmother who exemplified ideal Roman womanhood. Figure 6.6 depicts the
empress benevolently as the goddess Ceres, holding three poppy flowers in her
right hand and an overflowing cornucopia nestled in her left arm, both items
long-time symbols of fertility. Eastern kingdoms worshipped her as a goddess
in her lifetime, a practice the rulers could not establish in the West.

Likewise advancing their sons' careers were Livia's granddaughter,
Agrippina the Elder, and great-granddaughter, Agrippina the Younger,
mothers of the emperors Caligula and Nero, respectively. The Roman
historian Tacitus described Agrippina the Younger as gripped by a masculine

lust for despotic power. As wife of the Emperor Claudius, Agrippina the Younger established a colony of veterans in Germany, and defying age-old custom she sat beside her husband under the Roman standards to receive the homage of the conquered rulers of Britain.

King's Daughter

The other royal family relationship through which women might exert some influence was that of the king's daughter. Most commonly a daughter's influence was expressed not by her own agency, but through the valuable connection she provided to cement alliances between rulers of competing states. Vassal kings might pledge their daughters to become the wife of a greater king to signify the lesser king's allegiance. These princesses came with their full retinues and expected royal treatment, which they did not necessarily receive in their new home. One surviving letter from the Hittite king to the Egyptian pharaoh inquires after his daughter from whom they have had no word since she arrived at the Egyptian palace.

As with the other women in his life, King Zimri-lim of Mari invested his daughters with more than passive authority when he married them to vassal kings. Numerous letters regarding two of his daughters exhibit similar situations and complaints. After his conquest of Ashlakka, Zimri-lim confirmed Ibal-Addu as its king and married his daughter Inib-sharri to the king to insure his own ultimate authority. Inib-sharri performed official city duties in addition to her royal roles as its queen, a situation which pleased no one. Ibal-Addu preferred his previous wife and asserted his right to rule without an overlord. Inib-sharri objected to the arrangement from the outset, and once in Ashlakka, she repeatedly complained to her father that Ibal-Addu and his wife were mistreating her, that she was not receiving her expected allotments of servants, clothing, and food, and that they were plotting revolts. She begged to come home to Mari. Although her father counseled her to remain in her marriage, she fled to a nearby town, where she then decried her detention. What finally happened we do not know. Perhaps the fact that the letters stopped indicate that she did ultimately return to Mari.

Another daughter, Kiru, went through similar experiences. Married to a local king, Haya-Sumu, Kiru received formal authoritative offices, including possibly as mayor of the city. Kiru's status as daughter of the supreme ruler of Mari seems to have outweighed her position as wife of the local king. Consequently, those having matters of import came to Kiru rather than to her husband, anticipating that she would intercede for them with Zimri-lim. Kiru openly advised her father on political matters, chastising him for not listening to her on issues where she believed she was right. Like Inib-sharri, Kiru complained bitterly of abuse by her husband, who preferred another wife to Kiru, possibly even Kiru's younger sister or half-sister of lesser status who was married to Haya-Sumu at the same time as Kiru. Kiru felt Haya-Sumu had publicly insulted not only her but her father by disavowing her publicly in front of other vassal kings. She seems to have returned to Mari.

About 12 daughters of Zimri-lim emerge in the ancient records, several clearly married to vassal kings. Zimri-lim seems to have invested these daughters not only with the title of queen of these lesser kings but with real authority in their new cities. Clearly Zimri-lim attempted to stamp his rule over the lands he conquered by having his daughters execute this reigning authority. While marriage of royal daughters for political alliances was common, Zimri-lim exploited this custom far beyond that of other rulers. Virtually unique to Zimri-lim's reign is the extensive authority exercised by the women around him. What he may have learned from the powers wielded by his mother Addu-diri, he expanded into the vast powers he entrusted to his wife Shibtu in his absence from Mari. By investing his daughters with political authority Zimri-lim extended to the next generation this crucial power-sharing with his female kin, even as he retained the ultimate authority.

From one perspective Zimri-lim's daughters appear privileged to have had these authoritative positions in their communities. But the letters show that the women had no choice in these political marriages, and that even in the face of abuse and threats of revolt, their father preferred his own political ambitions to their best welfare. While few would seriously trade the wealth and privilege of royalty for the lot of the poor, royal women's high station nevertheless served to restrict their right to determine their own lives and often forced them into distant, loveless marriages. Interestingly, when asked by the Hittite king to send one of his daughters to that northern ruler just as he had sent his, the king of Egypt haughtily replied that others sent their daughters to him, but the Egyptian king did not send his daughters to marry foreign rulers. The Egyptian pharaoh thereby asserted his supremacy over these other kings, while this supreme standing insured that Egyptian princesses did not have to experience the unhappy separations from their families endured by other royal daughters.

WOMEN WHO RULED

Far fewer women ruled outright than enjoyed other influences upon the king. Documents from early Egypt and Mesopotamia indicate that women held greater governing authority in earlier eras before patriarchal ideologies became more firmly entrenched. The goddesses Egyptian Isis, Sumerian Inanna, and Babylonian Ishtar all were seen to legitimate the divine right of kings and to oversee the political harmony of the city. Female deities, especially Athena and Hera, continued to be the guarantors of the well-ordered civic polity for the Greeks. While a female deity serving such a role does not translate to women's actual rule in the society, many Mesopotamian images leave that impression. Several depictions of female figures in poses connoting worldly political power leave open the possibility that at some point in Mesopotamian history, the idea of a woman ruler may not have been so unusual. However, only one woman is listed in the kingship lists of the Early Dynastic period, Ku-Bau, who reputedly rose from a barmaid to ruler of Kish for one hundred years. Completely wrapped in the mists of early legend, Ku-Bau's reign exemplified to later rulers the disorder wreaked upon a society subjected to the unnatural state of female rulership.

Of these four ancient civilizations, only Egypt and surrounding African nations record ruling queens. Remarkably, evidence points to only six female rulers throughout Egypt's three-thousand-year dynastic history. To underscore the view that only men should rule, the few women actually recognized as rulers bore the title "Female King." Most came to the throne in times of great turmoil, and with one exception, none seems to have produced male heirs.

Early Ruling Queens

Lost in the legendary beginnings of Egypt's dynastic rule, and possibly serving as the third king of Egypt's first dynasty, was Meryt-Neith, early third millennium B.C.E. She enjoyed ceremonial and burial practices that typified male rulers, but we have no record of her royal deeds. In contrast, elaborated legends depict the rule of the "beautiful" Queen Nitocris in the sixth dynasty, circa 2150 B.C.E., although no archaeological records substantiate her rule.

Nitocris' ruling at the end of a dynasty typified two other Egyptian female rulers, Sobeknofru and Twosret, who ruled at the end of the 12th and 19th dynasties, 1789 and 1190 B.C.E., respectively. They were perhaps allowed to rule in order to preserve their line's dynastic power, but in effect each marked the end of her royal lineage. Two distinctive features attest to the importance of their rules. Diverging from the customary practice of burying queens in the Valley of the Queens, Twosret had an elaborate tomb in the Valley of the Kings. And it seems that Sobeknofru was accepted as a female monarch, openly depicted as a woman, without the male attributes that Hatshepsut would assume three centuries later.

Hatshepsut

Hatshepsut, the fifth ruler of the 18th dynasty, 1473–1458, was the principal wife of Thutmose II; after his death she functioned as queen regent of his son Thutmose III by a secondary wife. Although technically coregent with Thutmose III even after he reached majority, early in his reign she relinquished the titles and insignia of a queen and assumed the traditional titles of a king. A few early images of Hatshepsut as king show her in woman's dress, but visual images soon depicted her as a male king, including one as a sphinx, while texts continued to refer to her in the feminine. A row of engaged columns at her funerary temple at Deir el-Bahri on the west bank of the Nile opposite Thebes prominently depicts her as the bearded king (Figure 6.4). It is not known why Hatshepsut assumed these male insignia or what enabled her to maintain her rule until her death, even though Thutmose III had come of age to rule.

Figure 6.4 Hatshepsut as King, with chin piece. Photograph by and reproduced with the kind permission of Dr. Richard Wilkinson.

However Hatshepsut was able to acquire and maintain her hold on power—in which the force of her personality must have figured strongly—her reign was a successful and prosperous one. She mounted military campaigns, thereby fulfilling the king's traditional duty to maintain and extend the borders of Egypt. She embarked on an active, innovative building program for the gods, seen in the temple of Amun-Re at Karnak, Thebes, and in her own funerary temple at Deir el-Bahri. She recorded there an expedition to Punt, showing Egyptians bringing back "exotic" items, such as leopard skins and incense. If there was opposition to Hatshepsut's rule as king even while officially coregent with her stepson, it was not recorded. However, Hatshepsut herself in numerous texts went to great lengths to justify her unusual rule. These texts proclaimed her divine birth and rearing, the sine qua non of a pharaoh's divine right to rule.

Illustrative are the inscriptions on the shafts and bases of four obelisks Hatshepsut had erected for Amun-Re in Karnak, which proclaim her devotion to the god whose daughter she is and who sanctifies her right to rule. Hatshepsut had the obelisks made of solid blocks of pink Aswan granite and gilded in huge quantities of fine gold. The one obelisk still erect measures ninety-seven and a half feet high, the tallest obelisk standing in Egypt. In the speech inscribed on the obelisk, Hatshepsut stressed that she erected these expensive and richly decorated obelisks out of love for her father, she spelled out her divinely sanctioned status, and she identified herself like all pharaohs with Horus, the divine representation of the king:

As Amun, my father, favors me,
As I wear the white crown,
As I appear with the red crown …
As I rule this land like the son of Isis,
As I am mighty like the son of Nut …
As I shall be eternal like an undying star …
Amun, Lord of Thrones-of-the-Two-Lands;
He made me rule Black Land and Red Land as reward,
No one rebels against me in all lands.
All foreign lands are my subjects,
He placed my border at the limits of heaven …
My reward from my father is life-stability-rule,
On the Horus throne of all the living, eternally like Re.[2]

Over 20 years after Hatshepsut's death, Thutmose III erased her name from her monuments, which scholars once thought reflected her stepson's hostility to her rule. However, after so long a time other reasons may have motivated this erasure—namely, the desire to expunge any sign that contradicted cosmic order. Since a female ruler violated the natural order of the universe, *maat,* her memory had to be expunged, just as names of male rulers who acted contrary to *maat* were also erased from the official record. Nevertheless, Hatshepsut's powerful rule may have set the ground for the influential wives of kings, Tiye and Nefertiti, in another 150 years.

Makeda

Makeda, also known as Balkis or Belkis, Queen of Ethiopia, ascended to the throne upon her father's death in 1005 B.C.E. She may be better known to many by her biblical epithet, Queen of Sheba. Since the designations Ethiopia and Sheba variously referred to different lands including northeast Africa and parts of Arabia and the Near East, the territory over which Makeda ruled could have been quite vast. Both biblical and Ethiopian accounts record her acumen in establishing and building up trade networks. Like many other ruling queens, she built a new capital at Debra Makeda, "Mount Makeda."

Known mostly from the biblical account of her liaison with the Israelite King Solomon, whose romantic dimensions received primary focus in later versions, Makeda, as Kleopatra VII would do almost a millennium later, may well have been negotiating important economic and political agreements in her meeting with Solomon. Certainly, the hospitality Solomon lavished upon Makeda can be seen as a tribute to her position and influence. The biblical passage 2 Chronicles 9:12 states that "King Solomon granted the queen of Sheba every desire she expressed, well beyond what she had brought to the king. Then she returned to her own land, with her servants."[3] A trade agreement, diplomatic relations, and possibly a military alliance may have been some of the things Solomon gave Makeda.

Makeda also bore a son by Solomon, Menelik, to whom she passed on the rule of Ethiopia, while she remained as his advisor until her death in 955, fulfilling a customary role of queen mothers. Menelik began the Solomonid line of Ethiopian kings that lasted, with a 300-year interruption, until the deposition of Haile Selassie in 1974. (This 300-year interruption, incidentally, was due to the actions of another Ethiopian queen, Judith, possibly of Jewish ancestry, who conquered the Solomonid kings in 1000 C.E., after a 2,000-year dynastic rule.) Thus, the important rule of Makeda, whose 50 years as sovereign and queen mother formed the pivotal bridge between an old and new male dynastic line, has survived in legend, the strength of this legend testifying to the power of her rule.

Kleopatra VII

The legendary story of Makeda makes a fitting lead-in to the last female monarch of ancient Egypt, the Ptolemaic queen Kleopatra VII (69–30 B.C.E.,), who ruled mostly alone, sometimes as coregent with younger brothers or sons. Legendary already in her own time, virtually nothing is known of Kleopatra in Egyptian annals. What we do know comes mostly from the description of her in the *Life of Mark Antony,* by Plutarch, a second-century C.E. Greek biographer and historian, and from some probably contemporary portraits.

Recently, Afrocentrist interpreters, relying on African American oral traditions, have regarded Kleopatra as of a black African racial background. However, identification based on modern notions of racial distinction seem to have held little if any social or political significance in the ancient Mediterranean. Ancient evidence, which portrays Kleopatra as a daughter of the ruling Ptolemies, the Hellenistic Greek dynasty that ruled Egypt from the third to first centuries B.C.E, assumes Kleopatra's Greekness. Likewise, ancient artistic portrayals, which were not shy of depicting distinguishing physical characteristics, show her as Greek (Figure 6.5). The only ancient suggestion of non-Greek ancestry hints that her great-grandmother may have been of Persian descent, probably a royal marriage arranged between the Persian and Ptolemaic rulers.

However we view her ethnic make-up, Kleopatra distinguished herself from earlier Ptolemaic rulers in important ways. Powerful in both internal and external affairs, she actively sought the backing of the Egyptian people, supported traditional Egyptian rites, and was the first Ptolemy to speak Egyptian. She participated in the intellectual discussions of the Museum, the research center Ptolemy II had established in Alexandria. Expert in numerous languages, skeptical of interpreters, and renowned for her diplomacy, Kleopatra acted as her own ambassador with foreign diplomats.

Like Makeda before her, Kleopatra used her liaisons with powerful men of Rome—Julius Caesar and Mark Antony—to enlarge her realm, increase her resources, and secure defensive alliances. Still immortalized in modern books and films, Kleopatra apparently held a spellbinding influence over these powerful men. After seductively introducing herself to Julius Caesar in 47 B.C.E. and acquiring his support for her against her brother, Kleopatra began a liaison that both assured her rule and brought her to the attention of Mediterranean-domineering Rome. While still married to his Roman wife, Julius Caesar installed Kleopatra in her own living quarters in Rome, much to

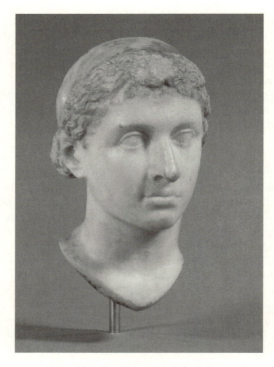

Figure 6.5 Kleopatra VII, marble bust. Before 31 B.C.E. Bildarchiv Preussischer Kulturbesitz / Art Resource, NY, Antikensammlung, Staatliche Museen zu Berlin, Berlin, Germany.

Caesar's political injury, where the Egyptian queen bore him a son, Ptolemy XV Caesar, known as Caesarion, "little Caesar."

After Julius Caesar's assassination in 44 B.C.E. and her brief attempt to help his followers, Kleopatra responded to Mark Antony's summons to meet him in Tarsus in southeast Anatolia. Plutarch describes the extravagance of Kleopatra's adornment, the outfitting of her ship, and the sensuous ambience of smells when Kleopatra sailed in for her rendezvous. Arriving in her own good time, Kleopatra

came sailing up the river Cydnus in a barge with a poop of gold, its purple sails billowing in the wind, while her rowers caressed the water with oars of silver which dipped in time to the music of the flute, accompanied by pipes and lutes. Cleopatra herself reclined beneath a canopy of cloth of gold, dressed in the character of Venus ... all the while an indescribably rich perfume, exhaled from innumerable censers, was wafted from the vessel to the river-banks.[4]

Antony was immediately smitten, and so began Kleopatra's second major liaison with a powerful Roman male. Antony forsook his wife Fulvia, who was fighting Octavian in Rome on his behalf, in order to follow Kleopatra to Alexandria, where the two flaunted their luxurious lifestyle with like-minded friends called the Inimitable Livers.

For Kleopatra, this extravagance accompanied political goals. As Julius Caesar had done before him, Antony helped Kleopatra to secure and extend her Egyptian rule. However, again like Julius Caesar, in the violent wrangling for control of Rome's political machine, Antony succumbed to the losing side of history. His rival Octavian, Julius Caesar's nephew and heir, defeated the combined naval forces of Kleopatra and Antony at the Battle of Actium in 31 B.C.E. Octavian then changed his name to Augustus, "the revered one," as he became the first ruler of the Roman Empire. In the following year, forestalling capture by Augustus, Kleopatra committed suicide to avoid being paraded through the streets of Rome as a conquered monarch. In a Romeo and Juliet-like preview, when Antony rushed into her fortified tower in Alexandria, Egypt, to find her dead, he killed himself by falling on his own sword. Kleopatra's death and the Roman conquest of Egypt brought to an end almost two hundred years of Ptolemaic rule in Egypt, the last of the Hellenistic kingdoms to fall to Roman rule.

Because of Kleopatra's association with powerful Roman political figures, her image has come down in Western history as an exotic, luxurious foreign queen who corrupted Roman morals. This popular view clearly influenced Vergil's portrayal of Dido in the *Aeneid,* his epic poem about the founding of the Roman Empire. The epic depicts a powerful foreign female ruler whose exotic and erotic ways undercut Roman morals and who must therefore be conquered in order that manly Rome might rule. This image has persisted, introduced to modern Western audiences by Shakespeare's play *Antony and Cleopatra* and by the 1963 Joseph L. Mankiewicz film starring the twentieth-century notorious Hollywood royal couple, Elizabeth Taylor and Richard Burton, the quintessential cinematic representations of the charismatic ancient queen and her virile Roman lover.

In whatever ways Kleopatra may have used female charms of seduction to achieve her ends, it is clear that her concern was always and foremost for Egypt. While hostile legend has turned her into a vamp, the evidence shows rather that like any successful ruler she shrewdly used whatever resources she had to accomplish her goals. If kings traded on the sexuality of their female kin to cement their political alliances, we may characterize Kleopatra as empowered to command her own sexuality for political purposes, which together with her other many talents she used superbly.

Figure 6.6 Empress Livia as Ceres, marble. Rome, 38 B.C.E. Réunion des Musées Nationaux/Art Resource, NY, Louvre, Paris, France.

Seven

Women and War—Symbol, Object, and Warrior

In 1892, a 12,000-strong Dahomean army battling combined French and Senegalese attacking forces included 2,000 regular female warriors. Begun in the eighteenth century as the king's elite ceremonial guard, this contingent of Fon women became a regular division of the Dahomean cavalry, renowned as expert sharpshooters with the latest military weaponry. This female fighting contingent seemed extraordinary to the western European men who engaged with them in nineteenth-century battles and who dubbed them Amazons, after the legendary ancient Greek figures.

Nor was this the first time European men named the women warriors they encountered Amazons. In the Americas, in a letter to King Ferdinand and Queen Isabella of Spain dated February 15, 1493, Christopher Columbus wrote of Carib women that they

use no feminine exercises, but bows and arrows of cane ... and they arm and cover themselves with plates of copper, of which they have plenty.[1]

Half a century later, in 1542, Francisco de Orellana bestowed upon the mighty waterway of South America its modern name, the Amazon, after the women warriors he found along the river. The Spanish chroniclers of the various encounters with women fighting alongside their men in defense of their villages could only situate these female warriors in mythical terms that placed them decidedly outside the bounds of appropriate "feminine" conduct. Moreover, fueling Spanish dreams of El Dorado, that golden promised land, descriptions of these female warriors were quickly elaborated into fanciful accounts of all-female villages whose activities suspiciously mirrored ancient portrayals of a mythic Amazon society. Interestingly, also in 1542, called "the Year of the Amazon in America" by one interpreter, the southwestern coast of North America also received its name after Spanish stories of "Califia and other Amazon dreams—California."[2]

Developing western European society inherited not only ancient stories about Amazons, but also the cultural and ideological attitudes about women warriors that these stories portrayed. The profusion of Amazon-naming of female combatants in Africa and the Americas underscores Western notions of the strangeness, until very recent times, of women serving as a regular part of their society's military forces. The fanciful Spanish elaborations of women-only societies hostile to men also serve to invalidate the reality of the female fighting forces and virtually erase them from the historical record.

Although war is considered a male endeavor in most societies, some women have always undertaken warrior roles. Like all other social aspects, women's engagement in warfare and how the society regarded women's battle activity varied considerably across cultures. Patriarchal nations have generally accepted women's participation in war only in extraordinary circumstances. Typically, these states have considered female warriors to be unnatural and unfeminine. But in other societies, frequently pre-state, but including even patriarchal states such as Dahomey, women have readily taken on combat roles for which they have received honor.

WAYS OF ANCIENT WARFARE

Ancient cultures held very different perceptions of warfare from modern Western notions. In short, war was a fact of life. People ate, they slept, adults had sex, women gave birth, men went to war. These last two were fatal activities for their respective genders. As has been noted, Sparta recognized the equivalency of these two activities by honoring equally women who died in childbirth and men who died in battle. Ancient documents may lament the horrors of war, the life-threatening wounds, the deaths, and the grieving mothers, widows, and daughters at home. But they rarely question the existence of warfare as a basic feature of life. When Greek documents call for Greeks to stop fighting, it is not on the principle, as might be espoused by modern Western democracies, that war itself as an institution is bad and must be avoided. Rather, it is that the diverse Greek communities should recognize their commonalities, stop fighting one another, and unite to fight their common external enemy, usually Persia. The divinely fashioned, elaborately decorated shield the Greek hero Achilles receives in Homer's story of the Trojan War, *The Iliad,* superbly illustrates the essential place of war in ancient perceptions. One half of the shield portrays all the joys of peace—people farming, herding, dancing at festivals, couples getting married. The other half depicts the horrors of war. Together they formed the totality of life.

Disputes over territorial expansion and colonization must reach deep into antiquity. However, initially, a primary purpose of warfare was less territorial than raids for goods—the looting for booty that comprised a principal form of income. The goal of these raids often included women, to be raped and carried off as concubines to produce children and as slaves to carry out needed work. Thus warfare has always entailed women in its practice, perceived not as active combatants or defenders, but as the vulnerable yet legitimate object of male sexual and military violence and conquest. Ancient Greek warriors used the pointed end of their spears to kill men and the blunt end to beat women into captive submission.

In earlier times these battle raids were probably not very frequent, nor did they generally significantly damage the opposing infrastructure, kill large numbers of the enemies, or abduct many women. Their goal was booty—charge or steal in, grab what you can and get out. However devastating to the ones who had been raided, in the eyes of the raiders these were legitimate aggrandizing missions. They were the means of accumulating wealth, women, and consequently status. Homer repeatedly calls the protagonist of his epic poem *The Odyssey* "raider of cities," revealing this to be an activity for which the hero wins acclaim.

Moreover, the thrill of battle and rush of adrenaline derived from combat and from killing figured as important components to men fighting. Men flourished on the excitement of battle and eagerly rushed into the fray of killing. All factors together—intensification of physiological sensations, and acquisition of goods, women, and status—made battle not only a necessary part of life, but enticing adventure to the men who desired to benefit from all its effects. At the same time, these were not professional warriors. Battle was only one part of these men's social duties, who mostly practiced the farming or pasturing life essential to their subsistence.

As with so many other features of life, the practice of warfare changed in the monarchical kingdoms. Besides acquiring wealth, conquest and territorial expansion propelled the imperial rulers, who established and maintained their reigns by warfare. Military exploits confirmed the king's superiority over all others and symbolized his rule in all iconographical and memorializing monuments. Through warfare ancient monarchies captured large numbers of people they enslaved to perform the tasks of an ever-expanding empire. And warfare was the means by which these states maintained a peaceful realm internally and guaranteed favorable trading status externally. To accomplish these military ends, these expanded centralized kingdoms employed large armies comprised of volunteers, mercenaries, and conscripts. Men who at one time went to battle intermittently over local disputes or periodic raids became part of vast armed forces in which they fought not for their own immediate interests but the king's.

Instead of *ad hoc* battles between small groups of warriors, warfare became an increasingly structured enterprise between huge numbers of opposing armies. These increasingly large and structured military endeavors required greater organization and coordination of efforts among soldiers, resulting in the development of military units comprised of groups of men fighting in coordination and not only as individuals. In actuality, such structure seems to have lasted only for the initial onset of battle, which quickly degenerated into individual action once fighting was engaged.

These organized armies led to the professional soldier who could distinguish himself through battle and conquest. In most military structures a man could rise through the military ranks to achieve high economic, social, and political status. Soldiers in the king's armies benefited not only from whatever booty they seized, but they often received land grants, citizenship, and other significant perquisites as rewards for their military service. Eventually in both Egypt's dynastic history and the Roman Empire, military command prevailed over royal lineage in determining the next pharaoh or emperor. At the same time that the military offered men in ancient empires these major benefits, many preferred not to be soldiers. Desertion rates were high, and often not only the deserters, but their families too incurred severe penalties that might include death, physical mutilation, disenfranchisement, and exile. Women were not typically considered part of the military forces, which meant they were also excluded from the economic, social, and political benefits men garnered from their military service.

Fundamentally, warfare formed the principal means by which a man achieved his identity in ancient Mediterranean cultures. War was a constant, accepted, and promoted part of life for men. Monuments glorified kings for their victories and conquests in war, while poetry and cultural ideologies transformed the horrors of war into the instruments by which men achieved glory and remembrance.

WOMEN AND WAR

Women as Victims of War

As noted, women's first connection with war was as its object and victim. In stark contrast to the men's experiences, war was not a way for women to achieve glory, but rather the means to terrorize and subdue them. Warfare offered men a legitimate social avenue by which to exercise their impulses to violence. However, this exercise of violence did not remain within the confines of the battlefield, but it spilled over to invade the domains and persons of the women. Moreover, violence against women seemed to spread from wartime situations to daily domestic circumstances, as accounts from all these ancient cultures refer to men beating their wives in order to force their obedience. Consequently, whether in war or not, violence was a fact of women's lives in antiquity.

Ancient Greek literature poignantly portrays women's suffering in war. In his play, *The Trojan Women,* the fifth-century tragedian Euripides staged in dramatic detail the misery experienced by the women of a conquered city, illustrated by the fate imposed on Troy's captive royal women. The aged queen Hekabe is assigned as a slave to one Greek hero, while her daughter Kassandra is raped on the altar of Athena by another Greek warrior. For being the wife of the Trojan hero Hektor, Andromakhe must endure rape, enslavement, and witnessing the murder of her son. Such sympathetic portrayals were rare, however, as most male-authored texts exhibit little concern with the feelings of the women thus victimized by men in war.

More commonly, male texts refer casually to women's status as booty, whether itemized in the records of conquering kings or objectified in literary illustrations. The first, and in the minds of many, the most enduring image of women in Homer's *Iliad* is of the captive Khryseis as a voiceless, live item of booty completely under male control. In the poem's opening scene, the men argue over her status as though she were an object, permitted no say in her situation.

The Iliad makes it clear immediately that this opening portrayal was not the only way women were perceived by the men of that society—igniting the men's argument is the plea by Khryseis' father to ransom his daughter back. Many scenes and references display the strength of familial love that included that of a father to daughter, son to mother, and husband to wife. However, in wartime, male perception of women as mute booty prevailed over familial affection in determining how men treated women. The predominance of references to women merely as the booty of war no doubt reflects the historical commonness of women trapped in such circumstances from the frequency of ancient wars and conquests.

Women as Martial Auxiliaries

While women of every class and background were subject to capture, rape, and enslavement in war, women were not only the victims of war's unbridled violence, but they actively supported their men's war efforts in various ways. Foremost, as the women themselves saw, was giving birth to the sons who would eventually go off to war.

Reputedly, Spartan women ardently championed their city's military endeavors and warrior code of ethics that honored the courageous warrior and humiliated the coward. Spartan mothers boasted of giving birth to sons who grew to be strong warriors defending Sparta, and Spartan women encouraged their menfolk to go to war with the phrase, "Return with your shield or on it." Men were to come home alive or dead as having fought bravely, but not return alive having fled from the enemy as a coward. Just as elite Spartan women benefited from the lifestyle Spartan military society upheld, they also suffered the disenfranchisement imposed on their men who defected on the battlefield. Clearly, concern for their own livelihood formed a crucial factor motivating Spartan women's strong backing of their men's militarism.

Women directly contributed to men's martial activities. Wives constructed their husbands' battle outfits, and women worked in state factories sewing the uniforms for the soldiers in the king's armies. Women's actions boosted morale by raising the victory cry, known in Greek as the *ololugmos,* the shrill, vibrato trilling of the tongue or throat that women of the Mideast and of indigenous American cultures still use to proclaim victory. For battles fought close to home, women probably participated in stripping booty from enemy corpses, and they had to gather their wounded and dead relatives in order to tend to them at home.

Men served as the official support staff of the imperial armies, but women probably functioned in this capacity for the smaller military forces. When the Romans defeated the Celtic forces in Britain, they also slaughtered the women and children attending to the warriors with the provisional wagons in back of the lines. Homer's *Iliad* portrays the Greek warriors who were besieging Troy as keeping captured women in their camps to carry out all the necessary domestic tasks they still needed in their wartime circumstances. The most common female camp follower was the prostitute, whose residence on the periphery of the troops assured her a steady income.

GODDESSES OF WAR

While a prostitute's association with men in the military centered on economic factors, the association between sexuality and war was a complex one. Several goddesses encompassed within their oversight attributes of war—Egyptian Hathor, Sumerian Inanna, Babylonian Ishtar, and Greek Athena. Images of the first three portray war as one aspect among the many they embraced, that included the realms of love, sex, fertility, women's and men's lives, the success of kings, and the prosperity of the community. As war goddesses they exhibited the same qualities of bloodthirstiness and ferociousness as male warriors. The iconography of Mesopotamian art regularly identified Inanna and Ishtar by their warrior attributes of a bow and arrows. These images lasted over fifteen hundred years, from the early Sumerian and Babylonian periods to the later Neo-Assyrian period (Figure 7.1). In Greek historical times, the goddess Athena represented less the violence of battle, which the male god Ares embodied, but rather the concept of victory in battle.

A selection of poems by Enkheduanna, the daughter of Sargon I, about 2350 B.C.E., develops the warrior aspects of the goddess Inanna. In a poem entitled "Inanna and Ebih," written at the dedication of a new temple to Inanna in celebration of her return from political exile, Enkheduanna described Innana's battle against the Mountain Ebih. The mountain, alone of all deities and forces, refuses to show Inanna deferential treatment, possibly

Figure 7.1 Official before Ishtar with weapons, green stone cylinder seal. Neo-Assyrian. 720–700 B.C.E. HIP / Art Resource, NY, The British Museum, London, Great Britain.

reflecting the political opposition to Enkheduanna's ruling family. From its opening, the poem vividly describes Innana's warrior aspects:

Lady of blazing dominion
clad in dread
riding on fire-red power …

flood-storm-hurricane adorned …
battle planner, foe smasher.[3]

Described throughout in the fiercest of terms, like any ancient warrior this Queen of Battle vaunts loudly over her fallen enemy:

I will wrench your neck
grab your thick horns
throw you in the dust
stomp you with my hatred
grind my knees in your neck … [4]

Animal imagery vividly portrays her fearsomeness, as she is called lioness, wild bull, and a snake spitting venom.

Embedded within a longer poem that praises Inanna for the wide range of powers she holds, one passage describes the aspects of the warrior goddess as integral to Inanna's being:

fighting is her play
she never tires of it …

a whirlwind warrior
bound on a twister …

wild bull Queen
mistress of brawn
boldly strong … [5]

The poems also reveal the cultural importance of Inanna's warrior aspects, praised for her martial deeds in song:

when you wear
the robes
of the old, old gods

when you slice heads
like a scythe cuts wheat swaths

then the black-headed [the Sumerians] praise you with song
the Sumerians sing in one voice
everyone sings sweetly a joy song.[6]

The poem first portrays Inanna as performing her killings as part of her divine ancient roots. Then, like the deeds of any battle hero, Inanna's warrior exploits are celebrated in song. Her worshippers praised Inanna precisely for her animal-like fierceness, her battle fury, her use of natural forces like hurricane winds, and her shrill destruction of her enemy. Song gives shape to and memorializes experiences; it is the vehicle for public praise and for celebration of heroic exploits. Enkheduanna's poetry praises the warrior goddess within this tradition of glorifying the killings of the victorious warrior in song.

Enkheduanna's descriptions show that Inanna's warrior qualities were not perceived as incidental attributes, but that they were fundamental to her divine powers. These integral warrior aspects were one facet of the goddess's widespread powers, which began as we saw with her being a goddess of sexuality, erotic desire, and fertility. The conjoining of all these aspects in the totality of the goddess suggests that Inanna's warrior activities were not contrary to the perception of her as a female deity. The issue of Inanna's gender in her warlike activities does not arise in the poems, where war appears unquestionably to be a part of female nature.

Like Egyptian Hathor, Inanna did not merely function as a divine figurehead for a range of human activities. She encompassed a spectrum of powers and energies which included the productive and creative as well as the destructive and fatal. Nor were these aspects perceived as entirely separate, for in her actions to initiate battle, Inanna invokes and becomes the power of the wind and other natural forces. The productive and destructive dimensions, regarded as mutually exclusive opposing forces in Western concepts of duality, appear in the characterizations of Inanna to form the interwoven texture of her full representation. Nor were her warlike aspects judged negatively or condemned by her ancient worshippers. Indeed, "the Sumerians sing ... sweetly a joy song" to this queen of battle, the warrior goddess for whom Enkheduanna wrote these celebratory songs.

Although ancient Greek descriptions of their goddess of war, Athena, appear as a pale echo of her Mesopotamian forebear, the Greeks similarly honored their war goddess for her martial representations. No longer associated with sexuality or with the totality of powers Inanna encompassed, Athena still retained an important complement of powers. While she was renowned as Athens's patron deity, ancient Greek art and literature portrayed Athena primarily as a goddess of war (Figure 1.10). Some Panathenaic vases, the coveted prizes awarded to winners in the contests held during the Panathenaia, depict Athena as striding into battle with her arm raised ready to hurl her spear. Homer's *Iliad* often describes Athena as waving her aegis, the mantle around her shoulders and chest, as part of her martial activity, an image that evokes the description of Inanna hurling down a storm from her widespread arms.

With such powerful images of goddesses of war, the question naturally arises of what connection these warrior images of a divine female being might have had with actual women's warrior roles. The answer seems to be little or none. Women did not form a regular part of Egyptian, Mesopotamian, Greek, or Roman military forces. Whether elegantly depicted, as are the images of Athena, or portrayed as ferociously as Inanna, these female warrior deities nevertheless represented anomalous gender roles for their societies, where war was emphatically defined as men's and not women's concern. This point leads to another question—why would a female deity be represented as a warrior goddess if women in the society had no actual role in warfare? Since the female warrior deities do not reflect women's actual practices, these divine female warrior representations must contain different cultural meanings.

The fiercest goddesses of war and of the wild emerge in the earliest layers of the historical record. These warrior goddesses may then evoke an earlier stage in society when women possibly assumed more active warrior roles. In contrast, the images of female warrior deities of later antiquity, like Greek Athena or Roman Minerva, lacked the active martial traits of their Egyptian and Mesopotamian avatars. Although the warrior goddesses were often perceived as unmarried females, their bellicose nature may reflect the spectrum of nurturing and punishing qualities that women might exhibit. Moreover, as divine beings, these goddess warrior images reinforced the distinction between the divine and mortal realms and the very different powers each gender can wield in their respective spheres. Certainly it accrues to her powers as a deity to demonstrate martial valor and to be endowed with abilities beyond those of mortal women but which show what women too might be capable of in the right circumstances.

In a profound way, a female deity of battle symbolically represented the reasons for which the men fight and thus served as a powerful inspiration to battle. The fact that Inanna was also the goddess of sex and fertility underscores the significance of this interpretation—it was literally the essence of life that the battle queen Inanna represented. For its preservation male warriors were exhorted to emulate Inanna's fierceness in battle. Besides inspiring male troops to martial valor, goddesses of war were also protective forces, personally guarding individual warriors and sometimes whole battalions. Ancient accounts describe visions of Athena appearing to an entire army auguring their upcoming victory. Similarly, by representing victory in battle as Athena Nike, the goddess Athena embodied the divine motivation that results in battle success.

The Greeks distributed the association with war and with love to the different goddesses Athena and Aphrodite, respectively. The mythological liaisons between the love goddess Aphrodite and the god of war Ares, expanded by their Roman counterparts Venus and Mars, further illuminates the symbolic value of the female as inspiration for war. Although they removed the power integral to warlike activities that the goddess Inanna exhibited, the affairs told between these apparently opposite deities perpetuated the connection between the two activities. Both the passions of erotic desire and of warfare overwhelm the individual. Likewise, both the joy of lovemaking and the outcome in future offspring make fighting for their sakes worthwhile. Early Syrian and Canaanite images of nude female figures, perhaps goddesses, frequently occur with a war god, possible forerunners to the Greek and Roman myths of love—really sexuality—serving as the inspiration for war.

Although they did not model women's actual martial activities, these powerful warrior goddesses must have left their imprint on both women's and men's minds. Their representations may have inspired only a very few women to engage in combat. In time, however, these images served to define women's appropriate roles in male-defined gender ideologies.

HISTORICAL WOMEN WARRIORS

Since women were not as a rule a regular part of their nation's military, those who fought did so under exceptional circumstances. History records names of women rulers, whose activities, as ruler, included warfare for both conquest and defensive purposes, such as the Egyptian ruling queens Hatshepsut and Kleopatra VII. Not actual combatants, however, these rulers directed their nation's military campaigns from the side, as male rulers did, exemplified by the Persian king Xerxes in his attacks against Greece. In contrast, later West African queens actively led their troops, male and female, into battle, such as Queen Amina of the Hausa, Queen Macario of the Mane, and several Asante warrior queens. Ancient Hebrew, Greek, and Roman sources spotlight several individual female battle leaders.

Biblical: Deborah and Jael

The Hebrew Bible hails the actions of two women, Deborah and Jael. Judges 4:4 begins by describing Deborah as a prophetess and a judge, who "used to sit under the palm of Deborah between Ramah and Bethel" where "the Israelites came up to her for judgment" (Judges 4:5). It then tells of her role as a military commander in a twelfth-century B.C.E. battle of confederated Israelite tribes against the Canaanites. Key to the victory was the action of Jael, who received the Canaanite General Sisera in her tent, killed him by driving a tent peg through his forehead with a hammer, and then delivered him to the Israelite general, Barak.

Judges 5 contains the Song of Deborah, which may be the oldest part of the Hebrew Bible, and which was likely Deborah's own composition. Her song first praises the Hebrew God for the victory. It then honors Deborah, who "arose as a mother in Israel" to marshal the Israelites to war. It especially celebrates Jael:

Most blessed of women be Jael,
the wife of Heber the Kenite …

She put her hand to the tent peg
and her right hand to the workmen's mallet;
she struck Sisera a blow,
she crushed his head,
she shattered and pierced his temple …
at her feet he sank, he fell;
where he sank, there he fell dead.[7]

Over a millennium later than Enkheduanna's poems, this biblical song of Jael's killing of Sisera recalls the ferocity of Inanna's defeat of Ebih. Even though these warlike actions by Deborah and Jael do not accord with ancient Israelite women's characteristic roles, the biblical narrative does not mark the women's actions as unusual. On the contrary, it implies an ordinary acceptance of Deborah's and Jael's actions as valuable contributions to their people's war efforts. This praise of Deborah's and Jael's crucial activities may be another sign of the female authorship of this passage.

Herodotos: Tomyris and Artemisia

In the late fifth century B.C.E., in his account of the Greek and Persian wars, Herodotos describes two warrior queens. When the founder of the Persian empire, Cyrus, tried to invade her realm, Queen Tomyris of the Massagatae first sent him several warnings to back off. When he attacked anyway, she defeated him in a violent battle which Herodotos calls the fiercest fight between non-Greek combatants. To celebrate her triumph, Herodotos describes Queen Tomyris as shoving the head of Cyrus' dead body into a wineskin she had filled with human blood and vaunting over him that she would quench his thirst for blood. Whatever her actual conduct, her story depicts a queen fully capable of leading her troops through the paces of a bloody and prolonged battle with a powerful opponent to ultimate victory. Moreover, while the imputation of bloodthirstiness brands her as monstrous in one way, in another it shows her to be fully a match to male warriors, whose victorious battle exploits are necessarily marked by the bloodiest fierceness.

In describing Persia's invasion of mainland Greece about fifty years later, Herodotos highlights for special commendation Artemisia, queen of Halikarnassos, a Persian ally who commanded her own ship at the naval Battle of Salamis, September 480 B.C.E. The Greek historian attributes to Artemisia the most trustworthy and valuable advice among the Persian king's council of war leaders. Probably of greater historical validity are the descriptions of her actions in the naval battle. Realizing the severe rout of the Persian ships, Artemisia fled, pursued by an Athenian ship. Seeing that her escape was blocked by the many Persian ships choking the straits, Artemisia rammed a Persian ally, sinking the ship and its crew immediately. This enabled her escape—the Athenian ship gave up the chase, believing her to be a Greek ally, and the Persian King Xerxes, observing from the shore, thought she had sunk a Greek ship and so commended her battle bravery.

Warrior Queens against Rome: Amanishakhete and Boudica

About five hundred years later, Romans encountered battle queens on both the northern and southern ends of their empire. In the 20s B.C.E., soon after Augustus defeated Kleopatra VII at the Battle of Actium and established the

Roman Empire, Roman forces attacked and destroyed the northern Kushite city of Napata, south of Egypt. Although the Kushite queen Amanishakhete, known to the Romans by her title, Candace, "Queen," was unable to save the city, she kept the Roman imperial troops from advancing further into Kush. She then forced the Romans to withdraw, and secured a treaty with Augustus to honor Kush's sovereignty.

Events went differently in the north, where historical accounts of Roman battles against the Celtic tribes in Britain record both female battle chiefs and regular female warriors. Notable was Boudica, queen of the Iceni in southeast England, whose land was pillaged by the Romans, she herself whipped and her daughters raped after her husband's death in 60 C.E. Boudica led a Celtic army in revenge that destroyed the Roman settlements at Colchester and London, and she defeated the first Roman legion sent against her, killing all Romans and Romanized Britons. Boudica's successes encouraged other Celts to revolt, terrifying the Romans left in Britain, the reverberations of her activities felt as far as Rome.

However, Boudica was ultimately overcome by a force of 10,000 Romans in a brutal defeat of her forces—the Romans slaughtered even the women, children, and cattle in the rear of the army. Despite this crushing defeat, the Boudica-led revolt caused the Roman emperor Nero to send a special envoy to secure a lasting peace with the Celts, and her name became a symbol for defense against tyranny. Eighteen centuries later, in 1856, Thomas Thornycroft erected a bronze statue of Boudica and her daughters on the Victoria Embankment in London.

These few examples of actual women warriors in antiquity, together with the indigenous American and African examples noted at the beginning of this chapter, show that, while they were certainly not the norm, women's warrior activities were not completely uncommon either. Even in cultures where women warriors were exceptional, nevertheless, those who did undertake military actions were highly praised for their successful exploits. Given that this was the case, one might ask why women's military activities loomed so fantastic in Greek, Roman, and later European accounts. Ancient portrayals of Amazons suggest an answer.

AMAZONS

Ancient Greek records of their own early history refer frequently to battles with Amazons, a non-Greek society reputedly comprised entirely of female warriors. Although one late source describes female warriors in north Africa, most accounts locate the Amazons in the same geographic area, northeast of the Black Sea. Thought at one time to be entirely fictional, as has happened for many other Greek myths, recent archaeological finds and modern historical investigation have uncovered a historical basis to the legendary tales. While the mythology transformed the Amazons into a female-only, man-hating warrior society, the earliest descriptions of the Amazons portrayed them as historical, not mythical, beings.

Ancient Greek historians depicted the Amazons as a historically credible group. Herodotos introduces the Amazons during his description of the Sauromatai, a tribe in northern Anatolia with whom the Scythians wished to ally themselves. Herodotos presents his accounts of the various tribes in the region, including the Amazons, with a mix of factual kernels and mythic elaboration. Herodotos states that the Sauromatai originated from the union of Amazon women with Scythian men, both of whom were warrior tribes. The catalyst for this story is a defeat of the Amazons by Athenian forces at the Battle of Thermodon on the south central coast of the Black Sea. In a debate with other Greeks at the end of the *Histories,* Herodotos has the Athenian speaker refer to their defeat of the Amazons at the Battle of Thermodon as one of Athens's early successful military exploits.

In his story of the Amazons, Herodotos claims that the escaped female captives from this battle landed on the coast near Scythian habitation, where their customary raiding quickly brought them into conflict with the Scythians. When, upon collecting the corpses, the Scythian men realized they had been fighting women, they ceased combat, changed their tactics, and encouraged the young men to befriend and marry the women. After some time the women allowed the men to approach them, had sexual intercourse with them, and lived together, with both women and men carrying out the same activities of hunting and warfare. Herodotos states that while the men were never able to comprehend the women's language, the Amazons learned the men's speech, which enabled them to communicate with one another. Although the men desired marriage, the women resisted, agreeing only after the men had met their conditions.

According to Herodotos, the women made the men recognize that they would not give up their warrior lifestyles to live as domestic wives, but that they would retain their hunting, raiding, and warring customs together with the men. Furthermore, the Amazon women convinced the Scythian men to move away from their paternal villages because of the hostility against them. Herodotos concludes this account by stating that the Sauromatian women have maintained their original Amazonian lifestyle—they hunt on horseback, with or without their husbands; they go to war; and they wear the same clothes as the men.

Passages from Homer's *Iliad* recall significant battles with Amazons in which earlier generations of Greek heroes fought. Recent archaeological excavations north and east of the Black Sea have unearthed numerous graves of females buried with weapons and other warrior insignia, which provide concrete evidence for the historicity of women warriors in this area. Similar finds in Ireland have also boosted the validity of the legendary and historical accounts of Celtic female warriors. These finds prove that Greek tales of female warriors have roots in a credible historical tradition.

From this historical foundation, Herodotos' account provides several insights into the Greek male perception of the Amazons as a society. First, Herodotos does not question their historicity, but he discusses them in the same way he does other ethnic groups. At the same time that the story acknowledges the unusualness of the Amazons' lifestyle as female warriors, it does not condemn or ridicule them, just as Herodotos does not condemn the actions of the warrior queens Artemisia or Tomyris that he relates. Rather, by having the Scythian men agree to the women's prenuptial conditions, the story reveals the men's respect for the Amazons' warrior customs. The story acknowledges other levels of power the women display besides their martial skills. Since they are able to learn the men's language, but the men cannot learn theirs, the tale underscores the women's superior intelligence to the men's, intellectually and conceptually. The strength of their identity and their reliance upon their own powers emerge in their convincing the men to accept their various terms for marriage, including relocating some distance away from their paternal homes.

Finally, it is noteworthy that the Scythian men were attracted to the war-like Amazons in the first place, that they were the ones who initiated the long process to befriend and court the Amazons, and that they agreed to abide by all the women's conditions. The men's conduct shows that these strong images of women fully steeped in their own power and capable of taking care of themselves *are* qualities that appeal to men. In patriarchal societies, however, such images of powerful, self-contained women undermined the cultural gender ideologies that required women to subordinate their powers to men's control. While Herodotos may have portrayed the Amazons in a favorable light, other Greek literature stressed the abnormality of the Amazons' lifestyle, which virulently threatened the foundations of civilized male Greek society. Greek mythological tradition mixed the perception of the Amazons as a historical society with the ideological purpose of using them to project a negative model of women's behavior.

Amazonomachies, "battles with Amazons," comprised a prevalent theme in early Greek literature and art that served to define Greek male identity. In particular, the tales of battles with Amazons characterized the exploits of the early Greek heroes—Herakles (Roman Hercules), Theseus, and Achilles—all of whose legendary tales contained historical kernels. The stories of the pan-Greek hero Herakles are filled with his famous labors, many of which are undeniably fantastic. In these tales, Herakles is *the* mythic culture hero, whose deeds make the world safe for civilization to exist. But other aspects of Herakles's legends may retain memories of early migrations of the Greeks, and stories relate that Herakles fought in a Trojan War about a generation earlier than the one made famous by Homer's poems. Since Trojan archaeology reveals several layers of destruction in the centuries of Trojan settlement, these tales may recall that Greeks had been battling Trojans long before the Trojan War of legendary fame.

Given the historicity of ancient Amazon society, it is possible that the tales of Herakles fighting the Amazons also have a historical basis. A frequent subject of early Greek vase painting depicts Herakles together with other warriors pursuing two or more Amazons. Some paintings portray Herakles alone defeating a single Amazon in battle, whose name is usually given as Andromakhe, "she who fights men," the same name as Hektor's wife in *The Iliad*. The mythology further elaborates these battles by including among Herakles's famous exploits the command to obtain the belt of the Amazon queen, Hippolyte. According to one version of the tale, Hippolyte voluntarily agrees to give Herakles the belt, but the goddess Hera, angered by the peaceful exchange, fires the Amazons to attack, leading to a full battle. In both literary and artistic media, Herakles' defeat of the Amazons and acquiring Hippolyte's belt signified his masculine power and superiority over women.

The cultural meaning of Herakles overcoming the Amazons changed from the earliest representations to the interpretation that quickly prevailed in Greek thinking. As a sixth-century black-figure vase painting represents (Figure 7.2), initial portrayals of groups of combating warriors echo the historically based accounts of battles between Greeks and Amazons. This one unusually portrays Herakles's Amazon opponent as still standing in equal combat with the hero, in contrast to most, which show the losing Amazon down on one knee. This painting also adds a unique touch by revealing one Amazon lifting her wounded comrade out of battle.

Notably, the object Herakles was to get from the Amazon queen was originally identified as a *zôstêr*, the belt warriors wore on the outside of their clothing as part of their defensive armor. The *zôstêr* emphasizes the martial aspect of the Amazons, who wore the same battle gear as male warriors. However, before long the object Herakles sought was called a *zônê*, the girdle women wore around their abdomens underneath their clothing. In particular, images described the *zônê* of Aphrodite as possessing magical, enchanting, love-inducing properties which the goddess of erotic desire lent to others when they wanted to avail themselves of its seductive charms. Changed from a war belt to an article of personal, erotic female attire, the different items

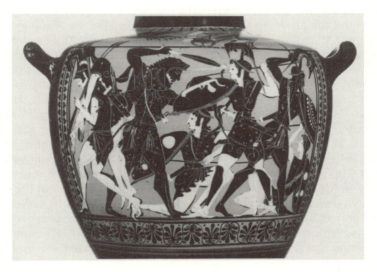

Figure 7.2 Amazonomachy—Herakles against Andromakhe, black-figure amphora. Athens, Greece. ca. 520 B.C.E. By permission of the Staatliche Antikensammlungen und Glyptothek, München, Germany.

Herakles seeks from the Amazon queen profoundly transform the meaning of his interactions. The warrior belt that signifies martial power may also project the Amazons as standing on a par with their male Greek opponents. Once the goal shifts to a personal item of female clothing with potent sexual connotations, the story dramatically highlights elements that may have been operating beneath the surface. But now the erotic dimensions of Herakles's exchange with the Amazon queen emerge as central to their interaction.

Vase paintings of the single hero Herakles defeating an Amazon warrior likewise eroticized the visual depictions of their combat. This literary and artistic eroticization of duels between Greek heroes and Amazon warriors undercut the women's military activities and accentuated instead their female vulnerability. The total effect reinforced Greek cultural ideology of male superiority over women. Similar images of Theseus and Achilles battling individual Amazons further intensified the erotic dimensions of these combat scenes.

In contrast to Herakles, Theseus was a specifically Athenian hero, who may credibly have existed, since he is considered one of the early kings of Athens, and many of the stories about him seem to have historical underpinnings. The stories of the war Theseus waged against the Amazons may also have a core of historical credibility. Theseus was among the Athenian forces who defeated the Amazons at the Battle of the Thermodon River, when he abducted the Amazon queen Antiope (Hippolyte in some versions). In revenge for the attack and capture of their queen, the Amazons invaded Athens, the subsequent battle and the Athenian victory recalled throughout Greek literature and art. Athenian legend memorialized their repulse of the Amazon attack into the very heart of the city, while both Theseus' capture of Antiope and the Athenian victory reinforced Greek gender ideology. In the third play of Aeschylus' monumental trilogy, the *Oresteia,* Athena recalls this victory, evoking the Athenian triumph over a force of unnatural women as a fitting foundation for the first court for murder trials she is establishing.

Athenian vase paintings and monumental art frequently depicted Theseus's capture of Antiope. These visual depictions both display Theseus's violence—he is often shown grabbing Antiope by her hair while plunging his sword into her chest—and eroticize their encounter. Rather than being portrayed in battle gear, Antiope is usually represented in a short, alluring skirt while her sleeveless chemise falls seductively off one shoulder, exposing a breast. This sexualization of the female warrior elides out her martial skills and power. Moreover, these eroticized portrayals do not present the female in her own sexual potency as might be seen in fertility festivals. Rather, these images project her as the sexual object of the male, whose control over the female is displayed through Theseus's violent abduction of Antiope. This eroticization also caters to the male viewer, for whose gaze these images are made.

Once the motif of Greek heroes killing Amazon warriors became an established feature of the Greek mythological tradition, stories of deadly encounters with Amazons proliferated for other heroes. Vase paintings frequently depict one other mortal hero in battle with an Amazon, Achilles, the principal warrior of the Greek forces at Troy. These images portray Achilles killing the Amazon queen Penthesileia, who led the Amazons as allies of Troy in that war, and with whom Achilles may have had a sexual affair. Some of the paintings of this scene portray Penthesileia as a warrior, often attired in a Persian warrior outfit. Other paintings display a scene of eroticized violence similar to many of the portrayals of Theseus and Antiope.

Alexander the Great also reputedly had a sexual liaison with an Amazon queen, Thalestris. However, by this point in antiquity, late fourth century B.C.E., factual investigators were on the ascendant. When one of Alexander's officers, Lysimakhos, was later asked about this liaison, he replied, "Where was I?" Lysimakhos' question implies the speciousness of this tale, one that Alexander himself may well have spread since he lost no opportunity to compare himself to past heroes, especially Achilles.

At the core of these tales about the Amazons rests a historical basis. Archaeological evidence confirms that female warriors lived in the area around the Black Sea where Greek stories situated them. Herodotos and other ancient Greek historians wrote of them as a real, distinct ethnic group. Their hostile encounters with Greek heroes occur in contexts of historical credibility—memorials recall these battles as worthy military victories of the past, on a par with other historically based battle monuments.

Besides war memorials, the Greeks commemorated the Amazons for furnishing elements of Greek heritage. The Greeks regarded the Amazons as the founders of many cities in Asia Minor, including the major centers of Mytilene, capital of Lesbos, and Ephesos, Priene, and Smyrna along the Ionian coast. At Ephesos, the Amazons were credited with setting up the wooden cult statue of Artemis and with originating the circular dance with weapons and shields maidens performed annually. Moreover, Amazon tombs and heroic cult centers existed throughout northern and central Greece, including Athens. These markers customarily identified the sites of people who had actually lived. Even if some of these may have had fanciful origins, the profusion of different types of historical memorials adds further support to the core of historical validity in the stories of the Amazons.

However, within the male-centered conceptual framework of the ancient Greeks, portrayals of the Amazonomachies could not remain battle tales equivalent to other war stories. To Greek men, women fighters displayed a perversion of female nature, and representations of successful female warriors posed a threat to the foundations of patriarchal social institutions. Consequently, in Archaic and Classical Greek literature and art, Amazonomachies served unmistakable ideological purposes to show Greek men's superiority over women and became increasingly important for defining Greek male identity.

As Amazon tales were elaborated, they grew increasingly fanciful. In the third century B.C.E. arose the notion that the name Amazon derived from the Greek word *a-mazos,* "without a breast." However, since "Amazon" was a foreign name, it could not have had this Greek meaning. Nevertheless the

Greeks frequently depicted the Amazons with one breast exposed, and they later believed that the Amazons cut off and cauterized their right breasts in order to shoot better, a notion completely contradicted by all practicing female archers. Tales also stressed the unnaturalness of female warriors, describing the Amazons as a man-hating, man-killing, woman-only culture. These extreme versions of female-only societies had the Amazon women mating with men only for procreation. But they raised only the girls, repudiating or even killing the boys. These fearsome, outlandish images persisted, thrusting aside the potentially historical remembrances.

Another Greek tale further underscores the cultural purpose of projecting the Amazons as unnatural models of female behavior. Although not including the Amazons per se, one version of the ancient Greek story of the abduction of Persephone by Hades makes explicit what happened to female warrior attributes within patriarchal cultural ideology. This tale relates that when Athena and Artemis, the two "maiden" goddesses of ancient Greece, heard Persephone's cry, they immediately jumped up from what they were doing, donned their armor, grabbed their weapons, and in female solidarity fought Hades to protect their sister. They would have beaten him too. Enter Zeus, who had "given" his daughter Persephone to her uncle Hades in the first place. Observing with consternation the scene from on high, Zeus hurls a lightning bolt in front of Athena and Artemis and summarily stops their short-lived successful combat to prevent Persephone from being abducted. The story shows that by this action Zeus saps the potency out of any female warrior activity, and he puts a stop to any questioning of his supreme male authority.

These early female avatars of the modern media idol Xena show that, however less common it may have been for a woman to choose the path of a warrior than for a man, some women did so choose. When a woman did, she clearly engaged in warlike activities with the same ferocity and the same intention to win as her male counterpart. While a few women were celebrated for their military exploits, the image of female warriors that prevailed depicted them as unnatural women, which was elaborated in time to project a vicious, man-hating, female-only society of women warriors. The historicity of ancient female warriors reinforces from one more perspective the potent images of women presented in earlier chapters, in this case where a very few women exercised their female powers through military activities.

Eight

In Her Own Voice 1—Women's Philosophical Writings

BACKGROUND

Overview of Ancient Women's Prose Writings

Ancient sources attributed a great variety of subjects to female authors, including astronomy, mathematics, philosophy, musical theory, social commentary, political advice, theology, and more. We know of many of these works only from brief quotations or references by others. Histiaia and Pamphile, for example, are both credited with authoring many books on diverse topics, including history, grammar, topography, and sex. Active during the third-century B.C.E. intellectual florescence in Alexandria, Egypt, Nikoboule wrote a history of Alexander the Great. Only two short fragments quoted by others that refer to the effects of Alexander's drunkenness remain. Nothing survives of the first-century C.E. family history written by the younger Agrippina, mother of the Roman emperor Nero. The Roman historian Tacitus acknowledged that he used her memoirs as a source for his history of the Roman imperial family, possibly quoting some sections.

Although elite Roman women were generally well educated, there are few examples of their writings. In the letter the elite matron Cornelia wrote to her younger son Gaius Gracchus, Cornelia speaks both as a mother anxious for her son and as a woman deeply concerned about the welfare of her country and the preservation of Rome. Written copies of the rousing speech Hortensia delivered in the Roman Forum were extremely popular and widely distributed, but only a late Greek version exists.

The Greek and Roman physicians Galen and Soranos acknowledged that some of their medical practices and understanding stemmed from the works of female doctors. Galen attributed various remedies to individual women writers on medical subjects—Kleopatra, Fabulla, Maia, Samithra, and Xanite. The Roman author of *Natural History,* Pliny the Elder, likewise cites several female authors for specific medicinal remedies—Salpe, Elephantis, Laïs, Olympias, and Sotira. Pliny claims that several were prostitutes, on the premise that prostitutes may have been more familiar with their bodies and felt freer to write on such subjects. Prostitutes also wrote pornography—two brief fragments by Philainis of Samos, fourth century B.C.E., exist.

Finally, two prose works by early Christian writers have survived. In one, *The Martyrdom of Perpetua,* a 22-year-old Christian convert, Vibia Perpetua, records her arrest, time in jail, and imminent death in Carthage during the persecution of Christians under the emperor Septimius Severus in 202–3 C.E. In this first known Christian text written by a woman, Perpetua describes her situation in jail and her concern for her baby and parents, and she speaks of encouraging visions. In her last entry she writes of seeing herself victorious against the devil—how she envisioned the wild animals she would have to fight in the games. Perpetua's testament to her faith made her appear blessed to others, and hence was widely published.

Less well known, and rediscovered in 1884, was the travel journal of Egeria, fifth century C.E., which records several journeys Egeria took from Istanbul to Jerusalem and through Egypt, Arabia, and Mesopotamia. Possibly a nun—she addresses her entries to her sisters—Egeria described the different biblical routes she followed, referring to the biblical passages and stories associated with them. She recounted the places she saw, the aid of local guides, and the kindnesses of her hosts at the churches and monasteries where she stayed along the way.

Background on Ancient Greek Philosophy

Women's philosophical texts comprise the largest number of surviving women's prose writings. Profound changes in ways of thinking developed in Greece in the seventh to fifth centuries B.C.E. Often referred to as a scientific or intellectual revolution, these shifts first emerged in the writings of Ionian thinkers, those living in the cities of eastern Greece, cultural centers stimulated by their interactions with ancient Near Eastern and Egyptian civilizations, where many of their mathematical, astronomical, and mystical ideas originated. A second wave resided in southern Italy and Sicily. Thus it was on the eastern and western frontiers of Greek habitation that innovative thinking began that set the foundation for Western rationality, what came to be called philosophy, "love of wisdom."

Principally, the ideas of these early thinkers privileged rational thought over other forms of perceiving and thinking about the world. These philosophers proposed naturalistic explanations for phenomena based on measured observation to counter traditional mythological etiologies for how the world worked. From the concrete and observable, these inquiries engaged theological issues by questioning traditional representations of the gods. They presented instead concepts of the divine that envisioned the godhead as a single, abstract, unmovable entity. These ideas further encompassed moral considerations, as these early thinkers argued that the concept of the divine must represent absolute qualities of goodness and justice, not the human weaknesses, immoralities, and crimes characterizing the stories of the Greek gods.

A major early figure, noteworthy for the significant role women played in promoting his ideas, was Pythagoras, early sixth century B.C.E., who established his philosophical school in Croton, southern Italy. Known to most moderns for his geometrical theorem, Pythagoras taught that number was the ordering principle of everything, and he introduced Egyptian-derived views on the immortality of the soul and reincarnation to the Greeks. At Croton women and men together investigated mathematics, theology, and morality abiding by the same rules of moral conduct. Pythagorean ideas profoundly impacted ancient Greek intellectual thought, lasting as Neo-Pythagoreanism until the early centuries c.e. Most writings by ancient Greek women philosophers come from female Pythagoreans.

The mystical, theological, and moral speculations of Pythagoras had a great influence on Plato, and in all likelihood on Plato's mentor, Sokrates. While Sokrates never wrote and only had informal followers for his intellectual and ethical inquiries, Plato wrote numerous dialogues that featured his portrayal of Sokrates typically besting other thinkers in a philosophical exchange. Some evidence suggests Plato's mother may have been a Pythagorean philosopher named Periktione, an intriguing notion.

The few times that Plato featured women in his dialogues he portrayed them as intellectually equal to men. In his *Republic* Plato radically proposed that women of the elite guardian class rule in his ideal society the same as men. In the dialogue Sokrates bases his argument on the concept that equal education of boys and girls yields both women and men capable of ruling their communities. Characteristically using an analogy from the animal world, Sokrates points out that one does not train hunting dogs differently according to their sex, but rather an owner trains both male and female dogs to perform the same tasks. The only difference is that the females sit out when they bear and are nursing their young. Although Plato did not maintain this radical proposition about women's civic roles in his last work, *The Laws,* two other dialogues accord women intellectual respect, the *Menexenus* and *Symposium*. In both, the character Sokrates praises an excellent female teacher, in the first, Aspasia on rhetoric, and in the second, Diotima on love—both to be examined below.

Plato's student Aristotle was a theoretician who applied his analytic methods to many fields, including biology, physics, metaphysics, ethics, politics, rhetoric, music, and poetry. He invented logic as a formal method of argumentation that has become integral to Western ways of thinking. In sharp contrast to Plato, Aristotle's works consistently situated women as inferior to men in every realm, but a few women did attend his lectures. Although the ideas of Plato and Aristotle proved central to the evolution of Western thought, in their own time they were only two among many other philosophical traditions. Their writings bear particular significance for understanding the role of women in ancient Greece, since they articulated in rational discourse the views about women that otherwise emerged in archaeological, artistic, or literary media.

A generation later, several women were among the followers of Epicurus, and women could readily associate with the freethinkers known as Cynics. Their name derives from the Greek word for dog, *kuôn*, since their flaunting of conventional modes of behavior likened them to dogs in the eyes of other

Greeks. Diogenes the Cynic held that human beings should live according to natural laws, which can be observed in how animals behave and which was how humans lived before the imposition of social mores. Hence, Cynics pursued a wandering life foraging for foods according to their seasons, begging, and eating, sleeping, urinating, defecating, and having sex in the streets or elsewhere in public—just like dogs. At the other pole, the Stoics perpetuated Sokrates's ethical ideas by advocating a life of moderation and self-control for both women and men. The first-century Roman Stoic philosopher Musonius Rufus supported educating women and stated that a wife who studies philosophy best shows her virtue.

GREEK WOMEN PHILOSOPHERS

All these ancient cultures had a tradition of female sages, often elderly. These elder female sages may have held more or less formal roles in various periods in ancient Egypt, Mesopotamia, and the Levant. The Greeks may also have recognized older women's wisdom. By late antiquity, the Greek concept of wisdom, *sophia*, was perceived as a deity. In Christian cosmology, Sophia was eventually identified with the spirit of God. Worshippers erected the magnificent fifth-century church of Hagia Sophia, "Holy Wisdom," in then Constantinople, modern Istanbul, in her honor.

This notion of women's wisdom emerged in other ways. Ancient traditions hold that the mothers of Thales, the first of the revolutionary Ionian thinkers, and of Plato were philosophers who influenced their sons' intellectual developments. If these stories are false, it is curious that male writers in ancient Greece's patriarchal culture would fabricate female progenitors of highly esteemed male philosophers. Especially if false, these biographies that identify a maternal source for major thinkers reveal a respect for female intellectuals that persisted in the face of growing hostile attitudes.

Female Pythagoreans
Who They Were

Women played prominent roles among the early Pythagoreans. An ancient historian of early Greek philosophers claimed that Pythagoras derived his ideas from the priestess at Delphi, Themistoklea. Although none of her works survive, writings attributed to Pythagoras's wife Theano do, as do some by their three daughters, Arignote, Damo, and Myia. Hence, among the earliest remaining Greek philosophical texts are those by women. The earliest material comes from the student and then wife of Pythagoras, Theano, who was the daughter of an aristocratic follower of Orphic mysticism in Croton. One fragment of her work *On Piety* and a number of shorter sayings called apothegms remain. Some may be by other women named Theano, a popular ancient Greek name.

The next wave of female Pythagoreans include Aisara, Phintys, and Periktione I, who may date from the late fifth to the first century B.C.E. Phintys was possibly from fifth-century Sparta and contemporary with Plato. Nothing connects the Periktione who was Plato's mother with the writings by women named Periktione. Most likely dating to the third to second centuries B.C.E. are Periktione II and Theano II, whose works differ linguistically and stylistically from those attributed to Periktione I and Theano I. These works exhibit fundamental similarities representative of Pythagorean thought.

The Pythagorean women's writings divide into two main groups. Some focus on abstract theoretical questions or concepts of the soul, law, and justice. The second, larger group addresses women's ethical issues and appropriate virtues. The first group of writings articulates the philosophical principles that underlie the functioning both of the cosmos and of the human society that reflects the cosmological. The second group illustrates how women's ideal ethical conduct is a key factor in maintaining the theoretical principles of order within the human realm and ultimately in the universal order.

Theoretical Ideas

Two works by Theano and her daughter Arignote discuss the concept of number, the fundamental principle of Pythagorean philosophy. A fragment of Arignote's, called one of the Pythagorean "sacred discourses," presents the metaphysical theory of number as the ordering principle of the entire universe and all that exists in it. Responding to some people's misunderstanding of Pythagorean number theory, in her book *On Piety* Theano explains that Pythagoras did not claim that the abstract concept of numbers could generate material reality. But rather, material objects come into existence according to the ordering principle of number. In his overview of earlier philosophers' ideas, Aristotle attributed the notion that numbers generate material bodies to the Pythagoreans without citing Theano's clarification.

Several apothegms, "short sayings," by Theano reveal ideas in a second major branch of Pythagorean investigation—the belief in the immortality and transmigration of the soul, ideas integral to the Pythagorean belief that a divine justice exists in the afterlife. The movement of souls from one life form to another expresses this divine justice—those who disrupted the essential harmony of society, and hence of the universe, by violating moral laws are punished by their souls transmigrating into bodies of animals considered to be lower than human. Their punishment thus restores universal harmony. If souls were not immortal, there would be no way to correct the violations committed by wrongdoers. Hence, the soul must be immortal and divine justice must exist in order to preserve cosmic order.

Possibly dating to the late fifth century B.C.E., Aisara's book *On Human Nature* elaborated the concept of justice in relation to the soul. Emphasizing the human dimension of universal order, Aisara regarded the dynamics that resulted in the well-ordered functioning of the individual soul to be the same as what on a larger scale led to the well-ordered functioning of the family and city.

Aisara described the soul as comprised of three parts that, like the male philosophers Plato and Aristotle, she organized hierarchically—mind on top, spirit in the middle, and desire on the bottom. This arrangement means that "the best part leads the others, the worst one is ruled, and the one in the middle holds a median position and both rules and is ruled." Aisara continues:

We can rightly call this arrangement the good order of the soul, since the better part ruling and the inferior being ruled brings strength to virtue. The inborn and kindred feelings of affection, love and friendliness will sprout from these parts.[1]

The proper functioning of the soul directly generates positive feelings that nourish the individual. By adhering to the well-ordered arrangement of their souls, individuals can apply this good order to the proper functioning of the family and city. This concept of *harmonia,* "harmony" or "balance," underlies individual, social, and universal order. It is fundamental to ethical discussions and to the relationship between women and men.

Aisara's *On Human Nature* reveals the ethical dimension of Pythagorean thought. Many of Aisara's ideas on the soul, its tripartite structure, and the analogous relation between the individual and the society are strikingly similar to those advanced by Plato in his *Republic.* Consequently, the uncertainty of Aisara's date prompts several tantalizing questions. Did Aisara and Plato both receive these ideas from common sources that they separately expressed in their writings? Did Aisara precede Plato, and did he derive his ideas from her work, or vice versa? Despite its brevity, this fragment, together with those of Theano and Arignote, shows that women fully participated in the abstract intellectual discussions of their day, of which they were frequently at the cutting edge.

From Theory to Ethics—Wisdom

Serving as a bridge between the two types of Pythagorean women's writings are several discussions of wisdom. Two fragments from *On Wisdom* by Periktione II articulate the role of wisdom in enabling humans to comprehend the order of the universe. Periktione II states that

Whoever has this analytic ability appears wisest and truest. These people have discovered a beautiful viewing point from which they can gaze upon divinity and see all things in a well-fitted order.[2]

Periktione II emphasizes the necessity of possessing wisdom as a key intellectual faculty that enables one to live a rewarding life, without identifying any gender distinction in this ability. This stress on self-awareness and prudent reflection as guides to one's conduct forms the hallmark of Pythagorean ethical thinking, and greatly influenced Sokrates, Plato, and other ancient Greek philosophical movements.

The extant fragment from *On the Harmony of Women* by Periktione I begins by making explicit the connection between women and wise, thoughtful behavior.

One should regard the harmonious woman as full of good judgment and prudence, whose soul keeps its awareness on virtue so that it will be just, courageous and wise, adorned with self-sufficiency and hating empty opinion. Noble things accrue to a woman from these things—for herself, her husband, her children, and her household; often too for her city, if a woman rules over cities and peoples, as we see in monarchies.[3]

In Periktione I's text, intelligent, self-reflective conduct is key to women's harmonious well-being, which is in turn fundamental to the well-being of all around her, from her immediate family to her royal subjects for ruling queens. This concept of elemental harmony underlies all ethical advice for women.

An apothegm of Theano's encapsulates the critical importance of women actively engaging their intellectual faculties in living their lives.

Better to be on a runaway horse than to be a woman who does not reflect.[4]

Fundamental was women's ability to bring their intelligence to bear on their conduct. This positive view of women's intelligence emerged throughout the writings of female philosophers who stressed the necessity of nourishing women's intellectual side. Only by actively using her intelligible abilities can a woman properly fulfill her crucial role within her family and the community.

This recognition of women as intelligent, thinking beings in these female-authored texts substantially corrects the predominating views of women in men's writings. As the Chorus of women in Euripides's play *Medea* sang, since Apollo silenced women's voices, the world hears only men's side. Moreover, the emphasis the female philosophers placed upon women using their intellectual faculties shows that, in spite of the legal and political stress on women's lack of subjectivity and voice, women did not just mutely fulfill male social projections. Women thought about their position in society, and they were aware of differences in women's roles in different cultures, as seen by Periktione I's comment on ruling female monarchs.

Women also communicated with each other about philosophical matters. In a letter from Theano II addressed to the philosopher Rhodope, Theano II explains that she has not sent Rhodope her copy of Plato's book, *Ideas on Parmenides,* because she wants to gain better understanding first about another philosopher named Kleon. The tone and words of Theano II's comments reveal a coterie of intellectuals, male and female, who met regularly to discuss philosophical issues.

Of further interest is how Theano II defined philosophy, speaking still of Kleon:

For I am so deeply in love with the soul of that man, which is the soul of a philosopher—one eager to do good, and one who fears the gods beneath the earth.[5]

Theano II identified philosophy in terms of moral conduct and reverential treatment of the gods, basic principles of the ethical philosophy associated with Sokrates. To be a philosopher was to perform good deeds wholeheartedly while paying due reverence to the divine world.

One other point in Theano II's comment is noteworthy. In speaking of her feelings for Kleon's soul, she used the erotic word for love, *erô,* rather than the word that connotes the deep bonds of familial love or friendship, *phileô.* Because of this erotic language, some scholars have interpreted the letter as a pastiche set between two *hetairai.* That *hetairai,* who were generally well educated, would participate in philosophical discussions is not in itself unusual—the fourth-century writer Xenophon says Sokrates conversed with the *hetaira* Theodote. Likewise, as we shall see below, philosophic texts frequently used erotic language to characterize the pursuit of wisdom. Theano II's use of this language reveals the depth of her passion for the pursuit of philosophy, for which she experiences the same intense sensory desire one feels from erotic passion.

Ethical Writings

Pythagorean women's ethical writings rested on two premises. First was the recognition of women's intelligence that they could apply to their moral conduct. Secondly, the female Pythagoreans identified women's virtue as essentially the same as men's. Phintys addresses both these points in her book *On the Moderation of Women.*

Many people perhaps think that it is not appropriate for a woman to philosophize, just as she should not ride horses or speak in public. But I think that some things are particular to a man and some to a woman. Specific to a man are military service, political activity, and public speaking, while managing the household, staying inside, and receiving and tending to her husband are specific to a woman. But I assert that courage, justice, and wise reflection are common to both. The virtues of the body and of the soul are equally fitting for both.[6]

That women and men have distinctive virtues was a common ancient Greek view. The idea that women and men may hold some virtues in common was far rarer and may itself reflect the perspective of a female author. Significantly, Phintys emphasizes the importance of mindful care of both body and soul.

Phintys affirmed the essential identity between women's and men's intellectual and ethical capabilities. At root, men and women operated by the same universal laws of wisdom, justice, and excellence. The gender-based differences in virtuous behavior elaborated the social distinctions between the sexes, but they did not efface the fundamental spiritual similarity between the two. As if to emphasize this identity, Phintys at first deems *andreia,* "courage," whose root meaning is "manliness," a virtue common to women and men. Phintys's attribution of this intrinsically male virtue to women indicates the extent to which she endowed women with empowering characteristics. The empowering effect remains, even though Phintys modified her initial assertion by claiming that bravery and wisdom were more suitable for a man to cultivate, while moderation was more fitting for a woman.

The Greeks deemed women's quintessential virtue to be *sôphrosynê*, frequently translated as moderation, but embracing prudent, thoughtful, and self-controlled behavior. For women, *sôphrosynê* specifically denoted sexual fidelity to her husband. Phintys enumerated five things from which a woman's virtue of *sôphrosynê* derives.

First is her most sacred and reverential treatment of her marriage bed. Second is the orderly care of her body. Third are her outings from her own household. Fourth is not participating in mystery rites or those of the Mother Goddess Kybele. And fifth is reverently and correctly performing the sacrifices for the gods.[7]

Maintaining strict marital sexual fidelity was the absolute bedrock of women's virtue. Phintys vehemently excoriated the sexually unfaithful woman, whom she believed wronged the gods by bearing illegitimate offspring. Phintys claimed that to commit these outrages for the sake of pleasure was unlawful and unforgivable, deserving the ultimate punishment. Other texts elaborated the severity of Phintys's comments on women's marital sexual infidelity. In *On the Harmony of Women* Periktione I applied the principles of Aisara's description of the soul to women's actual behavior and its consequences, both for good and ill.

The woman who rules over her desire and spirit will be reverential, pure and harmonious, so that unlawful passions will not pursue her, but she will maintain the deep bonds of familial love for her husband, her children, and her entire household.[8]

In contrast, an adulterous woman treats the members of the household, both free and slave, with enmity. She lies to her husband, deceiving him about all matters, and she may even pray for her husband to die and for the ruin of the home just so she can be with her lovers. These texts dramatically stressed that both the ruin and preservation of the household depend on the woman.

Periktione I likewise highlighted the benefits that accrued from a woman's virtuous conduct. Her first duty was not to herself but to live lawfully and honorably with her husband, whose marriage bed she preserved.

For everything depends on this. A woman must bear everything from her husband, even if he is unfortunate, errs out of ignorance, disease, or drunkenness, or consorts with other women. For this fault is excused in men, but in women never, on whom revenge is imposed... When a woman is loving to her husband and treats him honorably, harmony reigns... She thus will bring benefits not only to her husband, but also to her children, relations, slaves, the entire household with all its possessions, fellow citizens and foreign guest friends.[9]

In two letters addressed to women upset that their husbands were sleeping with *hetairai*, Theano II expanded on the importance of women putting up with their husband's extramarital affairs. Both letters use the word *hetaira*, which may imply some greater levels of intellectual or emotional engagement by their husbands than merely sexual gratification. Both letters stress the need to recognize that men's desire for multiple sexual partners is inherent in their nature.

In a letter to Nikostrate, Theano II unstintingly stressed the importance of women maintaining their highest ethical conduct regardless of their husbands' actions. While she called the husband's behavior of consorting with a *hetaira* madness, she focused on how Nikostrate should conduct herself in the situation. It was not right for Nikostrate to be jealous, closely watch her husband, or plot anything against him, for she made a bad situation worse if she condemned her husband or fought with the *hetaira* over her husband, which would only drag her down. She also should not make any decisions in her distraught state.

Since he is ill he bids you to suffer his pains. Because he trips up in his behavior, he wants you to err in your conduct, and because he is destroying his life he wants you to destroy the things that benefit you; but in punishing him you will be punishing yourself.[10]

Theano II underscores the idea that any condemnatory action Nikostrate might take against her husband would ultimately harm herself and her home. For her own well-being and the harmony of her household, Nikostrate should overlook her husband's sexual affairs. Instead, by patiently enduring her situation and by upholding her own proper conduct, Nikostrate will cause her husband to return to her.

Like Phintys, Theano II illustrates Aisara's theory of mind ruling over spirit and desires. Nikostrate's ability to forebear her husband's behavior superbly epitomizes the harmonious benefits of such internal order of the different parts of one's soul, or as we might say, of one's character. Relying on the notion that fundamentally all individuals will enact this principle in their behavior, Theano II believes that by presenting an exemplar of virtuous behavior, Nikostrate will cause her husband to reflect on his own injurious conduct and return to their marriage, where his true benefits lie.

The female Pythagoreans attended to other aspects of women's *sôphrosynê* with the same strictness as marital fidelity. Women should dress modestly, in plain white garments, not wear clothing that was diaphanous, intricately embroidered, or made from silk—the kind of clothing elite women favored and which women of lower classes probably emulated as much as they could. Pythagorean women also advised against using makeup or hair dyes or indulging in extravagant oils, baths, coiffures, jewelry, food, and drink. Phintys emphasized that the purpose of a simple appearance and moderate fulfillment of basic needs was that the woman maintain good order in her entire demeanor. Besides displaying extreme lack of self-control, foolishness, and female weakness, Periktione I thought that extravagance in personal grooming prepared women to indulge in other vices, notably illicit sex.

In her discussion of the body Phintys repeatedly used a form of the word *kosmos*, whose basic definition was order, as in our word cosmos for the order of the universe, and which could refer to the good order of the community as well as the individual. At the same time, among its many meanings, *kosmos* also meant adornment, especially when referring to women's clothing, jewelry, and makeup, whence our word cosmetics. Phintys may be deliberately playing upon these contrasting meanings in order to highlight her point that a woman's true adornment was her natural beauty and modesty.

Phintys added another reason why women should dress plainly. Luxurious display by wearing gold and emerald jewelry would cause envy and make the wearer appear haughty and ostentatious in front of ordinary women. That the masses envied the elite was a common trope in Greek literature. Far rarer was Phintys's consideration of the effect upon ordinary women of elite women's actions. Most philosophers, and indeed most Greek writing, unabashedly concerned themselves only with the elite class and gave attention to the lower social and economic classes only when necessary to prevent uprisings and maintain social order.

Phintys's statement may reflect a changing consciousness about social class distinctions. Since Epicurus's school was open to slaves as well, Phintys's ideas may reflect a larger intellectual movement that regarded class differences as superficial rather than the inborn marks of a person's quality, as Greek literature customarily expressed. Such views would be consistent with the emphasis the female Pythagoreans placed on development of a woman's inner virtue and beauty, and with their repeated exhortations to women to avoid concerning themselves with surface embellishments.

The letter to Phyllis by Theano's and Pythagoras's daughter Myia on the proper care of an infant (see chapter 3) well illustrates the pivotal importance of applying the principle of moderation to the raising of children. Myia stressed a moderate mean in room and bath temperature, bath frequency, and roughness of the infant's clothing. In a letter to Euboule, Theano II admonished Euboule for raising her children luxuriously and without moderation. Like any modern observer of child behavior, Theano II derided Euboule's indulging her child's every whim, feeding him the moment he cried or whined, encouraging his delicate, finicky eating habits, giving him whatever he wanted as soon as he wanted it, and allowing him to yell at and beat the servants and throw tantrums when he did not get his way. Permitting this behavior created an immature, undisciplined, useless adult who would be unable to handle adversity or live a productive life. Theano II contrasted the example of poor children who received none of these luxuries, but grew up none the worse for this lack; if anything they ended up more robust.

Phintys's inclusion of the proper occasions and means for women to go about outdoors offers some interesting glimpses into women's lives. Always maintaining the focus on women's proper decorum, Phintys asserted that women should make their expeditions from the house to attend the theater or games or to do the shopping after daybreak, but not after dark, and they should be attended unostentatiously by one, or at most two, servants. Phintys's remarks presume the normalcy of women's activities outside the household, including going shopping, which many researchers believe elite women habitually delegated to their slaves or servants. Likewise, the prevailing scholarly opinion has held that in fifth-century Athens women did not regularly go about in public, nor did they attend theatrical performances or other public spectator events. Phintys's statement reveals a different world of women's activities.

Connecting women's ritual activities with the reasons for her to leave the house, Phintys states that

a woman should conduct her processions out of the house to make public sacrifices to the founding deity of the city on behalf of herself, her husband and the entire household.[11]

Phintys's statement epitomizes the fundamental place women's ritual practices held for their own and their families' well-being. Moreover, to maintain *sôphrosynê* in carrying out their ritual roles, women should avoid the rites of the mystery religions and of the worship of the Mother Goddess Kybele, orgiastic rites which Phintys claimed led to drunkenness and madness. The Pythagorean women apparently set themselves against prevailing Greek belief by denouncing these fundamental fertility and transcendent rites. Besides condemning what they saw as the socially disruptive, licentious behavior of the mystery rites, the Pythagoreans may also be promoting their beliefs in the immortality of the soul over the blessedness mystery initiates received.

Finally, Periktione I presented the reverence a woman displayed to her parents as crowning her due respect to the gods. A woman should exhibit only the utmost respect towards her parents and obey them in every matter, even if they are crazed or act wrongly due to disease or deceitful intent. A woman who abhors her parents is in turn hated by other people, and for her irreverent treatment the gods of the underworld will punish her eternally. Periktione I claims that the greatest human fault is to treat one's parents disrespectfully. In contrast, she considered the sight of one's parents to be beautiful and divine, as was also a woman's care for them.

The Cultural Meaning of Pythagorean Women's Writings

Writing in a society with marked inequities in gender behavior, Pythagorean women emphasized woman's intelligence and inner strength, which enabled her to carry out her foundational cultural role. These works regarded women as active, thinking beings, who could choose to live lives based on virtue. All stress women's quintessential virtue of *sôphrosynê*, the quality of moderation she should display in all activities beginning with marital sexual fidelity to her husband, as the means by which women attained virtuous lives and brought honor to themselves, their husbands, and their families.

Some of their advice reflects the wisdom of a modern counselor or psychologist—striving to keep emotions such as anger, jealousy, or suspicion from harmfully controlling one's actions remains a laudable goal in personal behavior. To keep one's actions aimed at what the Greeks called the highest good appears a more daunting challenge. As Aisara expressed, by upholding these highest ethical standards in one's actions, a person created well-being in oneself, the family, and the community.

At the same time, Pythagorean women's emphasis on women upholding strict marital fidelity while accepting their husbands' extramarital sexual behavior may strike many modern readers as unjust and improper, whether seen from religious, humanist, or feminist perspectives. The Pythagorean women acknowledged that society was the way it was, nor did they seek to change the societal features they found unfair. To the contrary, they advised women to accept the sexual double standard, not to be envious of the greater sexual freedom men enjoyed, and not to be carried away by self-destructive feelings of anger, condemnation, or despair.

In ancient Greek society, which did not hold modern ideas of rights and freedom, everyone, men included, was far more constrained by social circumstances than is generally the case today. Acceptance of society's inequities by the Pythagorean women philosophers does not mean that they saw women as powerless. Rather, their writings emphasize the sources for women's empowered position and honored status within their socially construed and constricted roles. By actively choosing to live a life guided by the principles of female *sôphrosynê*, a woman created harmony within herself, her family, and the community. She was the bedrock upon which the proper functioning of the society and ultimately the universe depended.

Some may regard this responsibility for the well-being of the entire society as an unfair and unrealistic burden to lay upon the women, but the female Pythagoreans regarded it as a mark of woman's crucial and honored place within family and society. How she fulfilled this awesome responsibility could earn a woman praise or blame depending on whether she chose to conduct herself virtuously or immoderately. In these ways the Pythagorean women writers showed women how to fulfill their active moral potential within the constraints society imposed upon them. At the same time their approach enabled women to gain self-esteem and honor for their actions.

The writings by the female philosophers have been omitted from the Western philosophic tradition, which has not regarded these works as "philosophy," but rather as particular women's concerns removed from more universal philosophic issues. However, as the female Pythagoreans themselves asserted, their attention to matters important to women fully paralleled the attention male philosophers devoted to issues important to men. Recognition that the writings by the female philosophers rightly fit under the rubric of philosophy instead expands the definition of what we consider to be the appropriate subjects of philosophical discourse. Pythagorean women's writings show that women's concerns as well as men's are subjects worthy of philosophical treatment.

From this perspective, the Pythagorean women should be acknowledged for themselves recognizing women's own intrinsic worth and intelligence, and for advancing this esteem in their writings to other women. Their writings furnished an ethical basis to women's lives analogous to men's discussions of the ethical values underlying their realms of activity. In this way Pythagorean philosophy provided women with powerful validations for their roles in society. The terracotta might not directly portray a female philosopher, but the self-assured pose of the Tanagran woman (Figure 8.1) dramatically reflects the confidence in her female identity that the Pythagorean women philosophers advocated.

The Women Sokrates Admired—Aspasia and Diotima

Two other female philosophers are known only from their association with Sokrates. In Plato's *Menexenus,* Sokrates extols Aspasia, a known historical figure in the second half of the fifth century B.C.E., as a teacher of rhetoric. In the *Symposium* Sokrates claims to have learned all he knows about erotic matters from Diotima, about whom nothing else is known.

Aspasia

Aspasia, the Milesian-born spouse of the Athenian leader Perikles, was variously depicted by four fourth-century followers of Sokrates. One sharply denigrated her. Aeschines and Xenophon praised her positive qualities, which Plato may also have done. These authors portrayed Sokrates, Perikles, and others consulting Aspasia for what she had to teach them about politics, relationships, or public speaking. In Plato's *Menexenus,* for the occasion of a public funeral memorial, Sokrates recites for his friend a funeral oration he says he recently heard from Aspasia. In this rhetorical tour de force that exhibits the features expected of such public commemorations, Aspasia reminds the hearers of Athens's glorious past from myth-historical times to recent events. Plato may be transmitting a speech he believes originated with Aspasia, or he may be exercising his own rhetorical skill and experimenting with writing a funeral oration. Especially in the latter case, by attributing the speech to Aspasia, Plato pays rare tribute to the woman he identifies as excelling in rhetorical skill.

Both Sokrates' followers Aeschines and Xenophon describe Aspasia as highly respected for her intellectual, political, ethical, and psychological acumen; she was regarded as an expert on male-female relationships, and educated married couples on their proper marital roles. Relying on her knowledge of the truth, Aspasia advocated that marriages be made and sustained honestly with concerted mutual effort by both partners. In reflection of complementary gender roles, for Aspasia a marriage succeeded when each strove to be the best possible partner they could be, excelling at their particular tasks and in the qualities they shared in common—memory, care, and self-control.

Aspasia regarded *erôs* and the search for *aretê,* "excellence," as interwoven, which anticipated the fusion of the two seen in Theano II's expression of her love for Kleon's philosophic soul in erotic language. The Sokrates in both Plato's and Xenophon's works entitled *The Symposium* likewise merged the two. Although Aeschines portrayed Aspasia as a *hetaira,* he shows her giving her advice not to men and other *hetairai* in an atmosphere of open sexuality, but to respectably married couples. Moreover, in contrast to the Pythagorean women who limited their ethical comments to other women, Aspasia included both spouses in the scope of her remarks.

By combining *erôs* with virtue, Aspasia acknowledged the important place of sexuality within the marriage relationship. This interweaving situates both erotic and intellectual activities within the respectable realm of marriage. Her weaving together *erôs* and the search for excellence provided each partner in the marriage with an opportunity to strive to be their best. By infusing philosophic explorations with the sensory intensity and passion of eroticism, far from being a dry, passionless endeavor, the pursuit of wisdom, excellence, and virtue becomes a dynamic, enlivening affair.

Diotima

Plato's most literary dialogue, *The Symposium,* a men's "drinking party," presents a second learned female figure, Diotima, a priestess from Mantinea, in the northern Peloponessos: Sokrates says that Diotima once taught him all he knows about *ta erôtika,* "erotic matters." One symposium participant suggests that rather than merely getting drunk to the entertainment of flute girls, they should drink moderately and have a discussion on the nature of love, *erôs*—which they do. Speaking last, Sokrates opposes earlier descriptions of Eros, the male deity of Love, as embodying ideals of Beauty. As represented by Sokrates, Diotima first presents Eros as a figure who mediates between various dualities—beautiful-ugly, good-bad, wise-ignorant, divine-mortal. Sokrates claims not merely that he learned about love from Diotima, but that she initiated him into the mysteries of love. This language evokes worshippers' initiation into mystery rites from which they received the blessings of the presiding deities and often secret knowledge.

The initiation Sokrates presents in *The Symposium* is a philosophic one. Diotima first instructs Sokrates in her esoteric view of the birth and nature of Eros. In her genealogy, Eros's father was Resource, son of Metis, goddess of wisdom and cunning who was also the mother of Athena. His mother was Poverty, who lay down beside a drunken Resource at a feast for Aphrodite and conceived Eros. Although Poverty plotted to sleep with Resource, Diotima says Eros received his scheming nature from his father, who had inherited it from his mother Metis. Radically shifting the focus of discussion from the physical realm to the philosophical, Diotima describes Eros as

a clever hunter, always weaving some scheme in his spirited, resourceful pursuit of wisdom, as he philosophizes through his entire life, a clever wizard, sorcerer and sophist.[12]

Because wisdom is among the most beautiful things, by necessity Eros is a philosopher, between wisdom and ignorance, always seeking wisdom.

Diotima transfers the focus on Eros from one of sexual to philosophic pursuit. As seen in Aspasia's ideas, *erôs* forms the root of philosophical inquiry. Using language of male homoerotic activity, Diotima presents this transference in stages—first the lover appreciates the beauty of a particular adolescent which compels him to engage with the youth, both sexually and in order to direct his intellectual and ethical improvement. With maturity, the lover next recognizes that his love of an individual's beauty can be generalized to the beauty of all youth, which develops into an abstract, philosophic concept of Beauty. Diotima then explains how the philosophic Eros, as a lover of the ideal Beauty, produces the lover's desire to insure the goodness of his beloved's soul. For Diotima, in marked contrast to Plato's other views on the immortality of the soul, this desire means that the lover seeks to replicate the worthwhile qualities of his own character, seen as embedded in the *psykhe* ("soul"), in the soul of his beloved. This Eros, consequently, leads to the highest philosophic and ethical activity—identified as the good life—which results in the person's happiness.

In their descriptions of Diotima and Aspasia, Plato, Aeschines, and Xenophon attributed the idea that *erôs* was integral to philosophical inquiry to two women—one was identified as a priestess, the second was the politically influential, non-Athenian wife of Athens's leading statesman. Using somewhat different language, each woman addressed her remarks to different audiences. Aspasia spoke to married couples. In *The Symposium*, Diotima speaks to a single male in the context of Greek male homoerotic associations. Diotima thus stands in complete opposition to the female Pythagoreans, who intended their counsel for other women.

Diotima's focus reflects the masculine cast ascribed to her and other female philosophers, vividly illustrated in the small bronze relief plaques dating to 340–30 B.C.E., shortly after Plato's death, that were used to cover a wooden box holding a roll of *The Symposium*. These plaques depict Sokrates listening intently to Diotima who is seated on a stool, her right leg crossed over her left, her right elbow leaning on her right thigh as she expostulates her point to the attentive Sokrates standing opposite her. Above them flies a winged Eros, carrying the priestess's ritual headdress and the ritual box that holds the sacred objects. Although not considered feminine, an early interpreter considered Diotima's pose appropriate for a person completely absorbed in their intellectual discourse. It may be that if intellectual endeavor was conceptualized in male terms, a woman engaging in such activity could only appear as masculine. At the same time, there may be less emphasis on the gendered dimension of these portrayals than on the independence of the intellectual activity, which the ancient Greeks could only express in male-framed language.

Despite their differing status and philosophic approaches, both Aspasia and Diotima regarded the passion of eroticism as essential to philosophic pursuits. From the outset eroticism was acknowledged as fundamental to human life and as leading to great physical enjoyment. More importantly, erotic desire aimed at the betterment of oneself and of one's beloved, thereby first transferring the effect of eroticism into the realm of ethics, and ultimately into the realm of philosophic inquiry. The importance of the fundamental desire of love was preserved. For Aspasia it formed the ground for a married couple's philosophic endeavors. For Diotima, eroticism served as a first stage in the pursuit of wisdom, which, according to the example of Sokrates, diminishes as the pursuit of intellectual and ethical wisdom increases.

Other Greek Women Philosophers

History records the names of numerous women in the various Greek philosophical schools and refers to writings by some of them, though none survive. After her father's death in the late fifth century B.C.E., Arete of Kyrene in north Africa became head of the school of Hedonism, a philosophical practice dedicated to the idea that pursuit of pleasure should be the principal aim in life. However, the ancient definition of hedonism was concerned with nurturing not only the pleasures of the body, but recognizing the value of moral and intellectual pleasures as guiding principles of life that result in true spiritual and physical contentment. A Renaissance source asserted that Arete wrote 40 books and educated 110 philosophers. The known written works of the Kyrenaics may have been penned by Arete's son, Aristippos, who was called *mêtrodidaktos*, "mother-taught," a nickname which highlights once again the influential role of a mother-philosopher.

Other than two women, Lasthenia of Mantinea and Axiothea of Philesia, who studied at Plato's Academy dressed as men, women did not attend Plato's Academy or Aristotle's Lyceum. But women were openly welcomed to the garden established by Epicurus around 300 B.C.E. One, Leontion, wrote a rebuttal to the Aristotelian claim of women's natural inferiority to men, which has unfortunately not survived.

Women could also freely follow the Cynic Diogenes. Notorious was Hipparkhia, who preferred to share the nonconventional lifestyle of her lover Krates, publicly renouncing society's expectations that she marry, raise a family, and live according to social prescriptions. She reputedly ignored all other suitors to be with Krates, threatening her parents to kill herself if they stopped her. Upon her parents' urging, even after Krates tried to dissuade her from accompanying him, Hipparkhia was adamant. Krates reportedly then disrobed in front of her, saying effectively, "What you see is what you get. Prepare yourself."

But the girl chose him. She assumed the same dress and went around with him. She made love to him in public, and she accompanied him to dinner parties.[13]

A late epigram describes the basis for Hipparkhia's conduct. Written in Hipparkhia's voice, it proclaims,

I, Hipparkhia, have no use for the works of deep-robed women. I have chosen the Cynics' manly life. I don't need capes with brooches or thick-soled slippers, and I don't care for scented hair ties. I live by my staff and double cloak, the ground for my bed. My life outstrips that of Atalanta of Mainalos, because pursuit of wisdom is more valuable than racing over a mountain.[14]

Hipparkhia's actions show how vastly the scope of women's potential intellectual activities expanded during the Hellenistic period. While Pythagorean women were advocating women's strict marital fidelity without questioning the societal sexual double standard, Hipparkhia and others exemplified in word and deed a life of greater female autonomy. The epigram too identifies this life as a manly one, unable to find other language to characterize such independence of female action.

Besides these, sources name a few other female philosophers about whom nothing else is known—Thargelia, Euphrosyne, and Magnilla. In the late first century B.C.E., Queen Kleopatra VII was renowned for her learning and active participation in the Alexandrian Museum of higher learning. She thereby continued the practice begun by her forebear, Ptolemy II, who founded the Museum not only as a repository of books, but even more as a research center that attracted intellectuals from many lands to study and engage in intellectual discourse. Likewise, Julia Domna, 170–217 C.E., the Syrian-born wife of the Roman emperor Septimius Severus and mother of Caracalla, was called "the philosopher Julia." Interested in neo-Platonic ideas, Julia had a coterie of mathematicians and philosophers who consulted with her on intellectual and theological matters.

The works of two women expounded alchemical formulas. Only a diagram remains of an alchemical text, *The Chrysopoeia,* "Gold-making," by a later Kleopatra. Maria, who may have lived in the first century C.E., identified herself as Jewish, claiming that only someone of Jewish heritage could touch the philosopher's stone. The extant fragments furnish detailed recipes for specific chemical combinations, including diagrams for the instruments for the chemical reactions. In describing the distillate achieved from one reaction, Maria speaks of the heart of Saturn holding the tincture and the vessel of Hermes which the philosophers have hidden as manifest in the action of fire. Though Maria may have been Jewish, her mixing together Greek and Roman gods demonstrates the syncretism of beliefs prevalent in this period.

Finally, in the fifth century C.E., two women were prominent in two different centers of neo-Platonism—Asklepigenia in Athens and Hypatia in Alexandria, Egypt. This period witnessed escalating conflicts between followers of traditional Greek religious and cultural practices and devotees of increasingly powerful Christian sects. Although neo-Platonic ideas profoundly influenced the development of Christian theology, the pagan orientation of these two neo-Platonic schools put them at odds with the rise of Christianity.

After the death of her father in 430, Asklepigenia became director of the Neoplatonic Academy in Athens, which sought to reconcile the differing principles of Platonic and Aristotelian philosophies with Greek religious and magical beliefs. Asklepigenia taught the fundamental ideas of the Athenian school, exemplified by her student Proclus, late antiquity's major proponent of Neoplatonism. Accentuating the mystical strain of Platonic ideas, through intelligence, introspective contemplation on the nature of the self leads to mystical union with the One, the state of true happiness.

In the more scientifically oriented Neoplatonic school in Alexandria, Hypatia emerged as a paragon of intellectual accomplishment. She was born circa 370–75 C.E., the daughter of a mathematician and philosopher who taught at the Museum in Alexandria. Hypatia was renowned for her work in mathematics, astronomy, engineering, and Neoplatonic philosophy. By the age of 30 she was named head of the Museum, a rare honor for anyone at that relatively young age, and especially for a woman. Her commentaries were famous for correcting and contributing to Ptolemy's mathematical and astronomical theories, which held till Copernicus revolutionized Western ideas of astronomy in the sixteenth century. Her works also elaborated upon the algebraic and geometric theories of others. In one letter a devoted student, Synesius, asks her to build him an astrolabe, and in another he requests a hydrometer to measure the density of water, providing her the instructions for making one.

While ancient biographies are often filled with fantastical, unlikely details, one anecdote about Hypatia illustrates the depth of her adherence to intellectual pursuits. Exasperated by the persistent attention of a student who had romantic rather than philosophic designs, Hypatia reputedly threw a bloody sanitary cloth at him and proclaimed that the young fool was only interested in sex and not in what was truly beautiful.

While Hypatia was highly esteemed by her intellectual peers, her accomplishments made her an object of envy, especially in the area of astronomy, which seemed particularly to gall the Christian forces in Alexandria. Even though Synesius had some influence as a Christian, Hypatia fell victim to antipagan Christian violence in March of 415 C.E. Incited by the bishop of Alexandria, Cyril, a Christian mob, comprised largely of monks, dragged Hypatia from her chariot as she was on her way to deliver a lecture. They stripped her, flayed her skin with broken pottery shards, and then hacked her body to pieces, which they spread around Alexandria. Other than referring to the shame this brought upon the Christian element in Alexandria, sources provide no further information on the consequences of this horrendous attack.

To ancient observers, Hypatia's murder exemplified the violence that infected the Alexandrians during this period. At the same time, the brutal manner of Hypatia's death provides a gruesome commentary to the fate of women philosophers, scientists, and engineers in subsequent centuries. In the short term, the terror tactic used against Hypatia no doubt inhibited even the few women who might pursue intellectual careers. Over the long term, with the destruction of most of the writings by women philosophers, later shapers of Western cultural institutions were able to promote the fiction that intellectual matters were an exclusively privileged male concern.

Figure 8.1 Standing woman, terracotta. Tanagra, Greece, late 4th c. B.C.E. Réunion des Musées Nationaux/Art Resource, NY, Louvre, Paris, France.

Nine

In Her Own Voice 2—Women's Poetry

WOMEN AND THE DIVINE CRAFT OF POETRY

Women Create Immortal Poetry—Helen, Sappho, Nossis, and Erinna

Throughout these ancient cultures, women were integrally associated with the craft of poetry. The power of divine inspiration was typically conceptualized as female, familiar through the Greek images of the Muses, of whom Erato, "the lovely one," represented poetry. In the *Iliad*, Homer depicts Helen as the archetypal creator of poetry. Speaking to the Trojan defender Hektor, she proclaims that

Zeus imposed this evil fate upon us so that we would become
the subjects of song for people in the future.[1]

Thus Helen, the very figure who is blamed as the cause of the war, emerges as the poem's only character to reflect on the nature of poetic creation. Characteristic of oral traditional societies, Helen states that the reason they must endure their present experiences is so that these events might be transformed into song. This memorialization imparts meaning to events that may seem meaningless to those living through them, which in turn provides models of conduct for future generations.

Similarly, the Greek female poet Sappho, late seventh century B.C.E., recognized that her poetry immortalized her. In an ancient paraphrase, Sappho claimed that the Muses made her truly blessed and enviable so that even after her death she would not be forgotten. While oral traditional poetry memorialized the event, with the onset of writing, verse began to immortalize the poet, and Sappho's fragments repeatedly honor the Muses for granting her this divine memorial.

Sappho received great renown in antiquity for her poetry. Called the tenth Muse, of her nine books of poetry mostly tattered fragments and only one complete poem survive. She created her own distinctive metrical pattern, which came to be known by her name as sapphics. Her verse influenced many other Greek and Latin poets. The Latin love poet Catullus showed his great esteem for Sappho's poetry by translating some into Latin. He also experimented with sapphic meter, and he called his beloved by the learned pseudonym Lesbia, by which he accorded her honor to match Sappho's.

An ancient commentator on style said that Sappho's words ideally suited her meaning:

When Sappho sings about beauty, her language is beautiful and sweet. And if she sings about loves or spring or the halcyon, she weaves into her poetry all beautiful words, some of which she herself devised. [2]

Like other poets, Sappho was said to weave head wreaths out of myrtle, anise, and celery. Nor was she shy about proclaiming the superiority of Lesbian singers, those from her native island of Lesbos, over all others. Taken from a poem of hers, the phrase "after the Lesbian singer" became proverbial.

Two of the Hellenistic Greek female poets, early third century B.C.E., identified themselves as worthy inheritors of Sappho's poetic art. In an epigram written as though the voice from the grave were speaking to passersby, a common convention of grave epitaphs, Nossis, from Lokri, southern Italy, proclaimed:

Stranger, if you sail to Mytilene of the beautiful dances,
where the flower of the Graces enflamed Sappho,
say that the land of Lokri gave birth to one equally dear to the Muses,
and once you've learned that my name is Nossis, go on.[3]

An epigram describes another Hellenistic poet, Erinna, who may have been from Lesbos or another eastern Greek island, as comparable to Sappho, even though she followed another poetic Muse, that of epic verse:

This is the Lesbian honeycomb of Erinna.
Though small, it is wholly blended with the honey of the Muses.
Her three hundred lines are equal to Homer,
though she was only a maiden nineteen years old.
Whether spinning at her distaff out of fear for her mother or working at
the loom, she held fast as a servant of the Muses.
As much as Sappho bests Erinna at lyric poetry,
by that much Erinna outstrips Sappho in epic hexameter verse.[4]

Three hundred and more years after her time Sappho remained the standard for excellent poetic composition. Erinna can carry on this poetic heritage Sappho established—the Lesbian honeycomb—while pursuing it in her own distinctive way, heroic epic rather than love poetry.

Kleoboulina the Riddler—The Skill of Poetic Illusion

Possibly contemporary with Sappho, Kleoboulina from Lindos on the southeast Greek island of Rhodes displayed one type of women's association with wisdom that found expression in poetic verse. Highlighting dimensions of cleverness, Kleoboulina was known for her riddles, three of which survive. One riddle illustrates her clever imagination.

I saw a man deceiving and stealing by force,
And this act of force was most rightly done.
What did I see?[5]

The riddle alludes to artistic creation, which the Greeks regarded as an *apatê*, a "deception," or, in reference to mimetic arts, an illusion. Although Greek society generally did not condone deceitful conduct, they did tolerate deceit practiced for a higher purpose, such as to prevent a crazed individual from harming themselves or others.

At the same time the Greeks agonized over their perception that all artistic media produced an *apatê*, an illusion; the more successful the artist the greater the illusion created. Phintys, in accord with Plato, would ban all poets from the city for that very reason, that they created something superficial and unreal. Kleoboulina's riddle suggests that she supports the accomplished effect of *apatê* in artistic creation, where the best artist is the one who most successfully employs creative deception to fashion a work of art stunning in its mimetic truth.

Hymns—Women Honor the Deities

One way women exhibited their traditional association with poetry was by composing hymns to the gods. We have seen some of Enkheduanna's praise songs of Inanna, and it is likely that the Egyptian women who held the honored roles of temple singer also composed the hymns they sang. Sappho has hymns to several deities. One beseeches Aphrodite, frequently called Kypris because of her principal sanctuary on the island of Cyprus (Greek Kypros), and the female water spirits, the Nereids, to protect her brother:

Kypris and Nereids, grant that
my brother reach here unharmed,
and that all that his heart desires
be fulfilled.
Let him make up for all his past mistakes
and become a joy to his friends
and a menace to his enemies.
May he be willing to honor
his sister, no longer causing us
grievous pains and suffering.[6]

This appeal to Aphrodite for protection and to insure the moral improvement of her brother's conduct reveals a side to Aphrodite's worship not evident in the prevailing focus on her eroticism.

Hellenistic epigrams frequently invoked deities. Two by Nossis highlight aspects of women's lives seen earlier, including rituals of childbirth and women's woven dedications. In one, Nossis calls upon Artemis as goddess of childbirth:

Artemis, goddess of Delos and lovely Ortygia,
put your sacred arrows down in the lap of the Graces,

wash your body clean in the river Inopos,
and come to Lokri to free Alketis from her harsh labor pains.[7]

In an epigram to Hera, Nossis names herself and her mother as the dedicants of the goddess's robe. Nossis notably identifies her mother by her mother's name, thus recognizing three generations of her matriline:

Honored Hera, you often come down from heaven
to look at your incense-scented Lakinian temple,
accept this linen cloak which Theophilis, daughter of Kleokha,
wove for you together with her noble daughter Nossis.[8]

Several epigrams by the Hellenistic poet Anyte of Tegea in the northern Peloponessos identify a deity's sanctuary and describe their qualities, such as this one to Aphrodite:

This is the place of Kypris, where she always likes
to come to gaze out at the bright sea from the land
in order to secure the sailors a good voyage. The sea trembles
around as it looks upon her shining wooden image.[9]

Like Sappho's verses, Anyte evokes a protective side of Aphrodite who watches over those who travel the seas, the place of her birth. In addition, this epigram may refer to a ritual bathing or procession of the wooden cult image of the goddess to the sea. The Greeks thought that wooden statues were the oldest images of their gods—some were believed to have divinely materialized before their human worshippers.

Two prose epigrams by a first-century C.E. Roman priestess of Hera at Ephesos show the continued tradition of priestesses composing their own hymns as well as transmitting traditional ones. Likewise, attributed to Jesus's mother Mary is the Magnificat, sometimes called the Canticle of Mary (Luke 1:46), which Mary says in response to Elizabeth at the visitation. The hymn is still recited in daily or weekly Vespers and continues to be part of the liturgy in Advent, the winter liturgical season that concentrates on Christ's birth. Given the many priestesses throughout the millennia of Mediterranean antiquity, women's hymnal composition must have been commonly accepted devotional practice. In this tradition, it is noteworthy that as I write this, renowned contemporary American poet Maya Angelou has written a prayer for all people today.[10]

Hero Tales and Public Celebrations—Korinna

Another way women displayed their traditional poetic craft was by composing poems on mythological themes for public celebrations. Among her many poetic themes, several of Sappho's fragments evoke epic and heroic topics. One badly damaged fragment spotlights choral performance:

I shall go to enjoy the harmonies of the delightful
chorus ... their clear voiced song.[11]

Tattered fragments show that the fifth-century poets Praxilla and Telesilla wrote hymns and heroic poetry, and nothing remains of Erinna's renowned epic verse. Best illustrating the public celebration of heroic poetry is Korinna of Tanagra in Boiotia, central Greece, possibly fifth century B.C.E. Korinna composed choral poetry for public festivals that often treated legendary or heroic themes in which she proclaims that she sings of the excellences of heroes and heroines. These are the choral songs by which the ancient Greeks publicly celebrated their heritage.

In one poetic fragment Korinna validates her role as chosen by the Muse of Choral Poetry:

Terpsikhore summons me to sing
beautiful ancient heroic tales
to the white-robed Tanagraian women.
And the city rejoices greatly in my clear, sharp voice.[12]

Korinna identifies her role as divinely legitimated singer to the community, delighted by the city's admiration of her.

Several fragments of Korinna's poetry depict the mythological stories that form her poetic subjects. In stories about both gods and heroes, Greek poets interwove individual praise with legendary tales. After several broken lines and before the Terpsikhore fragment ends, Korinna recalls her many poems on the legendary background to her native region of Greece.

I begin to sing the stories of our fathers to the adolescent girls,
stories that I have embellished with my own skill.
Often have I adorned our ancestor the river god
Kaphisos with my tales.
Often too our ancestor the great Orion
and his fifty strong-man sons,
the offspring he begot after sleeping with the nymphs.[13]

This fragment emphasizes Korinna's important role in the poetic tradition. Like all great poets she was not merely a rote transmitter of her cultural lore. Rather, she enhanced the tradition by putting her own poetic stamp on the songs she received, thus bestowing greater honor upon both her ancestors and the songs. For her skill in doing so, she received great praise.

WOMEN'S PERSONAL, POLITICAL, AND SOCIAL POETRY

Enkheduanna—Personal View of Political Exile

From ancient Mesopotamia come the earliest writings by a known author anywhere in the world, Enkheduanna, daughter of Sargon I, ruler of Babylon, and High Priestess of the Moon God Nanna in Ur. Dating to the 2300s B.C.E., her poetry about the great Mesopotamian goddess Inanna, segments of which were cited in earlier chapters, stands out as remarkable for several

reasons. Her poems provide the first examples of signed literature. Remarkably, this earliest known, signed writing was by a woman in a culture whose
other recorded documents were primarily by, for, and about men. Nevertheless, Enkheduanna spoke unabashedly in a woman's voice, providing
thereby distinctive, female perspectives.

Previous chapters examined various aspects of Enkheduanna's poems
about Inanna, notably the goddess's erotic and warrior dimensions. This
chapter will look at those passages where Enkheduanna spoke in her own
voice and of her own situation in exile, where she was prevented from worshipping Inanna as was the goddess's due, and where she wished to regain
her former position as high priestess. Enkheduanna begins by addressing
Inanna, extolling the goddess's qualities and identifying herself:

Queen of all given powers …

INANNA
SUPREME IN HEAVEN AND EARTH …

to sing your praise is exalted
You of the bountiful heart
You of the radiant heart
I will sing of your cosmic powers …
I
the high Priestess
I
Enheduanna.[14]

Fundamental to Enkheduanna's role as the priestess/poet was to sing the
praises of the goddess, which she joyously fulfilled.

This glorification of Inanna was not the only goal of her poem but served
as a prelude to the circumstances of her exile, which Enkheduanna then
relates. In her anger, Enkheduanna prays that the chief male gods, An and
Enlil, destroy their, and her, enemies, including wrecking the city and curs-
ing babies to die in their mothers' arms. Enkheduanna then describes in
vivid language how she experiences her exile.

I am not allowed in my rooms
gloom falls on the day
light turns leaden
shadows close in
dreaded southstorm cloaks the sun
he wipes his spit-soaked hand
on my honey sweet mouth
my beautiful image
fades under dust.[15]

Enkheduanna characterized her exile as loss of her rightful space and
loss of the very light of the sun. Instead of maintaining her exalted, civilized
station, she was forced to wander the wilds. Although she named him

elsewhere, in these passages Enkheduanna contemptuously referred to the cause of her troubles as "that man," whom she considered repulsive next to her own beauty.

Enkheduanna ended these descriptions with glorifying praise of Inanna, as she appealed to the supreme goddess to restore her to her rightful place, which eventually occurred. Enkheduanna's poems of Inanna's battle with the mountain Ebih may metaphorically describe how Enkheduanna envisioned the turbulent period of her exile. Enkheduanna's poem celebrating Inanna's victory over the mountain with hymns composed for the dedication of a new temple to the goddess no doubt celebrated Enkheduanna's own restoration to her former position.

Biblical Victory Songs—Miriam and Deborah

Two songs in biblical literature celebrate Israelite victories. After their successful crossing of the Red Sea and escape from their pursuing Egyptian enemy, circa thirteenth century B.C.E.,

Then the prophet Miriam, Aaron's sister, took a tambourine in her hand; and all the women went out after her with tambourines and with dancing. And Miriam sang to them,

"Sing to the Lord, for he has triumphed gloriously;
horse and rider he has thrown into the sea."[16]

These two verses of Miriam's song are the oldest poetic couplet in the Hebrew Bible, possibly composed at the time of the event. The song Moses leads at Exodus 15:1 begins with this couplet of Miriam's song, which may indicate that the entire song he sings was Miriam's composition.

In the twelfth century B.C.E. Deborah's song in Judges 5 celebrated an Israelite victory (see chapter 7). Like Miriam's, Deborah's song is one of the oldest parts of the Hebrew Bible. Deborah sings her song together with the winning general Barak, whom she had appointed to his command in her capacity as judge of the community (Judges 4:4–10). Deborah twice refers to herself in the song:

The peasantry prospered in Israel,
they grew fat on plunder,
because you arose, Deborah,
arose as a mother in Israel.[17]

To celebrate the victory, the people called for Deborah:

"Awake, awake, Deborah!
Awake, awake, utter a song!"[18]

Her song recounts the story of the battle, culminating with Jael's capture of Sisera and dividing the enemy spoils after battle, for which Deborah praises her God.

Sappho—Family and Ethics

Sappho lived in the same period and region of Greece where early philosophic thinking originated. Two fragments raise ethical issues, which shows that women could voice their ethical concerns in various literary modes. Aristotle quoted a few lines in his *Rhetoric* that address the connection between feelings of shame and honorable action. When her contemporary poet Alkaios claimed that shame prevented him from telling her something, Sappho replied,

If you desired something worthwhile and good,
and if your tongue were not striking up some evil speech,
shame would not cover your eyes
but you would speak out justly.[19]

A second, quoted by the physician Galen, describes beauty in a way that anticipates Pythagorean women's views:

For he that is beautiful is beautiful as far as his appearance goes;
but he that is good will thereby also be beautiful.[20]

In both fragments Sappho treats topics central to later ethical philosophies. Both these fragments focus on inner qualities of moral justice and goodness that rightly shine forth in the value of one's words and the beauty of one's appearance.

Two of Sappho's fragments express her feelings about her daughter Kleis.

I have a beautiful daughter radiant as
golden flowers, beloved Kleis,
for whom I would not take all of Lydia or lovely.[21]

The fragment ends abruptly. Since Lydia in Anatolia was legendary for its wealth, Sappho demonstrates the depth of feelings for her daughter—nothing in the world was more precious than her own daughter. In a second tattered fragment, Sappho bemoans the fact that she cannot get an embroidered headband for her daughter, perhaps due to her own political exile.

Nossis—Dedications

Several epigrams by Nossis accompanied paintings, many describing the faithful likeness of the paintings and their effect on the viewer. One epigram draws out a moral meaning from the painting's aesthetic quality:

This is Melinna herself. See how her gentle face
seems to look at me sweetly.
How truly the daughter is like her mother in all ways!
It is beautiful when children are like their parents.[22]

Another epigram suggests the occasion for dedicating both the portraits and epigrams.

Kallo has set up her picture in the house of shimmering Aphrodite,
a portrait she had made that looks just like her.
How gently she stands; look at how much grace blossoms on her.
May she fare well, for her life carries no faults.[23]

Setting up these portraits for Aphrodite may have been part of coming-of-age rituals, as the adolescent moved into adulthood and the realm of sexuality. These dedications might have continued the Archaic practice of setting up dedicatory *kore* statues (see chapter 2).

One other epigram of Nossis's turns the realistic effect of these portraits to a more precious direction:

This picture reveals Thaumareta's beauty, it well captures
the status and youthfulness of the gentle-eyed one.
Seeing you, even the little house watchdog would wag its tail
thinking that it was seeing the mistress of the house.[24]

The image bestows high praise—the picture's verisimilitude is so lifelike that even her dog takes it for the real person.

Anyte—Funerary and Pastoral

Anyte wrote epigrams on a wide range of themes—dedications to gods, funerary epigrams, both solemn and amusing epitaphs, and vivid descriptions of pastoral landscapes that would influence the major male Greek pastoral poets of the Hellenistic period. The funerary epigrams frequently describe the young woman's death before marriage, a poignant reminder of the dangers young women faced:

Often wailing upon her daughter's tomb, her mother Kleina
cried for her dear child, her life cut short.
She invokes Philainis' soul, who before her marriage
crossed over the pale stream of the River Akheron.[25]

One of Anyte's funerary epigrams gives a sadder reason for young women's portraits:

Instead of a bridal bed and sacred marriage rites
your mother set up a maiden-like image on this marble tomb
that looks like you in size and beauty,
Thersis, so we can talk to you even though you are dead.[26]

Some of Anyte's funerary epigrams honored men who died as heroes. One ends by proclaiming:

But this beautiful poem on the stone above you sings
that you died fighting for your dear fatherland.[27]

Especially honorific is another which claims that the soldier "died holding his round shield over his comrade."[28] Throughout Greek literature, men fear an inglorious death from drowning or disease, as they proclaim their desire to die a noble death in battle. These two epigrams accentuate the men's heroic deaths. The first honors the dead warrior for defending their homeland. The second enhances this fundamental heroism by proclaiming he died while protecting his fellow soldiers, the highest accolade accorded a fallen warrior.

While Anyte's epitaphs display the solemnity expected of such memorials, other epigrams reveal a more humorous side as they commemorate dead birds, dogs, dolphins, and even a girl's dead pet grasshopper and cicada.

Anyte developed an innovative poetic genre—pastoral poetry, which evoked refreshing, idyllic landscapes, sanctuaries of nature deities, and places of respite for the hot, weary traveler.

Stranger, rest your tired legs under the elm,
a sweet breeze rustles through the green leaves.
Drink the cold spring water from the fountain. For indeed this is
a resting place dear to travelers in the burning heat.[29]

The Hellenistic poet Theokritos elaborated Anyte's pastoral epigrams into extended descriptions of idyllic country environments.

Erinna—Young Women and Death

Erinna's surviving poetry memorializes her childhood friend Baukis who died young. One reads like an epitaph on her tomb addressed to passersby:

Greet whoever passes by my tomb here,
whether they are citizens or come from another town.
And tell them this too, that this tomb holds me as a buried bride,
that my father called me Baukis, and that my family is from
Tenos, so they might know. And that my close friend
Erinna inscribed this poem on my tomb.[30]

In the fragmentary lines of the one longer poem of hers that is extant, "The Distaff," Erinna recalls the games young girls played that they put aside upon marriage, and the close emotional bonds the girls had developed.

maidens ... tortoise ... tortoise ... sea wave ...
from white horses ... I shouted ...
you leaped wildly through the garden of the large courtyard.
Poor Baukis, I cry these laments for you,
already in ashes lie our dolls in our bedrooms.
When we were little girls, the bogeywoman Mormo terrorized us—
big ears on her head, she ran on all fours
and kept changing her face.
But when you came to the marriage bed, you forgot everything
you heard as a child from your mother,
dear Baukis, the forgetfulness of Aphrodite.
tears my cheeks.[31]

The broken lines of this badly tattered fragment add to its poignancy. The beginning evokes a children's tag game called "torty-tortoise" the girls played running around the yard, while another bit recalls the monstrous figure that frightened them as girls. Erinna remembers the dolls they had to put away as they came to the age of marriage, which have now been burned. Erinna states near the end that she cannot view her friend's corpse; the reason for this is unknown. It could be her age, lack of familial relationship, unmarried status, or even priestly office. Erinna's lament for her close childhood friend Baukis is all the more wrenching since we know she was to die herself soon afterward.

TOURIST INSCRIPTIONS

In the second century C.E. five women's names are attached to the inscriptions engraved by Greek and Roman tourists on Egyptian monuments—one was carved on the pyramid of Cheops, and four on a colossal statue of Memnon. These inscriptions testify to the interest in tourist travel from the Hellenistic period on, when increasing numbers of Greeks and then Romans journeyed to the lands their leaders had conquered and were ruling. While tourists came from all classes, the women's poems identify them as Roman elite, highly educated in mythology and history, and skilled to write their poems in an elegant, literary Greek.

Sometime after 130 C.E., Terentia engraved on the pyramid of Cheops an epitaph to her dead brother, who had achieved the supreme rank of consul under the Emperor Trajan before the age of 30.

I saw the pyramids without you, sweetest brother,
and all I was able to do was to sadly pour forth
my tears for you.
And I carve this lament in memory of our mourning.[32]

As Terentia states in the poem, by carving her brother's epitaph upon the ancient Egyptian pyramid, she expected her tribute to his memory to last as long as the pyramid. By fortuitous chance it has. A German visitor recorded the poem in 1335; the surviving testimony of the inscription since the original was lost when the pyramid's limestone facing was removed.

Of a different sort are the poems four women inscribed on the one remaining colossal statue in front of the mortuary temple of the pharaoh Amenhotep III, 1468–38 B.C.E., near Thebes, Egypt. Associating Amenhotep III, whose principal wife was Queen Tiye, with their mythological hero from Egypt, Memnon, the Greeks, and later the Romans, called the colossus a statue of Memnon, son of the goddess of Dawn—Greek Eos, Roman Aurora— and her mortal lover Tithonos. The statue gained fame in antiquity due to damage caused by the Persian King Cambyses at the end of the sixth century B.C.E. Responding to changes in temperature, the cracked stone seemed to sing, which the Greek and Roman tourists interpreted as a good sign, that the ancient hero Memnon was speaking to them. Visitors, especially if they had heard Memnon "sing," inscribed their names on the statue, sometimes with dates and with lines of verse. The earliest inscription dates to 20 B.C.E., a decade after Rome wrested away rule of Egypt from the Ptolemaic Greeks.

Two of the women's inscriptions resemble spontaneous graffiti. One, by Dionysia, possibly dating to 122 C.E., reveals her reverence for the site and her expectation to return often to hear Memnon's voice. Besides this reverential attitude before the hero's statue, another one, by Caecilia Trebulla, before 130 C.E., reveals the writer's deep feelings for her mother, whom she thinks of during her visit.

By Trebulla.
When I heard Memnon's holy voice,
I yearned for you, mother, and I prayed that you might hear it too.[33]

Other inscriptions, however, reveal more elaborated verse that the authors have clearly polished before they were committed to stone. One by Demo, circa 200 C.E., provides a traditional poetic frame for these tourist inscriptions:

Son of Eos, greetings! For you rang out kindly to me,
Memnon, because of the Pierian Muses, my protectors,
song-loving Demo. And to show my gratitude,
my lyre will always sing of your power, oh holy one.[34]

Reminiscent of Archaic Greek poets, Demo formally greeted the hero of the shrine. She claimed Memnon spoke to her in recognition of her divinely sanctioned poetic talent. In return, still within the ancient tradition, Demo spoke of her songs as her honoring gifts to the hero. Situating the poems inscribed on Memnon's statue in this context of traditional dedicatory offerings shows that they were regarded as having greater significance than what we might consider incidental tourist graffiti.

Dedicatory in nature, the most extensive inscriptions on the colossus of Memnon come from Julia Balbilla, an aristocratic Roman woman who accompanied the Emperor Hadrian and his wife Sabina on a visit to the site, November 20, 130 C.E. Julia Balbilla commemorated this visit with four poems, which the emperor probably commissioned. At the head of the first poem, Julia Balbilla identified herself and the occasion for these inscriptions:

By Julia Balbilla,
when the August Hadrian
heard Memnon:
When he saw Hadrian, the king of all, before the rays
of the sun rose, he uttered his greeting as he was able.
And when Titan was driving through the air on his white horses—
when he held in shadow the second measure of hours—
like sonorous bronze Memnon sent out again
a piercing sound. And for a third time he sounded forth in greeting.
Then Emperor Hadrian himself warmly greeted
Memnon. And he left on stone for future generations

these writings that describe all he saw and heard.
It became clear to all that the gods love him.[35]

Julia Balbilla portrays the statue as honoring the emperor by singing out to him three times, weakly at first and more vigorously as the day warms. Hadrian in turn displays his esteem for the divine hero by having this poem inscribed upon it, which in its turn honors its composer, Julia Balbilla, which she acknowledges at the end of the second poem:

These words are mine, Balbilla, the pious.[36]

In the last two poems, Julia Balbilla requested that Memnon not keep silent before the queen Sabina, but that he sing for her also. She stressed the honor the queen deserved and Hadrian's anger should the statue persist in this silence. She ends the poems by affirming Hadrian's power and the tourist's delight in the statue's "song":

And Memnon, trembling before the power of the great Hadrian,
suddenly sang, which she heard with joy.[37]

WOMEN'S LOVE POETRY

By far, the theme of love formed the most prevalent subject in women's poetic writings. Love poetry exists from many ancient civilizations—Egyptian New Kingdom, circa 1300–1100 B.C.E.; Greece and Israel, seventh through third centuries B.C.E.; Rome, first century B.C.E. through third century C.E. Ancient love poetry by both women and men exhibited similar features—vivid, sensuous images, affinity with the natural world, open expression of erotic desire, and rich metaphoric descriptions of sexuality. The love poetry often ritually set erotic feelings and activities in honor of a goddess of love—Egyptian Hathor, Greek Aphrodite, Roman Venus. The love poetry also shows similarities with the sacred marriage hymns to Mesopotamian Inanna. While they express common erotic feelings, a crucial difference also exists. The poetry to Inanna celebrates her sacred union with her consort, presumably sung in a ritual setting with overt ritual and community-promoting dimensions. The love poetry, whatever ritual associations it may have had, was to, by, and about the personal desires of human lovers.

Egyptian New Kingdom

Although Egyptian love poetry is mostly anonymous, many poems speak in a woman's voice and were likely written by women. Displaying the features characteristic of love poetry, these poems sensuously paint the gardens that form the typical settings for love scenes, under or near a tree, with the garden's vivid appeal to all the senses. The poems portray trees as encouraging to lovers, evoking palm, sycamore, fig, and apple trees for this amatory, sensory pleasure. The images often evoke the tree's association with a goddess, customary throughout these ancient cultures.

Many of the poems in one sequence of Egyptian love poetry, called Songs of the Orchard, speak in the voice of the tree.

"Come and pass the time
where the young are gathering.
The meadow celebrates
its day …
Spend the day in delight …
reclining in my shade."[38]

By giving them human speech, the poems present the trees as freely offering their shade as welcome trysting places for young lovers.

Other poems use the natural world as settings for eroticized pursuits of fishing and hunting. One delights in sensuous, watery double-entendres.

Love, how I'd love to slip down to the pond,
 bathe with you close by on the bank.
Just for you I'd wear my new Memphis swimsuit,
  made of sheer linen, fit for a queen—
Come see how it looks in the water!

Couldn't I coax you to wade in with me?
 Let the cool creep slowly around us?
Then I'd dive deep down
  and come up for you dripping,
Let you fill your eyes
  with the little red fish that I'd catch.[39]

The narrator of the poem uses the occasion of the natural world to call up her own sensuous images of herself emerging dripping from the water in her new fitted linen swimsuit—no doubt sheer and clinging when wet. She then elaborates the imagery of caressing the fish to entice her lover to her.

Another poem uses imagery from hunting to express the woman's love as the girl describes herself as caught in her lover's trap.

Your love
ensnares me. I can't let it go.
 I shall take home my nets,
but what shall I tell my mother,
 to whom I return every day
laden with lovely birds?
 I set no traps today,
ensnared as I was by love.[40]

Thinking of love as a game, an endeavor like hunting that entails capture and pursuit, characterized much ancient love poetry, which Greek and Roman love poets greatly elaborated.

Much of the Egyptian love poetry related the aches of young lovers whose attraction to one another was forbidden by their parents, the social order, or their young age. It is tempting to think that these poems reflect a more permissive attitude to premarital, adolescent sexuality in a society that for much of its ancient history seemed more comfortable with female sexuality. But these may simply be the ancient equivalents to today's adolescent love songs. Whether revelatory of actual sexual practices or merely teenage mooning, these poems provide a glimpse into women's sexual feelings and how they expressed their erotic desires, whether or not they actually acted upon these desires.

One final Egyptian poem illustrates both delight in passion and one far rarer element—deep, lasting, affectionate marital love.

Your love, dear man, is as lovely to me.
As sweet soothing oil to the limbs of the restless,
 as clean ritual robes to the flesh of gods,
As fragrance of incense to one coming home
 hot from the smells of the street …

While unhurried days come and go,
Let us turn to each other in quiet affection,
 walk in peace to the edge of old age.
And I shall be with you each unhurried day,
 a woman given her one wish: to see
For a lifetime the face of her man.[41]

Although not as prevalent as the images of erotic love and desire, ancient literature and art do provide occasional examples of this deep love between a married couple. Other rare examples include the enduring love between Penelope and Odysseus in Homer's *Odyssey* and in the representations of the dead couple on Etruscan sarcophagi and tomb paintings. An Egyptian painting at Deir-el-Medina, of a couple listening to a harper visually illustrates the sentiments of long-lasting love this poem presents (Figure 9.1).

The Biblical Song of Songs

Commonly acknowledged to have been written by a woman, the biblical Song of Songs displays similarities to both Mesopotamian sacred erotic poetry and Egyptian love poetry. A collection of oral traditional songs, the poem's origin may date back to its dramatic time, during the rule of the Israelite King Solomon, about 1000 B.C.E, although it was not written down until the fifth century B.C.E. Its authorship is often attributed to King Solomon due to a misunderstanding of the song's subtitle, in Hebrew, *Shir ha Shirim asher l'Schlomo*, "The Song of Songs which is to/for Solomon." Somehow this subtitle gave rise to the mistaken interpretation that *asher l'Solomon* meant that the poem was written by, not for, Solomon, which has resulted in the conventional naming of this book as the "Song of Solomon." However, since one meaning of the word *asher* is "praise," the phrase would more correctly be rendered as "The Song of Songs [which I sing] in honor of Solomon." This translation accords the opening of the biblical book with ancient

Figure 9.1 Couple listening to Harper, Ramesside tomb of Inherkha. Deir-el-Medina # 359. Photograph by Dr. L. H. Lesko, as published in *The Remarkable Women of Ancient Egypt* by Barbara Lesko (Berkeley, CA: B.C. Scribe Publications, 1978). By permission of Dr. Barbara Lesko.

Mediterranean praise poetry, which similarly highlighted the poet's *singing* their song in honor of the king or hero being celebrated.

Several features underscore the poem's female authorship. The poem's principal voice is female, which serves as the focal point uniting all poetic elements, even when the male voice is speaking. Female perspectives permeate the poem in ways not seen in male-authored texts, especially in the poem's repeated, extensive descriptions of the male lover. Finally, the poem displays a deep grounding in a female-oriented world through the prominent woman's voice and her frequent appeals to the Daughters of Jerusalem, the chorus-like community of women the protagonist addresses.

The Song presents its love poetry in a loosely arranged dramatic text centering on the dialogue between the two lovers. It begins with the sensuous evocation of her lover's kisses by the female persona who then identifies herself:

Let him kiss me with the kisses of his mouth!
For your love is better than wine,
your anointing oils are fragrant,
your name is perfume poured out …

I am black and beautiful,
O daughters of Jerusalem …
Do not gaze at me because I am dark,
because the sun has gazed on me.

My mother's sons were angry with me;
they made me keeper of the vineyards,
but my own vineyard I have not kept![42]

The poem's narrator first imagines the luscious erotic sweetness of her lover—his kisses, touch, even name. She acknowledges her dark complexion, which results from toiling in the vineyards, and asks the women not to look at her as different for that reason. Although women worked outdoors more commonly than the Song suggests, the poem portrays her field labor as a punishment. The chief consequence of this outdoor work distinguishes her appearance from the typically pale look of women who remained indoors, the visage that set the standards for feminine beauty. At the same time, her calling herself black has led some to identify her with the Queen of Sheba. The Song would then describe her famous liaison with King Solomon, who is named several times in the poem, as both a king and a shepherd. If this association is valid, then the Song's heritage would derive from the area of Ethiopia, which makes its connection to Egyptian love poetry all the stronger.

The Song's images evoke the sensuousness of the springtime landscape, both wild and cultivated. Like the Egyptian love poetry, the Song of Songs describes the lover's entry into a sensuous garden, one filled with fountains of flowing water and orchards of trees teeming with pomegranates, select fruits, spices and incense, and it expands the significance of the tree for the lovers' union:

As an apple tree among the trees of the wood,
so is my beloved among young men.
With great delight I sat in his shadow,
and his fruit was sweet to my taste.[43]

Now the tree serves also as a metaphor for the delight of being with the lover, enjoying the fruit of his kisses and lovemaking.

Images from both the natural and human constructed worlds permeate the lovers' descriptions of each other, which the king's praise of his female beloved vividly illustrates:

How beautiful you are, my love,
how very beautiful!
Your eyes are doves …
Your cheeks are like halves of a pomegranate
behind your veil.
Your neck is like the tower of David …
Your two breasts are like two fawns,
twins of a gazelle,
that feed among the lilies.[44]

Amidst the profusion of sweet fruits and gentle animals, the comparison of the woman's neck with the tower of David stands out sharply, perhaps suggesting her proud bearing.

Here and in the woman's description of her beloved the poet seamlessly blends delightful, alluring images from both the natural and human worlds, which function harmoniously to support the lovers.

As if to confirm the text's female authorship, only the woman voices her desire for her beloved, while images replete with sexual double entendres evoke graphic sensual visions:

My beloved thrust his hand into the opening,
and my inmost being yearned for him.
I arose to open to my beloved,
and my hands dripped with myrrh,
my fingers with liquid myrrh,
upon the handles of the bolt.
I opened to my beloved.[45]

The poem, however, does not fulfill immediate sexual expectations, but elaborates the mutual praise and sexual innuendoes.

Before it ends, the Song of Songs expresses the inextinguishable fiery power of love.

Its flashes are flashes of fire,
a raging flame.
Many waters cannot quench love,
neither can floods drown it.[46]

To many, the Song of Songs is an anomaly among the books of the Bible. The name God never appears, and its focus on erotic passion seems contrary to the principal image the biblical texts project of a patriarchal, asexual divinity. The most evident similarities, in both language and imagery, are with Mesopotamian sacred marriage poetry, where the sexual union of the king with the priestess representing the goddess Inanna/Ishtar assures the fertility of the earth, of animals, and of humankind. Although nothing identifies the woman in the Song as a priestess, the poem's depiction of the couple's union as a "marriage" and its pervasive evocation of the fertility of the natural world underscore this association.

The meaning of this openly sensual writing within the religious biblical corpus has raised many questions. The Song of Songs profoundly challenges the prevalent societal views about erotic passion. By extensively praising the joys of sexuality and desire—not only as a formal duty married men must fulfill for their wives—the Song opposes the very basis of conventional biblical sexual mores. The other books of the Bible endorse the expectation of women's strict marital fidelity and reveal severe punishments for female adultery. But the sexuality evoked in the Song is not within societal norms since there is no indication that the lovers are married.

These anomalies have led both Jewish and Christian theologians to interpret the Song as an allegory for the people's love for God, arguing that human passion serves as a metaphor for spiritual love—an interesting development of the plaiting of eroticism with the pursuit of wisdom noted among the Greek philosophers. Even if this interpretation were valid—which seems a strain given the Song's open, vivid sensuality—it still leaves the question of why the spiritual love of God would be expressed only in this book in such erotic terms. This portrayal of sensual erotic love stands in striking contradiction to the depictions elsewhere in the Bible of humans standing in fear or awe of the supreme divinity.

If the Song of Songs holds a sacred meaning, it is dramatically distinct from that of the rest of the Bible. Its sensibilities, like those of Mesopotamian, Egyptian, and Greek erotic poetry, emerge in the open celebration of love, erotic desire, and sexual pleasure in a world where nature and city and male and female stand in harmony, not in opposition. The poetry of these other Mediterranean cultures could openly proclaim the blessings of love and desire in honor of their goddesses of eroticism Inanna, Hathor, or Aphrodite. The biblical Song of Songs reflects those same praises in a world where, even while omitting any direct reference to deity, nevertheless sings its praises in honor of a divine concept of love and sensuality in tune with that of the Mediterranean cultures surrounding it. As a female-authored text, the Song demonstrates the correspondences in women's sensual perceptions across the diversity of the ancient Mediterranean world.

Sappho

The sensuous images in the Egyptian and biblical love poetry find a florescence in the first recorded female Greek poet, Sappho, who describes the sanctuary where they await the goddess of erotic desire Aphrodite with now familiar, pansensory appeal:

Come to me here from Crete to this holy
sanctuary—your delightful grove of apple-trees,
where incense perfumes the altars.
Cold water gurgles through the apple branches,
roses shade the grove
and sleep drifts down from shimmering leaves.[47]

As before, a shady grove of apple trees, the sounds and touch of cold flowing water, the heady fragrance of ritual incense, the natural perfume of roses, and the tingle of cool breezes characterize the goddess of love's sanctuary, a place to delight the senses and relax the body and mind. Sappho's poems often reveal a ritual dimension in the occasions for their composition and performance, and many refer directly to young women's ritual choral song and dance groups.

Sappho's love poetry spans a range of erotic subjects. Many honor Aphrodite or the male deity of erotic passion, Eros. These vividly describe the passionate sensations of love through the activity of Eros, who causes lovers to go weak in the knees. In one fragment the sound and rhythm of the Greek words replicate the mountain wind rush of Eros' power:

Eros shook me to the quick,
like the mountain wind swooping down the oak trees.[48]

Another fragment, unusual among Sappho's poems for expressing passionate adolescent heterosexual desire, attributes this power to Aphrodite:

Sweet mother, I am unable to weave my web;
Slender Aphrodite has conquered me with desire for a boy.[49]

Other fragments recall the woman who has left Sappho's poetic circle with both tenderness and the intensity of feeling that characterized women's affections.

" ... I simply wish I were dead!"
She left me weeping,
"Sappho, I leave you completely against my will."
And I answered her,
"Go in good cheer and remember
me, for you know the bonds we formed,
the beautiful things we shared.
You wore many woven garlands made of roses and crocuses,
you lavished on much flowery scent, like a queen,
and on a soft bed
you expressed your tender desire.[50]

In this poem Sappho's sensuous images underscore the ways women expressed their mutual love in playful delights and tender lovemaking. The lines hint at what other sources also portrayed—Sappho was the poetic and musical educator of groups of adolescent girls during their period of *partheneia* before they married. Many of Sappho's poetic fragments evoke the depth of feelings the girls shared with one another during this time, often recalling these feelings after the girl has already left to get married.

In contrast to the heterosexual emphasis in love poetry from most other cultures, but typical of most ancient Greek erotic poetry by both women and men, Sappho's love poetry was primarily homoerotic, celebrating women's love associations. Because it was an accepted part of cultural practice, this homoeroticism was not regarded as being in opposition to heteroerotic love and desire, since marriage was a prerequisite for everyone's status as an adult, male and female. Rather, this acknowledgment of homoerotic desire reflects the fundamentally gender separate, homosocial settings for expressing affection, love, desire, sexuality, and creativity in ancient Greece. While the word "lesbian" with a small "l" is commonly used today to refer to female homosexuals, in antiquity, "Lesbian" with a capital "L" identified someone from the island of Lesbos. Thus Sappho alluded to other Lesbian singers, including her well-known male contemporary poet from Lesbos, Alkaios.

However deep and long-lasting the women's feelings for each other may have been, these were not the only goal of the women's affections. These poetic verses illustrate that the feelings the women shared characterized their stage of adolescence from which all would normatively proceed to marriage. Our incomplete knowledge about ancient women's lives does not indicate whether women continued their adolescent friendships into their adult, married lives. Given the homosocial nature of ancient Greek society, some were probably able to maintain their friendships and loving associations. However, for the women remembered in Sappho's poems, who have left not only the circle of adolescent girls but also the island of Lesbos to live their married lives elsewhere, maintaining these friendships would have been more difficult. It is here that Sappho's poems may have provided the threads of connection in writing not directly possible in their lives. As she herself states, "remember me and the bonds we formed."

Battle imagery emerges in Sappho's one complete remaining poem. Contrasting with the tender remembrance of the above lines, the poet now appeals for Aphrodite's help in her pursuit of her present amatory quest in a women's game of love. The poem begins in typical hymnal form, as Sappho invokes Aphrodite and describes the goddess's characteristics. As was also customary, Sappho grounds her particular pleas on the goddess's previous benefices. Sappho then proceeds to express humorously the game of love and Aphrodite's former part in it.

Immortal Aphrodite, intricate deceit-weaving
child of Zeus, I beseech you, Lady,
come, if ever before you heard my voice,
and asked why again I called,
"Whom should I entice again into your affections,
Sappho?
For if she flees, soon she'll pursue you;
if she will not accept your gifts, soon she'll give them;
and if she doesn't love you, soon she'll be loving,
even if she's unwilling."
So come to me now too,
whatever my heart desires,
accomplish it. And you will once again
be my battle ally.[51]

In the goddess's response to Sappho's appeal, Aphrodite assures Sappho she will be successful in her love pursuit, even if her beloved presently rejects her advances. While this line can reflect the lover's conquest of an unwilling beloved, it more importantly highlights the depth of Aphrodite's power, who can transform the person fleeing unwanted amorous attention into one who now chases her former pursuer. As the Song of Songs portrays, the power of love is invincible, sweeping all other images before it.

The final line of Sappho's poem brings out an analogy found in other Greek love poetry, that the game of love corresponds to battle maneuvers. The Mesopotamian goddess Inanna encompassed the spectrum of love and war as elemental passions that engaged people's lives. While some of this elemental force may still be operative, Sappho's language, "battle ally," emphasizes the similarity of the two as scheme-driven activities. The poetry portrays the game of love as the pursuit of a target, which requires strategy, allure, and deceit, and where winning is a conquest.

Written for a different purpose, Sappho's wedding songs, *epithalamia,* celebrated both the bride and the groom. In general, the songs sung on the wedding night were quite bawdy, as friends of both the bride and groom raucously cheered the couple on their first night's lovemaking. One source suggests that one purpose of the women's songs was to cover the bride's screams at her first intercourse. Sappho's wedding poems often humorously magnify the groom's size:

The doorkeeper's feet are seven fathoms long.
It took five ox-hides to make his sandals,
which ten cobblers toiled to make.[52]

Another fragment speaks of the groom in gentler imagery, comparing him to a slender sapling.

The fragments that address the bride often refer to her loss of virginity, one humorously and in two voices:

"Virginity, virginity, where have you gone away to, leaving me?"
"I'll no longer come to you, no longer will I come."[53]

Other fragments evoke this loss in poignant metaphors:

Just like the sweet apple that reddens on the top-most branch,
the very highest tiptop branch, and the apple pickers have forgotten it.
No, they haven't forgotten it, they couldn't reach it.[54]

These fragments express the sense of loss a girl experiences at marriage. However, this is not the focus of the wedding songs.

Other fragments tenderly praise the happy wedding couple on this joyous day.

Fortunate bridegroom, here is the marriage you prayed for,
you have the girl you prayed for.
[To the bride:]
Your shape is lovely, and your eyes gentle like
honey, Eros pours down over your beautiful face
Aphrodite has superbly honored you.[55]

As seen in Chapter 2, Aphrodite embodied the sexually mature qualities which she bestowed on the bride. The bride in turn was now regarded as epitomizing Aphrodite's qualities of beauty and sexual allure. Other fragments also congratulate the groom for the excellence of the woman he is marrying.

Finally, a one-line fragment must reflect the characteristic ending of most wedding poetry:

Farewell, bride, farewell, honored groom, many.[56]

And so the wedding poems fittingly conclude with good wishes to the newly married couple.

Because of Sappho's importance in the development of ancient Greek and Roman lyric poetry, and because of her continued significance to our modern appreciation of ancient culture, we can rightly conclude our examination of her poetry with a farewell to her great artistry in her own words. We may justly apply to Sappho the image of one four-word fragment that apparently addresses the evening star: "the most beautiful of all stars."[57]

Nossis

About three centuries later, from the opposite end of Greek habitation, Nossis considered herself Sappho's descendant as a composer of erotic love poetry, making her views explicit in one epigram.

Nothing is sweeter than erotic love. All other delights are
second. I even spit the honey out from my mouth.
This Nossis claims: whoever Kypris has not loved
does not even know what kind of flowers roses are.[58]

Although little of Nossis' poetry remains, as seen above, several epigrams accompanied young women's portraits set up in Aphrodite's temple. One epigram provides a sexually explicit reason for these dedications:

Let us go to the temple to look at the statue of
Aphrodite, how it is intricately worked in gold.
Polyarkhis erected it, with the great wealth she
gained from the splendor of her own body.[59]

As previously noted, *hetairai* might be both educated and wealthy. As this epigram shows, like other individuals in the society, *hetairai* expressed their appreciation for their successes with dedications to the gods appropriate to their means. And they would have formed a ready audience for erotic poetry. Perhaps characterizing the lyric activity of such poets as Sappho and Nossis is the early third century terracotta figurine of a woman playing the kithara, which she may have used to accompany her poetic verses (Figure 9.2).

Sulpicia 1

Only a few erotic poems by two Roman female poets, both named Sulpicia, survive, while sources name a few other poets otherwise unknown. As many as 11 poems may remain by the first Sulpicia, who possibly wrote in her late teens in the second half of the first century B.C.E. Through her uncle Messalla, a major patron of Rome's premier poets, Sulpicia may have enjoyed the privilege of participating in his literary salons. Her poems follow the pattern of Roman male love elegy established by Catullus by presenting a narrative overview of the tumultuous course of her love across several poems.

Roman love elegy embroidered the game of love into an elaborate art—the elite male poets described hot, steamy affairs with highly educated, elite married women. The poets spoke of themselves as enslaved to their mistresses, whom they called their *domina,* "mistress." Like a master over a slave, the poems describe the *domina* as enjoying full command over the men, who are so stricken with passion that they are willing to endure the most abject humiliations. These images deliberately juxtaposed the presumed gender and class relations of the society for purposes of erotic pursuit. The poets emphasized their beloved's erudition by referring to her as *docta puella,* "learned girl," and endowing her with a literary pseudonym. Catullus called his beloved Lesbia, alluding to that island's acclaimed poet, Sappho.

Sulpicia presented comparable scenarios of the game of love that she experienced from a distinctly female perspective. She called her beloved Cerinthus, from the Greek word for wax, referring to the wax writing tablets poets used. The short sequence of her poems begins with appeals to different deities to protect her beloved. Dedicated to the Roman war god Mars on the first of March, his month, it highlights her participation in the ritual chorus that was celebrating the god's day. At the same time, Sulpicia immediately sets the poem in the context of the mythological love affair between the Roman goddess of love Venus and Mars, and for most of it she tantalizingly describes her own erotic appeal.

From Sulpicia's eyes,
 fierce Love lights his twin torches.
And she, whatever she does, wherever she goes,
 Allure stealthily adorns her and follows behind her.
If she loosens her hair or if she arranges it, she sets hearts aflame.

Let her possess whatever the wealthy Arab, who tills the scented crop,
 reaps from his fragrant fields,
and whatever jewels the black Indian, close to the waters of Dawn,
 gathers from the red shore. [60]

Sulpicia's description of her sensual allure, the erotic passion radiating from her eyes, clad in expensive robes, and adorned in exquisite, imported jewels and perfumes, echoes the sensual adornment of the goddess before the sacred marriage rituals in Mesopotamian and Greek hymns. In the differing cultural and literary milieu of Latin love elegy, Sulpicia likewise alluringly adorns herself in a ritual context before the presentation of her game of love. Just as Sappho invokes Aphrodite as her battle ally to help her in her love pursuits, it may be fitting that Sulpicia sets the ritual context for her adornment in honor of the god of war Mars, honored for his military might. If Sulpicia's poetic description validly reflects actual practice, Mars may also have been worshipped from a very different perspective as the lover of the goddess of love, Venus.

The rest of her poems describe Sulpicia's feelings for Cerinthus at different stages of their affair. In one, after expressing her gratitude to Venus for bringing her together with her beloved, Sulpicia joyously proclaims their first lovemaking:

Love has come at last, and such a love as I
 should be more shamed to hide than to reveal ...
The sin is sweet, to mask it for fear of shame is bitter.
I'm proud we've joined, each worthy of the other. [61]

Sulpicia expresses both her wish to proclaim her love openly and her awareness that social proprieties render such open declarations impossible. Although as the poem's persona Sulpicia finds nothing wrong with expressing her sexual passion, the society will take a harsher stance. She then defies this social condemnation, exulting in the joys of their mutual love and dismissing those who would denounce her as themselves untouched by love's passion.

In the course of their passion Sulpicia voices a lover's delights and fears, and like the male poets she frequently incorporates mythological allusions. In one she fearfully imagines Cerinthus in the woods hunting a boar, and she appeals to the wild animal to spare her beloved. Although Diana, goddess of the hunt, led her lover to the woods, Sulpicia invokes Amor, Love, to protect him. After questioning what madness would induce someone to track savage beasts and get their tender legs torn up by brambles, Sulpicia imagines herself accompanying Cerinthus on the hunt:

Oh, Cerinthus, just so I can wander with you,
 I myself will carry the twisted nets through the mountains ...
Then the forests would delight me, light of my life, if I can lie
 with you in front of the hunting nets themselves.

Any woman who secretly sneaks up on my beloved,
 let her fall, to be torn to pieces, among fierce beasts.
But you leave the desire for hunting to your parent,
 and quickly come back to my embrace.[62]

Imagining her beloved on a hunt, Sulpicia fears for his physical safety, envisions the woods as a place for their lovemaking, and then fears for the opportunities the hunt presents him for other sexual liaisons. Her concern that Cerinthus' delicate skin not be torn by the dangers of the hunt turns to savagery as Sulpicia prays for wild beasts to tear apart any rival for his love.

Several poems revolve around the importance of birthdays. In one Sulpicia praises the day of Cerinthus' birth:

When you were born the Fates sang of a new form of love's slavery
 for women and granted you proud realms of power.
I burn more than all other women. This thrills me, Cerinthus, that I am ablaze,
 if you burn with a like fire sparked by me.
Do not be unfair, Venus; either let each of us submit equally
 in bondage to love's slavery, or remove my own bonds.[63]

Similarly, in another poem addressed to Juno as goddess of birthdays, which she begins by calling herself *docta puella*, Sulpicia declares that both she and her beloved equally merit to be enslaved by the bonds of love.

Sulpicia thus subtly alters the male poets' scenarios of being the slaves to their learned mistresses' bonds of love. She does not automatically reverse these gendered associations, which would result in replicating the unequal gender dynamics of the society. Instead, she identifies herself both as the learned mistress to whom the male poets dedicated their love, and, by being equally worthy of being held by love's chains, as the talented poet who can describe in verse form the intensity of erotic passion she as well as he experiences.

Two other short birthday poems express an adolescent's impatience with birthday plans made for her without her consultation and contrary to her desires.

My hateful birthday is here, which I'll be celebrating miserably,
 out in the boring country—without Cerinthus!
What is more exciting than the city? Is a country place with a chilly river
 running through it suitable for a girl?[64]

Her dreaded country outing rescinded, in the next poem Sulpicia jubilates over getting to celebrate her birthday in Rome with her beloved.

These two poems swing from melancholy to joy as the adolescent persona is first denied and then receives what she wants for her birthday, mood swings that also characterize the erratic course of her love. The final poem in the sequence expresses Sulpicia's regret that Cerinthus may no longer love her.

I wish, my light, that I was still your passionate desire
 as I thought I was just a few days ago.[65]

Sulpicia's few poems exhibit the same wit and interplay between erotic passion and poetry as emerges in the male elegiac poetry. Even if she composed this poetry in her teens, it does not prove she enjoyed any greater sexual freedom in her life than other elite Roman girls. On the contrary, several poems indicate that she remained firmly under her uncle's tutelage, and her desire to proclaim her love openly was strongly couched in her awareness of the social disapproval she would incur if she made her love publicly known.

It is probably safer to view Sulpicia's poems as expressions of adolescent desire that she voiced in the medium of Latin love elegy established by the poets in her uncle's literary patronage, without any implication of what these poems say about her actual life. Through these few poems Sulpicia shows not only her poetic ability to employ this verse form, but even more so her superb talent at being able to adapt this genre of male poetry to her distinctively female voice.

Sulpicia 2

Because of her use of a rare word, two lines of a poem by a second Sulpicia who lived in the late first century C.E. have been preserved. Beginning with the later commentator's introduction, these two lines state:

By *cadurcum* the female genital is understood, since it is the covering of the female genital. Or as others claim, it is a strip on which a bed is stretched. Whence Sulpicia says

If, after the straps of my bed frame have been put back in place,
it would show me lying naked with Calenus.[66]

Known as a writer of satirical and erotic verse, both the double entendre of her language use and her graphic punch line display the raucous nature of her poetry.

At the same time, two epigrams written presumably after her death about 96 C.E. assert that Sulpicia focused her erotic passion on her husband, Calenus. One proclaims this conjugal love as the principle of Sulpicia's verse:

Let all girls read Sulpicia
 who desire to please one man alone;
let all husbands read Sulpicia
 who desire to please one wife alone ...

she teaches chaste and proper loves,
games, delights, frivolities.
 One who judges her songs rightly,
will say no woman is naughtier,
will say no woman is holier.[67]

If the second Sulpicia framed her portrayal of erotic passion in the context of conjugal love, she would be virtually unique among Greek and Roman love poets to do so. In this regard her poem would approach most closely the Egyptian love poem honoring the married couple, and it provides another rare voice extolling the delights of marital love. Sulpicia is also the only known ancient Greek or Roman female writer of satiric verse. As such, she may be tweaking both the genre of Latin love poetry and the social censors by projecting images of her erotic passion through the love shared by a married couple. In either case, these two lines of bold and possibly satiric language offer the merest glimpse of how much has been lost.

Figure 9.2 Woman playing a kithara, terracotta. Aigina, Greece, ca. 275 B.C.E. Erich Lessing/Art Resource, NY, Louvre, Paris, France.

Epilogue

With these polyphonic women's poetic voices echoing in our ears, we conclude our excursion through the rich, diverse tapestry of women's lives in these four pivotal ancient Mediterranean cultures that have proved fundamental to the cultural development of the West and elsewhere. We have seen ways women from all these cultures and time periods participated in all social arenas, prominently emerging in their societies' domestic, religious, economic, governmental, intellectual, creative, and even military spheres. Enjoying deep cultural support for their roles, women's activities contributed to the formation of their own confident identities that empowered them to be active agents in their own lives. Often not content with merely accepting social limitations, many women pushed against the boundaries of their societies' restrictions and applied their intelligence and creativity to improve their own lives and to contribute to their communities. A few even achieved historical recognition for their endeavors. While elite women could take advantage of greater material opportunities, women of lower social-economic classes and slave women would have had to struggle with all their mental, emotional, spiritual, and physical resources to survive. At the same time, social customs and marital arrangements based on financial or political considerations might restrict elite women's activities in ways not expected of women of other classes. These contrasting features reveal repeatedly the complexity of women's lives in antiquity.

As seen in the progression from the earlier periods of Egyptian and Mesopotamian history to the developments in Greece and Rome millennia later, in general women received greater cultural valuation and enjoyed greater social standing in earlier times than in later. This diminishment over time is closely tied to the expansion of patriarchal ideas in ancient perceptions and social systems. Awareness of these ancient historical shifts has long been familiar to scholars of women in ancient Egypt and Mesopotamia, but it differs sharply from most modern historical approaches, which, based primarily on recent European history or on the restricted lives of women in ancient Greece and Rome, regard women's positions in every past culture as having been far more inferior and restricted than those of many contemporary women.

Figure 10.1 Three women at toilette, red-figured kylix (cup). Etruscan, Italy, ca. 350 B.C.E. The British Museum/Art Resource, NY, London, Great Britain.

But the picture of our female forebears is far more complex and dynamic than this simple linear progression suggests. While most of us would probably not trade our modern lives, with their many amenities and opportunities, for those lived by most women throughout antiquity, we enrich our own understanding, both of women in the past and of ourselves today, by recognizing the ways ancient women actively shaped their own lives within their society's social framework. The desire to determine one's own life is neither a modern invention nor do contemporary women have to totally reinvent the wheel of female-empowered identity. While much knowledge may have been deeply buried over the millennia, the sparks of women's intelligence, creativity, and resourceful capabilities have not been lost. The indestructible thread from our ancestresses is still being spun into present and future generations of proud, vibrant Daughters of Gaia.

Glossary

abortifacient   Abortion causing.

aiskhrologia   Greek, "shame talk," feature of fertility rites.

amenorrhea   Lack of menstruation.

androcentric   From Greek, "focusing on men."

archetype   The original model for something; for example, Isis is the archetype of the nursing mother.

aretê Greek,   "excellence" or "virtue."

emmenagogue   Promoting flow of the menses.

erotophobic   Fearful or scornful of sensuality and sexuality.

etiology   Cause or origin, as in etiological myths that give the origin of the seasons.

heteroerotic   Sensual and sexual enjoyment between opposite-sex individuals.

homoerotic   Sensual and sexual enjoyment between same-sex individuals.

homosocial   Same-sex environment as for domestic activities, education, or religious practices.

iconography   The symbolic, cultural meaning of artistic images.

kore, **sg.,** *korai*, **pl.**   Greek, "daughter" or "girl," often refers to statues of young women.

kourotrophos   Greek, "child-nourisher," often refers to images of nursing mothers.

ma'at   Egyptian, "order," referring to the principal order of the universe and of society.

matriarchy   From Greek, "rule by mothers"; historically, societies where women's concerns are central to the functioning of the society, often complementary and egalitarian in gender roles.

205

menarche   Onset of menstruation.

misogynist, -ic   Someone who hates women.

monotheism   Belief in one deity.

mystery religion   Secret, ecstatic rites that offer initiates blessedness in this world and the next.

naditum   Akkadian, a certain order of priestess dedicated to the deity.

Panhellenic   "All Greek."

pantheon   Greek, "all the gods"—the assemblage of the important deities.

partheneia   Greek, "maidenhood," a girl's adolescence between menarche and marriage.

parthenos   Greek, "maiden," an unmarried, adolescent girl, usually presexual.

patriarchy   From Greek, "rule by fathers"; historically, societies where men have imposed their authority over women in all aspects of social endeavor.

patrician   Member of the Roman aristocratic elite.

peplos   Greek, "robe," "dress."

plebeian   Member of the Roman common people.

polis, sg., *poleis*, pl.   Greek, "city" referring to the sovereign Greek city-states.

polytheism   Belief in many deities.

prehistoric   Referring to the time periods before the introduction of writing.

puberty   Physical changes that signify maturation into a fertile adult.

sistrum   The hand-held percussive instrument of Egyptian Hathor.

syncretism   The merging together of different religious beliefs.

univira   Latin, "of one man"—the Roman ideal of a woman staying faithful to one husband.

Notes

INTRODUCTION

1. Except where otherwise noted, all translations from ancient Greek and Latin throughout the book are mine. B.V.

2. I present the value of this comparison for ancient women's lives in my article, "The Primal Mind: Using Native American Models for the Study of Women in Ancient Greece" (under the name Zweig), 1993, which looks at how indigenous American cultures conceptualize women's identity and roles in ways radically different from Western perceptions.

CHAPTER ONE

1. Marilou Awiakta, *Selu: Seeking the Corn-Mother's Wisdom* (Golden, CO: Fulcrum, 1993), 9.

2. Paula Gunn Allen, *The Sacred Hoop: Recovering the Feminine in American Indian Traditions* (Boston: Beacon Press, 1986) 14.

3. Barbara Lesko, *The Great Goddesses of Egypt* (Norman: University of Oklahoma Press, 1999), 57.

4. Ibid., 40.

5. James B. Pritchard, ed., *The Ancient Near East: An Anthology of Texts and Pictures,* vol. 1 (Princeton, NJ: Princeton University Press, 1958), 232.

6. Ibid., 232.

7. Betty De Shong Meador, *Inanna, Lady of the Largest Heart: Poems of the Sumerian High Priestess Enheduanna* (Austin: University of Texas Press, 2001), 102, 107.

CHAPTER TWO

1. Diane Wolkstein and Samuel N. Kramer, *INANNA: Queen of Heaven and Earth* (New York: HarperCollins, 1983), 37.

2. Aristophanes, *Lysistrata,* lines 642–47.

3. "Homeric Hymn to Demeter," lines 480–82.

4. Aristophanes, *Frogs,* lines 440–46.

CHAPTER THREE

1. Mary Ellen Waithe, ed., *A History of Women Philosophers: Ancient Women Philosophers, 600 B.C.–500 A.D.,* vol. 1 (Dordrecth: Nijhoff,1987), 16, translation by Vicki Lynn Harper.

2. Sarah B. Pomeroy, *Spartan Women* (Oxford: Oxford University Press, 2002), 37–42.

3. Homer, *Iliad,* Book 3, lines 156–58.

4. Paula Gunn Allen, *The Sacred Hoop: Recovering the Feminine in American Indian Traditions* (Boston: Beacon Press, 1986), 227.

5. Homer, *Odyssey,* Book 5, lines 118–20.

CHAPTER FOUR

1. Gay Robins, *Women in Ancient Egypt* (Cambridge, MA: Harvard University Press, 1993), 82, quoting J. F. Borghouts, *Ancient Egyptian Magical Texts* (Leiden: Brill, 1978), 39–40, no. 62.

2. Karen Nemet-Nejat, "Women in Ancient Mesopotamia," in *Women's Roles in Ancient Civilizations: A Reference Guide.* ed. Bella Vivante (Westport, CT: Greenwood, 1999), 92.

3. Mary R. Lefkowitz and Maureen B. Fant, eds., *Women's Life in Greece & Rome: A Source Book in Translation,* 2nd ed. (Baltimore: Johns Hopkins University Press, 1992), 255, excerpt 356.

4. Ibid., 263, excerpt 365.

5. Ibid., 263, excerpt 366.

CHAPTER FIVE

1. *The Epic of Gilgamesh,* trans. N. K. Sandars (London: Penguin, 1960), 102.

2. "Homeric Hymn to Demeter," lines 208–9.

3. Homer, *Iliad,* Book 3 lines 125–242.

4. Homer, *Odyssey,* Book 2 lines 115–22.

CHAPTER SIX

1. Norman H. Russell, "Two Circles," in Geary Hobson, ed., *The Remembered Earth: An Anthology of Contemporary Indigenous American Literature,* Albuquerque, NM, 1981, p. 123.

2. Miriam Lichtheim, *Ancient Egyptian Literature: A Book of Readings,* vol. 2 (Berkeley: University of California Press, 1976), 28–29.

3. All Biblical citations in *The New Oxford Annotated Bible,* ed. B. M. Metzger and R. E. Murphy (New York: Oxford University Press, 1991).

4. Plutarch, "Life of Mark Antony," in *Makers of Rome: Nine Lives by Plutarch,* trans. Ian Scott-Kilvert (New York: Penguin, 1965), 293.

CHAPTER SEVEN

1. Samuel Eliot Morison, *Christopher Columbus, Mariner,* (New York: Little, Brown and Company, 1942), 17.

2. Abby Wettan Kleinbaum, *The War Against the Amazons* (New York: McGraw-Hill Book Company, 1983), 118.

3. Betty De Shong Meador, *Inanna, Lady of the Largest Heart: Poems of the Sumerian High Priestess Enheduanna* (Austin: University of Texas Press, 2001), 91.

4. Ibid., 101.

5. Ibid., 118–19.

6. Ibid., 92.

7. Judges 5:24, 26–27 in *The New Oxford Annotated Bible,* ed. B. M. Metzger and R. E. Murphy (New York: Oxford University Press, 1991).

CHAPTER EIGHT

1. Aisara, *On Human Nature,* 1.357.2–6.

2. Periktione II, *On Wisdom,* 3.87.5–10. (Thesleff, 146).

3. Periktione I, *On the Harmony of Women,* 4.688–689.3. (Thesleff, 142–43).

4. Mary Ellen Waithe, ed., *A History of Women Philosophers: Ancient Women Philosophers, 600 B.C.–500 A.D.,* vol. 1 (Dordrecht: Nijhoff, 1987), 15.

5. Theano II, "Letter to Rhodope." (Thesleff, 200).

6. Phintys, *On the Moderation of Women,* 4.589.3–11. (Thesleff, 152).

7. Ibid., 4.590.3–7. (Thesleff, 152).

8. Periktione I, *On the Harmony of Women,* 4.689.3–5. (Thesleff, 143).

9. Ibid., 4.691–692.3, 7–8, 693.1–4. (Thesleff, 144).

10. Theano II, "Letter to Nikostrate," section 6. (Thesleff, 199-200)

11. Phintys, *On the Moderation of Women,* 4.591.13–15. (Thesleff, 154)

12. Plato, *Symposium,* 203D5–7.

13. Diogenes Laertius, 6.97.

14. Palantine Anthology, 7.413.

CHAPTER NINE

1. Homer, *Iliad,* Book 6 lines 357–58.

2. Sappho, frag. 195. Standard references to numbering of Sappho's fragments, as in *Greek Lyric I: Sappho and Alcaeus,* ed. and trans. David A. Campbell, Loeb Classical Library (Cambridge, MA: Harvard University Press, 1982).

3. Gr. Anth. 7.718. References are to the ancient collections known as the Greek Anthology and the Palatine Anthology. See *The Greek Anthology,* 5 vols., ed. and trans. W. R. Paton, Loeb Classical Library (Cambridge, MA: Harvard University Press, 1916–18).

4. Gr. Anth. 9.190.

5. I. M. Plant, trans., *Women Writers of Ancient Greece and Rome: An Anthology* (Norman: University of Oklahoma, 2004), 31.

6. Sappho, frag. 5.

7. Gr. Anth. 6.273.

8. Gr. Anth. 6.265.

9. Gr. Anth. 9.144.

10. Maya Angelou, "Prayer," *Parade Sunday Newspaper Magazine,* December 25, 2005, p. 5.

11. Sappho, frag. 70.

12. Korinna, frag. 655.1–5. References to Korinna's poetry may be found in *Greek Lyric IV: Bacchylides, Corinna, and Others*, ed. and trans. David A. Campbell, Loeb Classical Library (Cambridge, MA: Harvard University Press, 1992).

13. Korinna, frag. 655.9–22.

14. Betty De Shong Meador, *Inanna, Lady of the Largest Heart: Poems of the Sumerian High Priestess Enheduanna* (Austin: University of Texas Press, 2001), 171, 174, selections. The different spellings of Enkheduanna's name reflect different ways of transcribing the ancient texts.

15. Ibid.,174–75.

16. Exodus 15:20–21.

17. Judges 5:7.

18. Judges 5:12.

19. Sappho, frag. 137.

20. Sappho, frag. 50.

21. Sappho, frag. 132.

22. Gr. Anth. 6.353.

23. Gr. Anth. 9.605.

24. Gr. Anth. 9.604.

25. Gr. Anth. 7.486.

26. Gr. Anth. 7.649.

27. Gr. Anth. 7.724.

28. Gr. Anth. 7.232.

29. Gr. Anth. 16.228.

30. Gr. Anth. 7.710.

31. Erinna, "The Distaff."

32. Terentia, pyramid inscription.

33. Trebulla, colossus inscription.

34. Demo, colossus inscription.

35. Julia Balbilla, colossus inscription.

36. Julia Balbilla, colossus inscription.

37. Julia Balbilla, colossus inscription.

38. Barbara Hughes Fowler, trans., *Love Lyrics of Ancient Egypt* (Chapel Hill: University of North Carolina Press, 1994), 52–53, selections.

39. John L. Foster, trans., *Ancient Egyptian Literature: An Anthology* (Austin: University of Texas Press, 2001), 20.

40. Fowler, *Love Lyrics,* 17.

41. Foster, *Ancient Egyptian Literature,* 18; my substitution of "man" for his last word, "lord."

42. Song of Songs 1:2–3, 5–6.

43. Song of Songs 2:3.

44. Song of Songs 4:1, 3–5.

45. Song of Songs 5:4–6.

46. Song of Songs 8:7.

47. Sappho, frag. 2.

48. Sappho, frag. 47.

49. Sappho, frag. 102.

50. Sappho, frag. 94, condensed.

51. Sappho, poem 1, condensed.

52. Sappho, frag. 110a.

53. Sappho, frag. 114.

Figure 10.2 Seated woman, steatite. Temple of Ishtar, Mari, Syria, early dynastic period II, Ur I, ca. 2645–2460 B.C.E. Erich Lessing/Art Resource, NY, National Museum, Damascus, Syria.

54. Sappho, frag. 105a.
55. Sappho, frag. 112.
56. Sappho, frag. 116.
57. Sappho, frag. 104a.
58. Gr. Anth. 5.170.
59. Gr. Anth. 9.332.
60. Sulpicia 1, poem 3.8, condensed. My translation based upon the one by Judith P. Hallett, "Women in the Ancient Roman World, in Bella Vivante, ed., *Women's Roles in Ancient Civilizations: A Reference Guide* (Westport, CT: Greenwood Press, 1999), 280, with modifications.
61. Jon Corelis, trans., *Roman Erotic Elegy* (Salzburg, Austria: University of Salzburg, 1995), 97, poem 3.13, lines 1–2, 9–10.
62. Sulpicia 1, poem 3.9, condensed.
63. Sulpicia 1, poem 3.11, condensed.
64. Sulpicia 1, poem 3.14.
65. Sulpicia 1, poem 3.18.
66. Judith P. Hallett, "Women in the Ancient Roman World, in Bella Vivante, ed., *Women's Roles in Ancient Civilizations: A Reference Guide* (Westport, CT: Greenwood Press, 1999), 284.
67. Amy Richlin, "Sulpicia the Satirist," *Classical World* 86, no. 2 (1992): 125–40, p. 126, translation of epigram 10.35 by the second century C.E. epigrammatist Martial.

Figure 10.3 Double Hathor earring, gold, enamel. Egypt, Nubian, Meroitic Period, ca. 270 B.C.E.–320 C.E. Museum of Fine Arts, Boston.

Further Readings

TRANSLATIONS OF COMMONLY REFERENCED ANCIENT WORKS

Aristophanes, *Lysistrata*, trans. Sarah Ruden. 2003. Indianapolis: Hackett.
The Epic of Gilgamesh, trans. N. K. Sandars. 1960. London, New York: Penguin.
Hesiod, *Theogony*, trans. A. Athanassakis. 1983. Baltimore, MD: The Johns Hopkins University Press.
Homer, *The Iliad*, trans. Robert Fagles. 1996. New York: Oxford University Press.
Homer, *The Odyssey*, trans. Robert Fagles. 1990. New York: Viking.
The Homeric Hymns, trans. Diane Rayor. 2004. Berkeley: University of California Press.
The New Oxford Annotated Bible, ed. B. M. Metzger and R. E. Murphy. 1991. New York: Oxford University Press.

INTRODUCTION

Christ, Carol. 1997. *Rebirth of the Goddess: Finding Meaning in Feminist Spirituality*. New York: Addison-Wesley. Valuable presentation of the significance of goddess worship in modern women's lives.
Doherty, Lillian. 2001. *Gender and the Interpretation of Classical Myth*. London: Duckworth. Good introduction to how different theories about myth have treated gender.
Lefkowitz, Mary R. 1986. *Women in Greek Myth*. Baltimore: The Johns Hopkins University Press. Introduction to various themes relating to women in Greek mythology.
Lerner, Gerda. 1986. *The Creation of Patriarchy*. New York: Oxford University Press. Good introduction to the principle of patriarchy and how early patriarchal societies established themselves.
Zweig [Vivante], Bella. 1993. "The Primal Mind: Using Native American Models for the Study of Women in Ancient Greece." In *Feminist Theory and the Classics*, ed. N. S. Rabinowitz and A. Richlin, New York: Routledge, 145–80. Provides critical new models for examining ancient Greek women based on indigenous American women's roles.

CHAPTER ONE

Allen, Paula Gunn. 1986. *The Sacred Hoop: Recovering the Feminine in American Indian Traditions.* Boston: Beacon Press. Good introduction to indigenous American concepts of the feminine and female ways of thinking.

Awiakta, Marilou. 1993. *Selu: Seeking the Corn-Mother's Wisdom.* Golden, CO: Fulcrum Publishing. A personal exploration of the importance of the Mother Corn goddess to a contemporary Cherokee woman.

Dexter, Miriam Robbins. 1990. *Whence the Goddesses: A Sourcebook.* New York: Teachers College Press, Athene Series. A survey of literary images of Indo-European goddesses from the ancient Near East through Europe.

Frymer-Kensky, Tikva. 1992. *In the Wake of the Goddesses: Women, Culture and the Biblical Transformation of Pagan Myth.* New York: Fawcett Columbine. Examines the status of women and concepts of the feminine in Mesopotamian goddess-worshipping societies and the demonization or erasure of these in the biblical tradition.

Gimbutas, Marija. 1991. *The Civilization of the Goddess.* San Francisco: Harper and Row. Focus on the gynocentric values of Neolithic goddess-worshipping societies.

———. 1999. *The Living Goddesses.* Berkeley: University of California Press. A posthumous summary of earlier works showing the still-living traditions derived from these ancient beliefs.

Goodison, Lucy, and Christine Morris, eds. 1998. *Ancient Goddesses: The Myths and the Evidence.* Madison: University of Wisconsin Press. A refreshing modern exploration of the archaeological evidence for ancient goddess worship from Mesopotamia, Egypt, and Europe.

Lesko, Barbara S. 1999. *The Great Goddesses of Egypt.* Norman: University of Oklahoma Press. Comprehensive examination of the history, powers, and worship of Egyptian goddesses.

Marinatos, Nanno. 2000. *The Goddess and the Warrior: The Naked Goddess and Mistress of Animals in Early Greek Religion.* New York: Routledge. Examines the Near Eastern association of the naked goddess of sexuality with the male warrior.

Meador, Betty De Shong. 2001. *Inanna, Lady of the Largest Heart: Poems of the Sumerian High Priestess Enheduanna.* Austin: University of Texas Press. Vivid translation with insightful interpretations of Enkheduanna's poetry about Inanna.

Pritchard, James B., ed. 1958. *The Ancient Near East: An Anthology of Texts and Pictures,* vol. 1. Princeton, NJ: Princeton University Press. Valuable resource with clear explanatory notes of ancient Near Eastern documents.

Roberts, Alison. 1995. *Hathor Rising: The Serpent Power of Ancient Egypt.* Totnes, Devon: Northgate Publishers. Comprehensive, readable exploration of the many aspects of Hathor throughout ancient Egyptian history.

Spaeth, Barbette. 1996. *The Roman Goddess Ceres.* Austin: University of Texas Press. Comprehensive exploration of the worship and images of the goddess Ceres throughout Roman history.

Van Sertima, Ivan, ed. 1988. *Black Women in Antiquity.* New Brunswick, NJ: Transaction Books. Insightful essays on women in mostly north African antiquity.

CHAPTER TWO

Calame, Claude. 1997. *Choruses of Young Women in Ancient Greece: Their Morphology, Religious and Social Functions,* trans. J. Orion and D. Collins. Lanham, MD:

Rowman & Littlefield Publishers, Inc. Detailed examination of young women's ritual choruses in archaic Greece.

Foley, Helene P., ed. 1994. *The Homeric Hymn to Demeter.* Princeton, NJ: Princeton University Press. Translation of the hymn with notes and various modern interpretations.

Kerényi, Carl. 1967. *Eleusis: Archetypal Image of Mother and Daughter,* trans. Ralph Manheim. Princeton, NJ: Princeton University Press. Presentation of the Eleusinian Mysteries with a Jungian interpretation.

Kraemer, Ross S. 1992. *Her Share of the Blessings: Women's Religions among Pagans, Jews, and Christians in the Greco-Roman World.* New York: Oxford University Press. Comprehensive overview of women's major religious practices in the Greek and Roman worlds.

Larson, Jennifer. 1995. *Greek Heroine Cults.* Madison: University of Wisconsin Press. Detailed examination of the widespread heroine cults throughout ancient Greece.

Neils, Jenifer. 1992. *Goddess and Polis: The Panathenaic Festival in Ancient Athens.* Princeton, NJ: Princeton University Press. Visual exploration of the goddess Athena's great festival through vase paintings and sculpture.

Sissa, Giulia. 1990. *Greek Virginity,* trans. Arthur Goldhammer. Cambridge, MA: Harvard University Press. Examines the changing concept of virginity in Greek, Roman, and early Christian times.

Wolkstein, Diane, and Samuel N. Kramer, 1983. *INANNA: Queen of Heaven and Earth.* New York: HarperCollins. Vivid translation with enlightening interpretations of the sacred marriage poetry featuring Inanna and her consort Dumuzi.

CHAPTER THREE

Blundell, Sue. 1995. *Women in Ancient Greece.* Cambridge, MA: Harvard University Press. Good, comprehensive survey of women in ancient Greece with sharp illustrations.

Brulé, Pierre. 2003. *Women of Ancient Athens,* trans. Antonia Nevill. Edinburgh: Edinburgh University Press. Engaging exploration of Athenian women's lives through poetry and art.

Cantarella, Eva. 1992. *Bisexuality in the Ancient World,* trans. Cormac Ó Cuilleanáin. New Haven, CT: Yale University Press. Examines the concepts and practice of homosexuality in Greece and Rome.

Clark, Gillian. 1993. *Women in Late Antiquity: Pagan and Christian Lifestyles.* Oxford: Clarendon Press. General overview of women's roles in late European antiquity.

Demand, Nancy. 1994/2004. *Birth, Death, and Motherhood in Classical Greece.* Baltimore: The Johns Hopkins University Press. Extensive examination of these aspects of Greek women's lives.

Dixon, Suzanne. 1992. *The Roman Family.* Baltimore: The Johns Hopkins University Press. Comprehensive examination of the shape and status of the Roman family.

Ehrenberg, Margaret. 1989. *Women in Prehistory.* Norman: University of Oklahoma Press. Examines women's roles and status in prehistorical societies.

Fantham, Elaine, et al. 1994. *Women in the Classical World: Image and Text.* New York: Oxford University Press. General overview of Greek and Roman women with numerous illustrations.

Fraschetti, Augusto, ed. 2001. *Roman Women,* trans. Linda Lappin. Chicago: University of Chicago Press. Detailed biographies of nine outstanding Roman women.

Gaca, Kathy L. 2003. *The Making of Fornication: Eros, Ethics, and Political Reform in Greek Philosophy and Early Christianity.* Berkeley: University of California Press. Provocative exploration of the transformation in concepts of sexuality in the late antique, early Christian period.

Golden, Mark. 1990. *Children and Childhood in Classical Athens.* Baltimore, MD: The Johns Hopkins University Press. A rare comprehensive examination of attitudes to and treatment of children in the ancient world.

Harris, Rivkah. 2000. *Gender and Aging in Mesopotamia.* Norman: University of Oklahoma Press. Examines women's life course in Mesopotamian society and literature.

Hawass, Zahi. 2000. *Silent Images: Women in Pharaonic Egypt.* New York: Harry N. Abrams, Publishers. Thorough, readable overview of women's lives with a wealth of color photographs and lively literary translations.

Holst-Warhaft, Gail. 1992. *Dangerous Voices: Women's Laments and Greek Literature.* New York: Routledge. Significance of women's laments in Greek society and literature.

Keuls, Eva C. 1985. *The Reign of the Phallus: Sexual Politics in Ancient Athens.* Berkeley: University of California Press. Provocative examination through art and myth of negative effects on women of Greece's phallic-oriented culture.

Lefkowitz, Mary R., and Maureen B. Fant, eds. 1992. *Women's Life in Greece & Rome: A Source Book in Translation.* 2nd ed. Baltimore, MD: The Johns Hopkins University Press. Extensive documentary sources on ancient Greek and Roman women.

Lesko, Barbara. 1978. *The Remarkable Women of Ancient Egypt.* Berkeley, CA: B.C. Scribe Publications. A brief visual and narrative excursus on distinguishing characteristics of Egyptian women.

Lichtheim, Miriam. 1973, 1976, 1980. *Ancient Egyptian Literature: A Book of Readings.* 3 vols. Berkeley: University of California Press. Translations of many Egyptian texts from the Old Kingdom through the Late Period.

Lightman, Marjorie, and Lightman, Benjamin. 2000. *Biographical Dictionary of Ancient Greek and Roman Women.* New York: Checkmark Books. Good biographies of all known Greek and Roman women.

Oakley, John Howard, and Rebecca H. Sinos. 1993. *The Wedding in Ancient Athens.* Madison, WI. Explores Athenian wedding customs through the visual arts.

Pomeroy, Sarah B. 1975, 1995. *Goddesses, Whores, Wives, and Slaves: Women in Classical Antiquity.* New York: Schocken Books. Basic comprehensive examination of women's lives in Greece and Rome.

———. 2002. *Spartan Women.* Oxford: Oxford University Press. Major examination of the distinctiveness of Spartan women.

Rabinowitz, Nancy Sorkin, and Lisa Auanger, eds. 2002. *Among Women: From the Homosocial to the Homoerotic in the Ancient World.* Austin: University of Texas Press. Explores the various artistic and literary portrayals of women's associations in Greece and Rome.

Robins, Gay. 1993. *Women in Ancient Egypt.* Cambridge, MA: Harvard University Press. Comprehensive examination of Egyptian women's lives with many sharp illustrations.

Rowlandson, Jane. 1998. *Women & Society in Greek & Roman Egypt: A Sourcebook.* Cambridge: Cambridge University Press. Extensive documentary sources on women in Greek and Roman Egypt.

Sealey, Raphael. 1990. *Women and Law in Classical Greece*. Chapel Hill: University of North Carolina Press. Readable examination of women's legal status and its cultural significance in several ancient Greek cities, the Roman Republic, and literature.

Skinner, Marilyn B. 2005. *Sexuality in Greek and Roman Culture*. London: Blackwell Publishing. Lively examination of the concepts and practices of sexuality in ancient Greece and Rome.

Tyldesley, Joyce. 1994. *Daughters of Isis: Women of Ancient Egypt*. New York: Penguin. Extensive readable introduction to women's roles in ancient Egypt with many illustrations and line drawings.

Vivante, Bella, ed. 1999. *Women's Roles in Ancient Civilizations: A Reference Guide*. Westport, CT: Greenwood Press. Readable informative introduction to women's roles in 12 ancient civilizations.

Watterson, Barbara. 1991. *Women in Ancient Egypt*. Stroud, England: Sutton. General overview of Egyptian women's lives with many sharp illustrations.

CHAPTER FOUR

King, Helen. 1998. *Hippocrates' Woman: Reading the Female Body in Ancient Greece*. London, New York: Routledge. Detailed examination of the treatment of the female body and conditions in ancient Greek medical texts and their influence on later practices.

CHAPTER FIVE

Barber, Elizabeth W. 1994. *Women's Work: The First 20,000 Years. Women, Cloth, and Society in Early Times*. New York: Norton. Importance of weaving to the economy, including techniques and myths.

Schaps, David. 1979. *Economic Rights of Women in Ancient Greece*. Edinburgh: University of Edinburgh Press. Detailed examination of Greek women's various economic roles.

CHAPTER SIX

Arnold, Dorothea. 1996. *The Royal Women of Amarna: Images of Beauty from Ancient Egypt*. New York: The Metropolitan Museum of Art, Harry N. Abrams, Inc., distributor. Beautifully illustrated presentation of the artistic depictions of royal Egyptian women in one period of Egyptian art.

Bauman, R. 1992. *Women and Politics in Ancient Rome*. New York: Routledge. Detailed examination of various forms of Roman women's political actions.

Burstein, Stanley M. 2004. *The Reign of Cleopatra*. Westport, CT: Greenwood Press. Engaging, comprehensive account of Kleopatra's life, reign, and the global effects of her rule.

Carney, Elizabeth D. 1999. *Women and Monarchy in Macedonia*. Norman: University of Oklahoma Press. Extensive examination of royal women's activities in Macedonia.

Flamarion, Edith. 1997. *Cleopatra: The Life and Death of a Pharaoh*, trans. Alexandra Bonfante-Warren. New York: Harry Abrams, Discoveries. Handy-size highlights of Kleopatra's life with many ancient and modern paintings, literary quotations, and dramatic references.

Foss, Michael. 1997. *The Search for Cleopatra*. London: TimeWatch. Lively, readable account of Kleopatra's life.

Henry, Madeleine. 1995. *Prisoner of History: Aspasia of Miletus and Her Biographical Tradition*. New York: Oxford University Press. Extensive readable examination of the historicity and misrepresentations of this outstanding woman in Athenian life.

Hughes-Hallett, Lucy. 1990. *Cleopatra: Histories, Dreams and Distortions*. San Francisco: Harper & Row. Explores different aspects of the ancient and modern images of Kleopatra.

Jackson, Guida M. 1999. *Women Rulers throughout the Ages: An Illustrated Guide*. Santa Barbara, CA: ABC-Clio. Biographical sketches of virtually all women rulers.

Kleiner, Diana, and Susan Matheson, eds. 1996. *I Claudia II: Women in Roman Art and Society*. Austin: University of Texas Press. Portrayal of powerful women through Roman art.

Leacock, Eleanor. 1978. "Women's Status in Egalitarian Societies: Implications for Social Evolution." *Current Anthropology* 19: 247–75. Pivotal essay on the egalitarian, complementary roles of women and men in pre-state societies and their larger cultural significance.

Plutarch, "Life of Mark Antony," in *Makers of Rome: Nine Lives by Plutarch*, trans. Ian Scott-Kilvert. 1965. London, New York: Penguin.

Samson, Julia. 1990. *Nefertiti and Cleopatra: Queen-Monarchs of Ancient Egypt*. London: Rubicon. (Orig. pub. 1985.) Thorough, readable accounts of these two queens.

Tyldesley, Joyce. 1996. *Hatchepsut: The Female Pharaoh*. London, New York: Penguin. Extensive readable account of the famous Egyptian female king with many illustrations and line drawings.

———. 1998. *Nefertiti: Egypt's Sun Queen*. London, New York: Penguin. Extensive readable account of the famous Egyptian queen with many illustrations and line drawings.

Zweig [Vivante], Bella. 1993. "The Only Women Who Give Birth to Men: A Gynocentric, Cross-Cultural View of Women in Ancient Sparta." In *Woman's Power, Man's Game: Essays on Classical Antiquity in Honor of Joy King*, ed. Mary DeForest, pp. 32–53. Wauconda, IL: Bolchazy-Carducci. Examines the empowering features of Spartan women's lives.

CHAPTER SEVEN

Alpern, Stanley B. 1998. *Amazons of Black Sparta: The Women Warriors of Dahomey*. New York: New York University Press. Introduction to the roles women played in Dahomey's military.

duBois, Page. 1982. *Centaurs and Amazons: Women and the Pre-History of the Great Chain of Being*. Ann Arbor: University of Michigan Press. Explores the meaning of images of females and animals in early Greek myth and art.

Kleinbaum, Abby Wettan. 1983. *The War Against the Amazons*. New York: McGraw-Hill Book Company. Overview of the various forms of hostility to Amazons from antiquity to the present.

Newark, Tim. 1989. *Women Warlords: An Illustrated Military History of Female Warriors*. London: Blandford. Good illustrated examination of powerful female warriors from different world cultures.

Salmonson, Jessica Amanda. 1991. *The Encyclopedia of Amazons: Women Warriors from Antiquity to the Modern Era.* New York: Paragon House. Comprehensive resource on actual and mythical female warriors throughout history.
Tyrrell, William B. 1984. *Amazons: A Study in Athenian Mythmaking.* Baltimore, MD: The Johns Hopkins University Press. Examines the significance of Amazon myths in Greek thinking.
von Bothmer, Dietrich. 1957. *Amazons in Greek Art.* Oxford: Clarendon Press. Comprehensively examines the portrayals of Amazons in Greek art.
Wilde, Lyn Webster. 2000. *On the Trail of the Women Warriors: The Amazons in Myth and History.* New York: Thomas Dunne Books, St. Martin's Press. Compelling imaginative associations of Amazons with other powerful female images; excellent maps of Amazon habitation.

CHAPTER EIGHT

Cavarero, Adriana. 1995. *In Spite of Plato: A Feminist Rewriting of Ancient Philosophy,* trans. S. Anderlini-D'Onofrio and A. O'Healy. New York: Routledge. A gynocentric approach to ancient Greek philosophic ideas through four distinctive female perspectives.
Dzielska, Maria. 1995. *Hypatia of Alexandria,* trans. F. Lyra. Cambridge, MA: Harvard University Press. Readable examination of the life, ideas, and intellectual environment of the philosopher Hypatia.
Kersey, Ethel M. 1989. *Women Philosophers: A Bio-Critical Source Book.* Westport, CT: Greenwood Press. Valuable encyclopedia of Western women philosophers from antiquity to the present.
Okin, Susan. 1979/1992. *Women in Western Political Thought.* Princeton, NJ: Princeton University Press. Readable examination of the portrayal of women in Plato's and Aristotle's political writings.
Waithe, Mary Ellen, ed. 1987. *A History of Women Philosophers: Ancient Women Philosophers, 600 B.C.–500 A.D.,* vol. 1. Dordrecht: Nijhoff. Informative, readable presentation and interpretation of the works of many ancient female philosophers.

CHAPTER NINE

Bing, Peter, and Rip Cohen, trans. 1991. *Games of Venus: An Anthology of Greek and Roman Erotic Verse form Sappho to Ovid.* New York: Routledge. Lively translations of much of Greek and Roman erotic poetry.
Churchill, Laurie J., Phyllis R. Brown, and Jane E. Jeffrey, eds. 2002. *Women Writing Latin: From Roman Antiquity to Early Modern Europe,* vol. 1. New York: Routledge. Insightful articles on Roman women writers with full translations of several.
Corelis, Jon, trans. 1995. *Roman Erotic Elegy.* Salzburg, Austria: University of Salzburg Press. Lively translations of select Roman erotic poetry.
Foster, John L., trans. 2001. *Ancient Egyptian Literature: An Anthology.* Austin: University of Texas Press. Lively translations of a broad range of Egyptian poetry.
Foster, John L., trans. 1974. *Love Songs of the New Kingdom.* Austin: University of Texas Press. Lively translations of select Egyptian love poetry.

Fowler, Barbara Hughes, trans. 1994. *Love Lyrics of Ancient Egypt.* Chapel Hill: University of North Carolina Press. Lively translations of select Egyptian love poetry.

The Greek Anthology. 5 vols. Ed. and trans. W. R. Paton. 1916–1918. Loeb Classical Library. Cambridge, MA: Harvard University Press. Includes the poetry of many Greek female poets.

Plant, I. M., trans. 2004. *Women Writers of Ancient Greece and Rome: An Anthology.* Norman: University of Oklahoma Press. Lively translations of almost all the writings by Greek and Roman women.

Rayor, Diane J., trans. 1991. *Sappho's Lyre: Archaic Lyric and Women Poets of Ancient Greece.* Berkeley: University of California Press. Lively translations of poetry by Sappho and several other Greek women.

Sappho and Alcaeus, ed. and trans. David A. Campbell. 1982. Loeb Classical Library. Cambridge, MA: Harvard University Press. Complete Greek texts and addenda with modern, literal translations.

Snyder, Jane McIntosh. 1989. *The Woman and the Lyre: Women Writers in Classical Greece and Rome.* Carbondale: Southern Illinois University Press. Readable examination with lively translations of the poetry and philosophy by many Greek and Roman women writers.

SOME MODERN LITERARY AND MEDIA TREATMENTS OF ANCIENT SUBJECTS

Boudicca: Warrior Queen. 2006. The History Channel. DVD. A stirring historical portrayal of Boudicca's leading the Iceni revolt against Rome.

Brindel, June R. 1981. *Ariadne.* New York: St. Martin's Press. An imaginative telling of the transition from sacred, matriarchal values to materialistic patriarchal ones on the island of Crete.

Cleopatra. 1963. Twentieth Century-Fox Corp., director, Joseph L. Mankiewicz, starring Elizabeth Taylor, Richard Burton, and Rex Harrison. An epic cinematic portrayal of the spectacular life of this remarkable queen.

A Dream of Passion. Director, Jules Dassin, starring Melina Mercouri and Ellen Burstyn. A provocative portrayal of the interactions between an actress' intellectual approach to the stage role of Medea and the passions of a woman imprisoned for killing her children.

Egypt's Great Queen. 2005. The History Channel. DVD. A historical exploration of Hatshepsut's unique role as a powerful Egyptian pharaoh.

Grahn, Judy. 1982. *Queen of Wands.* New York: The Crossing Press. A poetic envisioning of the multiple powers of Helen in ancient and modern metaphors.

H. D. (Hilda Doolittle). 1961. *Helen in Egypt.* New York: Grove Press. An eloquent modern epic poem about Helen from a decidedly female perspective by this superb imagist poet.

———. 1968. *Palimpsest.* Carbondale: Southern Illinois University Press. A moving portrayal of an educated Greek woman forced to live with her unsophisticated Roman captor.

Medea. 1983. Director, Robert Whitehead, starring Zoe Caldwell, Dame Judith Anderson, Mitchell Ryan. Kennedy Center production. The Robinson Jeffers' adaptation that explores Medea's psycho-sexual motivations.

Medea. 1970. Vanguard Cinema in association with Sceneries Distribution, director, Pier Paolo Pasolini, starring Maria Callas. In Italian with English subtitles.

Using little dialogue the opening visually and dramatically portrays Medea's primal, sorcerous background before following Euripides' play.

The Trojan Women. 1971. A Josef Shaftel production, director, Michael Cacoyannis, and starring Katharine Hepburn, Vanessa Redgrave, Genevieve Bujold, and Irene Papas. A moving rendition in English of Euripides' play about the conquest of Troy through the devastating impact on the women.

Wolf, Christa. 1984. *Cassandra: a novel and four essays*, trans. Jan van Heurck. New York: Farrar, Straus, Giroux. A modern woman's reflections upon singular divine gifts and punishments Cassandra has had to endure.

———. 1998. *Medea: a modern retelling*, trans. John Cullen. New York: Nan A. Talese. A modern woman's reflections on how Medea dealt with the experiences imposed upon her.

WEB SITE ON WOMEN IN ANTIQUITY

Diotima: Materials for the Study of Women in the Ancient World, http://www.stoa.org/diotima/. Various resources from course material, to essays to bibliographies.

Figure 10.4 Dancing girl/acrobat, painted limestone ostracon. Egyptian New Kingdom, 17th dynasty, 16th c. B.C.E. Erich Lessing/Art Resource, NY, Museo Egizio, Turin, Italy.

Figure 10.5 Funerary monument of Aththaia, daughter of Malchos, limestone. Palmyra, Syria, Roman imperial period, ca. 150–200 C.E. Museum of Fine Arts, Boston.

Figure 10.6 "Mistress of the Animals," goddess feeding two goats, ivory. Minet-el-Beida, Syria, Mycenaean, mid-late 2nd mil. B.C.E. Erich Lessing/Art Resource, NY, Louvre, Paris, France.

Index